The White Devil

THE NEW MERMAIDS

General Editors
PHILIP BROCKBANK
BRIAN MORRIS

The White Devil

JOHN WEBSTER

Edited by ELIZABETH M. BRENNAN

A New Mermaid

A MERMAID DRAMABOOK
HILL AND WANG • NEW YORK

© *Ernest Benn Limited 1966*
All rights reserved
ISBN (clothbound edition): 0-8090-9700-1
ISBN (paperback edition): 0-8090-1110-7
Library of Congress catalog card number: 68-30766
First American Edition September 1968

TO
MURIEL LOWDEN

Manufactured in the United States of America
234567890

CONTENTS

ACKNOWLEDGEMENTS

In the preparation of this edition of *The White Devil* I am indebted to those previous editors whose names are listed on p. xxxii. In particular I should like to acknowledge the debts that I owe to F. L. Lucas's and J. R. Brown's editions of the play; to Dr. Brown's bibliographical studies of the play; to Dr. Gunnar Boklund's work on its sources and R. W. Dent's book on John Webster's borrowing.

I am grateful to the General Editors of the series, and in particular to Dr. B. R. Morris, for sympathetic criticism and guidance. I have pleasure in thanking the Council of the University College of North Wales for the award of a research grant while this work was in progress.

ELIZABETH M. BRENNAN

Westfield College,
(*University of London*).
October, 1965.

INTRODUCTION

THE AUTHOR

VERY LITTLE is known about John Webster. He was born free of the Merchant Taylors' Company, probably about 1580. There was a John Webster admitted to the Middle Temple on 1st August, 1598. If this were the dramatist, the fact might explain the many legal allusions in his plays and the inclusion of trial scenes in *The White Devil*, *The Devil's Law Case* and *Appius and Virginia*. Ben Jonson's are the only Elizabethan or Jacobean plays which contain more legal allusions than John Webster's.

The earliest records of Webster's employment as a playwright are found in the diary of the theatre manager and financier, Philip Henslowe. Among the payments which Henslowe noted in his diary in 1602 were those made to Webster, Munday, Middleton, Dekker, Chettle, Thomas Heywood and Wentworth Smith for their work on the plays *Caesar's Fall*, *Lady Jane* and *Christmas Comes but Once a Year*. It is thought that *The Famous History of Sir Thomas Wyatt* which was published in 1607 contains the contribution of Webster and Dekker to the second play. The other two plays, like so many mentioned in Henslowe's diary, including Webster's tragedy, *The Guise*, have been lost.

In 1604 Webster wrote the Induction for John Marston's *The Malcontent* and collaborated with Dekker on *Westward Ho!*. The following year they wrote *Northward Ho!*. Webster's first tragedy, *The White Devil*, was performed and published in 1612. Despite *The White Devil's* apparently unsympathetic reception in the theatre, Webster seems to have lost no time in writing *The Duchess of Malfi*. An assiduous reader and borrower, Webster incorporated in his second tragedy some material which had only been published in 1612. Though the play cannot have been completed before late 1612, it must have been performed before December, 1614, when William Ostler, the actor who first played Antonio Bologna, died.

Webster's elegy on the death of Prince Henry, *A Monumental Column*, was published in 1613. The sixth edition of Sir Thomas Overbury's *Characters* (1615) contained thirty-two new 'characters', including that of 'An Excellent Actor', which were probably contributed by Webster. The dates of Webster's other extant works are uncertain. *The Devil's Law Case* was performed about 1617.[1] It is

---

[1] G. E. Bentley, *The Jacobean and Caroline Stage*, V (Oxford, 1958), 1250–51 urges that *The Devil's Law Case* may belong to 1610. R. W. Dent has found in the play two borrowings from Burghley's *Certaine Precepts* (1617) and concludes that 'Some such date as 1617 is surely right.' (*John Webster's Borrowing* (Berkeley and Los Angeles, 1960), p. 59.)

thought that Webster collaborated with Middleton on *Anything for a Quiet Life*, probably about 1621, and with Rowley and possibly Thomas Heywood on *A Cure for a Cuckold* between 1624 and 1625. *Appius and Virginia*, first published in 1654, may belong to the same period. The lost tragedy of *The Guise* was written some time before 1623 and another lost play, *The Late Murder of the Son upon the Mother, or Keep the Widow Waking* which Webster wrote in collaboration with Dekker, Ford and Rowley, was performed in September 1624. It has been suggested that *The Fair Maid of the Inn*, published in the 1647 Folio of plays by Beaumont and Fletcher, was written by Webster, Massinger and Ford.

Webster appears to have written no other plays, though he is known to have composed a Lord Mayor's Pageant and he wrote some occasional verses. He probably died in the sixteen-thirties.

THE PLAY

EARLY PERFORMANCES OF WEBSTER PLAYS

Caesar's Fall and *Lady Jane* were written for the Admiral's Men and the Earl of Worcester's Men respectively. The citizen comedies *Westward Ho!* and *Northward Ho!* were written by Dekker and Webster for the company of Paul's Boys who presented them in their private theatre. Upon the accession of James I the Earl of Worcester's Men changed their name to Queen Anne's Servants or the Queen's Men, and it was as the Queen's Men that they acted *The White Devil*, *The Devil's Law Case* and *Keep the Widow Waking* at the Red Bull, their theatre in Clerkenwell.

Webster's address to the reader of *The White Devil* speaks of the unfavourable conditions under which the play was first staged. It was acted 'in so dull a time of winter', in 'so open and black a theatre' that the audience was both small and unappreciative. The reference to the time of year, taken in conjunction with other evidence, enables us to date the first performance sometime in the early months of 1612.[1] It would indeed have needed a sturdy as well as enthusiastic audience to go to a public theatre whose auditorium was open to the wintry sky to see a play which, in its intellectual content and attitude to life, was remarkably different from other plays in the repertory of the Queen's Men at that time.[2] Nearly twenty years later the title of the second quarto (1631) could refer to *The White Devil* as 'diuers times Acted by the Queenes Maiesties seruants, at the Phoenix, in Drury-lane.' Samuel Pepys attended two performances of the play given by the King's Men in October, 1661. John Downes, in *Roscius Anglicanus, or an Historical Review of the Stage: After it had*

---

[1] See J. R. Brown, 'On the Dating of *The White Devil* and *The Duchess of Malfi*', *Philological Quarterly*, XXXI (1952), 353–62 [especially pp. 353–8].
[2] *Ibid.*, p. 355.

been Suppres'd by the late Unhappy Civil War, . . . (1708) included
'*Vittoria Corumbona*' in a list of twenty-one old plays which were
revived from time to time by the King's Men between 1663 and 1682.
The title pages of the third and fourth quartos refer to performances
by the King's Men at the Theatre Royal[1] in 1665 and 1672. In 1691
Gerard Langbaine in his *Account of the English Dramatic Poets* wrote
of '*Appius and Virginia, Dutchess of Malfy*, and *Vittoria Corrombona*'
as examples of plays by Webster which had gained applause 'even
in our Age.'

The *Duchess of Malfi* was first acted by the King's Men both in
their private theatre in Blackfriars and in their public theatre, the
Globe, between 1612 and 1614. They also presented *Anything for a
Quiet Life* at the Blackfriars theatre in 1621.

THE SOURCES OF THE PLAY

John Webster's tragedy, *The White Devil,* first performed in Jacobean
London, is based on the story of a beautiful woman who had been
murdered in Padua about twenty-seven years earlier. Vittoria
Accoramboni was born in Gubbio, in Northern Italy, on 15th
February, 1557, and the events which led to her murder at the age of
twenty-eight were surrounded in reality, no less than in Webster's
dramatization of it, by an atmosphere in which treachery, murder
and piety were strangely mingled.

The Accoramboni were an old and respected family, with property
in Umbria and Rome, but they were not wealthy. Vittoria, one of
eleven children, and extremely beautiful, came to Rome as a young
girl and at the age of sixteen was married to Francesco Peretti, the
nephew of Cardinal Montalto. Childless, and perhaps not very happy
in her marriage, Vittoria met the Duke of Bracciano about 1580.
Some twenty years Vittoria's senior, Paulo Giordano Orsini had
been betrothed to the child Isabella de Medici four years before
Vittoria was born. Their marriage was celebrated in June, 1558, when
Isabella was sixteen. A few days later the Pope created the bride-
groom Duke of Bracciano. Between 1560 and 1572 they had three
children, including the son Virginio who later succeeded to the dukedom, but in fact the couple did not often live together. The Duchess
of Bracciano preferred to remain at her father's court in Florence
while her husband lived chiefly in Rome. By 1576 it became known

---

[1] Between 1660 and 1663 the King's Men played at the Theatre Royal in Vere
Street, a theatre which had been converted from an indoor tennis court by
Thomas Killigrew. In 1663 Killigrew and a syndicate built a Theatre Royal
in Bridges Street and it was used by the King's Men till 1672 when it was
burnt down. For a short time the company acted in the Lincoln's Inn Fields
theatre. They finally moved to the Theatre Royal in Drury Lane in 1674 and
played there till their amalgamation with the Duke's Company to form the
United Company in 1784.

that Troilo Orsini was Isabella's lover. During one of the Duke of
Bracciano's rare visits to the Medici court Isabella died. She was
probably strangled by her husband himself.

Vittoria's brother Marcello was in the Duke of Bracciano's service
and he encouraged her relationship with the wealthy and magnificent
widower, who quickly fell in love with her. On the night of 16th
April, 1581, Francesco Peretti received a letter from Marcello which
urged him to come immediately to a meeting-place near Monte
Cavallo. As Francesco and a single torchbearer approached the
appointed place Francesco was first shot down and then, the torchbearer having fled, was finished off with a dagger. He was buried
quietly in a near-by church. Rather oddly, the Cardinal Montalto
made no great inquiries into the death of a nephew whom he had
loved and who had been his heir.

Vittoria went to her father's home in Rome, but within a fortnight
of her husband's death she was secretly married to the Duke of
Bracciano. With her chambermaid acting as sole witness, the Duke
placed a ring on Vittoria's finger. This wedding ceremony–*per verba
de presenti*–was the same as that performed by the Duchess of Malfi
and Antonio Bologna, *circa* 1505, and presented on the stage in
Webster's second tragedy.[1]

Paulo Giordano took the new Duchess to his villa at Magnanapoli,
and later told Pope Gregory XIII of their marriage. Vittoria was
promptly informed that any marriage contracted by her without the
Pope's consent would be considered null. She was ordered by Papal
injunction to return to her own home and the Duke was forbidden
to have anything to do with her. The health of both lovers suffered
during their separation and in November, 1581, the Duke took his
wife back to live with him. By this time enough had been learnt of
the circumstances of the death of Francesco Peretti to cause the
Pope to intervene more directly to prevent Vittoria from having the
Duke of Bracciano as her second husband. At the beginning of
December the Duke was ordered once more to send her home.
Paulo Giordano obeyed, and as Vittoria was on her way she was
arrested and confined to a nunnery whence, on 20th December, she
was removed to the Castle Sant Angelo.

At first the Duke, treating Vittoria as his lawful Duchess, tried
hard to have her released; but in June, 1582, he promised the Pope

---

[1] *Per verba de presenti* means 'by words about the present.' Two articles, not
always in agreement, which throw light on the significance of such a marriage
are: D. P. Harding, 'Elizabethan Betrothals and *Measure for Measure*',
Journal of English and Germanic Philology, XLIX (1950), 139–58 and Ernest
Schanzer, 'The Marriage Contracts in *Measure for Measure*', *Shakespeare
Survey* 13 (1960), 81–89. See *The Duchess of Malfi*, I.ii, 389–406. All references and quotations from this play are taken from the New Mermaid
edition (1964).

and Francisco de Medici, Grand Duke of Tuscany and brother of
his dead wife, that he would renounce Vittoria. When Vittoria received the cold letter in which he declared that he was releasing her
from all ties to him, she tried to commit suicide. It was not until
November, 1582, that she was released from prison, upon condition
that she would return to Gubbio.

Vittoria dutifully visited the Pope and Cardinal Montalto before
going to Gubbio, where she remained for several months while
Paulo Giordano stayed in Bracciano. On 7th September, 1583, he
set out to make a pilgrimage to Loretto and to inspect the forti-
fications at Ancona. On his return he appointed a meeting with
Vittoria, brought her home to Bracciano and married her quietly,
but with religious ceremony, on 10th October.

For over a year they lived in happiness and splendour which were
diminished only by the Duke's illness in the summer of 1584, caused
by a malignant ulcer in the leg. The doctors would have amputated
the limb, had the Duke not been unhealthily corpulent; but, in fact,
by the autumn he seemed to be quite recovered and in December
he and Vittoria took up residence together in Rome, though the fact
of their marriage was not revealed. In February, 1585, the Duke told
not only the Pope, but his first Duchess' relations, that he was
actually married to Vittoria. The news was not well received, and
the lovers were once more in danger of being separated. When the
Pope died suddenly on 10th April, Paulo Giordano assumed that
the theological objections to his marriage had died too. He married
Vittoria publicly, in Rome, on 24th April, 1585. Only an hour or so
after this wedding the election of the new Pope was announced. He
was Cardinal Montalto, who took the name of Sixtus V.

The impossibility of achieving a reconciliation with the new Pope
became immediately obvious and within two days the Duke, his
Duchess and her brother Marcello had left for Bracciano. A few
weeks later they went to Venice. Paulo Giordano was often very ill
on the journey and in July they went to Padua where he underwent
a course of treatment. By late October he was much worse, and made
his will. They left Padua for Salò on Lake Garda where the first Duke
of Bracciano died on 13th November, 1585, aged about forty-eight.

His will had made lavish provision for Vittoria and left the remainder of his lands to his son Virginio, but neither the Medici nor
the Orsini families would accept Vittoria's right to her husband's
property. After the Duke's funeral she set out for her beautiful home
in Padua. On the journey she was overtaken by Lodovico Orsini, a
distant cousin and former confidant of her husband's. Considering
that he was acting on behalf of the young Duke Virginio and
Francisco de Medici, Grand Duke of Tuscany, Lodovico accompanied Vittoria to Padua, forced her to surrender the will and give

up all claims to Paulo Giordano's property. He then returned to Venice. Vittoria was able to use an earlier document to make the authorities of Padua recognize her right to a large share of her late husband's property. Hearing of this, Lodovico Orsini returned to Rome, bringing with him a company of reliable *banditti*, some of whom were gentlemen.

On the night of Sunday, 22nd December, 1585, the eve of her own saint's day, Vittoria was at prayer before a crucifix, her young brother Flamineo was singing the *Miserere* in an adjoining room when Lodovico's *banditti*, armed and fantastically masked, surrounded and entered her palace. Flamineo was shot and, when he had crawled to his sister's room, stabbed to death. Two men held Vittoria while Tolomeo Visconti murdered her brutally and with obscene jests.

Apparently Lodovico Orsini himself took no part in the murders. None the less, the assassins had set out from and later returned to his house, and two days later the combined Paduan and Venetian authorities had it besieged. He surrendered on Christmas Day and two days later was strangled in prison. Most of the *banditti* were publicly executed. Finally, Marcello Accoramboni, who had not been found on the night of his sister's murder, was beheaded by order of the Pope in June, 1586.

WEBSTER'S TRAGEDY OF THE WHITE DEVIL

The relationship between John Webster's tragedy of 'Paulo Giordano Ursini, Duke of Brachiano, With The Life and Death of Vittoria Corombona' and the real people concerned is not simple, for no single known source could have supplied all the details of the play, and so any theory concerning the selection of extant sources which he could have used must be based on probabilities, not certainties. A pamphlet published in London in 1585, called *A Letter Lately written from Rome, by an Italian Gentleman, to a freende of his in Lyons in Fraunce....* [1] gave a detailed description of the election of Cardinal Montalto as Pope Sixtus V, and told something of Duke Bracciano's relationship with Vittoria and of the suspicion of his responsibility for the death of Vittoria's husband, the new Pope's nephew. An early sixteenth-century Italian pamphlet, *Il miserabil e compassionevol caso, succeso nella città di Padova*, related the death of Vittoria and described how, when captured and questioned about her death, Lodovico Orsini's reply contained the Virgilian tag *manet altamente repostum*. This was echoed, perhaps consciously, in *The White Devil*, II.i, 262. Between 1596 and 1612 five historical works, two published in Venice, the others in Padua, Paris and London respectively, contained accounts of the death of the Duke of Brac-

[1] The translator was I.F., i.e. John Florio, who may in fact have written it.

ciano and the murder of Vittoria,[1] while over a hundred manuscripts circulated different versions of the facts around Europe from the late sixteenth century onwards.

In his detailed and invaluable study, *The Sources of 'The White Devil'* (Uppsala, 1957) Dr. Gunnar Boklund concludes that he has established beyond reasonable doubt that the account of Vittoria's life given in a manuscript news-letter written in German for the Fugger banking house in Augsburg[2] was a main source of Webster's play, 'although by no means necessarily or even probably in the form with which we are now familiar. . . . The search for the Italian original should continue.' (p. 122). Webster probably utilized information provided by the early pamphlets, *A Letter Lately written from Rome* and *Il miserabil e compassionevol caso*. He also seems to have known another version of Vittoria's story, found either in what Dr. Boklund calls the 'Claudio Accoramboni' group of manuscripts,[3] –behind which was an author well acquainted with her life in Rome, but badly and inaccurately informed about her life in Northern Italy and her death in Padua,–or in one of the two early Venetian histories: Cesare Campana's *Delle Historie del Mondo* (Venice, 1596) and Giovanni Doglioni's *Historia Venetiana* (Venice, 1598). These latter accounts of Vittoria contain a knowledge of Marcello Accoramboni's murderous activities in Rome, but they say nothing of his later life and do not identify the brother who died with Vittoria at Padua.[4]

The information revealed by Dr. Boklund's research into the sources of the play is essential for a full appreciation of Webster's treatment of characterization, plot and construction. Indeed, though it may be admitted that Webster did not give his play a completely unified action, a comparison of the disparate elements of narrative and characterization provided by the sources with their treatment by Webster will demonstrate his concern to provide its world and action with as much unity as possible. So the figure of Francisco de Medici, colourless in Webster's sources, became both a powerful character and one means of unifying the elements of the plot.[5] Flamineo's deeds and personality were not simply based on those of the historical and villainous Marcello: through Flamineo Webster comments to the audience on the life and atmosphere of the play and, moreover, on any life–in the world in general–in which expectation exceeds reward, the natural attributes of youth and vigour are treated

[1] There were also brief references to Vittoria in some other works. See Gunnar Boklund, *The Sources of 'The White Devil'* (Uppsala, 1957), p. 54 n.
[2] This is now in the Nationalbibliothek, Vienna: MS. 8959. It is reprinted in Victor von Klarwill, Ed., *The Fugger News-Letters 1568–1605*, translated by Pauline de Chary (1924), pp. 85–89.
[3] Gunnar Boklund, *op. cit.*, pp. 36–38.   [4] *Ibid.*, p. 129.
[5] *Ibid.*, pp. 149–50; 167–8.

as saleable commodities, and great men, deserted by their parasites, have to face death alone.[1]

The difference between the real first Duchess of Bracciano and Webster's saintly Isabella is caused by accident as well as design. The dramatist was probably quite ignorant of the facts of the adulterous Duchess' death four years before the Duke met Vittoria. In the Fugger News-Letters' account of the relationship of the Duke with his Duchess and with Vittoria, what was probably true is juxtaposed with speculation and with falsehood. It is implied that the separation between Paulo Giordano and Isabella may perhaps have been caused by emotional and temperamental difficulties; and it is this implicit reason for their unsatisfactory marriage that leads to the Duke's interest in Vittoria:

> But as the said Prince had but little sexual intercourse with the former Duchess of Florence, he was induced by fleshly desire to break his marriage vows.

Vittoria's unwillingness to be unfaithful to her husband is given as the reason for the latter's murder at Paulo Giordano's command, and her subsequent refusal to yield to the Duke because his wife is still living leads to Isabella's murder.[2]

John Webster's Isabella lives apart from her husband, but is cold and saintly. Moreover, Webster's Camillo is not the young Francesco Peretti to whom Vittoria would not be unfaithful: he is old and almost certainly impotent, so unresponsive to and unappreciative of her youth and beauty that he, no less than her lover the Duke, would employ her brother Flamineo to bring them to bed together.[3]

His sources, not his powers of selecting, compressing or altering events, are responsible for Webster's lack of reference to the two early marriage ceremonies of Vittoria and Paulo Giordano; for the idea that Bracciano died of poisoning;[4] for his heir being called Giovanni instead of Virginio; and for the quite unhistorical refusal of the new Pope to pursue Vittoria or take vengeance for his nephew's death.[5] The sources would have led Webster to make Lodovico per-

---

[1] For detailed examinations of the relevance of Flamineo to the play's action see Gunnar Boklund, op. cit., pp. 158–61 and B. J. Layman, 'The Equilibrium of Opposites in The White Devil: A Reinterpretation', PMLA, LXXIV (1959), 336–47.

[2] The Fugger News-Letters 1568–1605, pp. 85–86.

[3] Webster's awareness of the temptations resultant upon the physical and emotional tensions of a sterile union between a pretty young woman and an impotent old courtier is made more explicit in his treatment of the relationship between Julia and the Cardinal of Aragon in The Duchess of Malfi. See The Duchess of Malfi, II. iv, 27–36.

[4] See Gunnar Boklund, op. cit., pp. 116 n. and 135 n.

[5] A full account of 'what Webster probably knew' is given by Gunnar Boklund, ibid., pp. 135–7. Dr. Boklund makes the point that this was, indeed, largely unhistorical.

sonally responsible for Vittoria's death, and to characterize him as a
villainous murderer; but not to associate him with the pirates who
marauded the Italian coast[1] or to present him as in love with Isabella.
They could not have contributed much to the delineation of Vittoria's
brothers. Marcello was revealed as implicated in Francesco Peretti's
death and was supposed to be in Bracciano's employment; 'a certain
Duke Flamineo'[2] was the brother who died with her. Rupert Brooke's
suggestion that Webster switched the brothers' names because
Marcello was more appropriate for a pure young hero, Flamineo for
an amazing villain,[3] may be correct. The accurate description of one
method of electing a Pope – a method which, in fact, is not that described in detail in *A Letter Lately written from Rome* – was derived
from Webster's reading of Jérôme Bignon's *A Briefe, But an Effectuall
Treatise of the Election of Popes*, translated into English in 1605;[4] but
the magnificent central scene of the play, that of Vittoria's arraignment, is Webster's own. None of the sources which we think he knew
refer to any kind of trial of Vittoria, though her confinement to a
nunnery is mentioned.[5]

Whether Webster's sources told the story of Vittoria and Bracciano
accurately or not, they told it briefly, thus leaving him almost entirely
free to transform narrative into drama through characterization, and
to order the action of his play according to certain patterns formed
by the establishment of relationships between characters: for example, between Francisco de Medici and Count Lodovico; Lodovico
and Zanche; Zanche and Flamineo. His sources presented Vittoria
Corombona's career as beginning with her resistance to Bracciano's
importunity and concluding with her being brutally murdered while
at prayer. Yet this seemingly pious woman was apparently to some
extent involved in the murders of her own husband and the first
Duchess of Bracciano. Far from attempting to reconcile these con-
flicting aspects of his heroine's personality, Webster made her even
more elusive of analysis than she must have been in real life. He reduced to a mere hint[6] her unwillingness to be unfaithful to her husband, but stressed her religious fortitude in the face of death. He
gave his audience some reason to pity Vittoria as the neglected wife of
Camillo and the saleable goods to be prostituted to her brother's
desire for advancement, yet showed her in the last scene capable of
cheating her brother to save her own skin and of attempting to
murder him by the brutal, animal method of trampling him to death.
It is obvious from the large number of accounts of her life that
Vittoria must have excited curiosity and speculation among her con-

---

[1] See II, i, 142–3 n.   [2] *The Fugger News-Letters 1568–1605*, p. 87.
[3] Rupert Brooke, *John Webster and the Elizabethan Drama* (1916), p. 237.
[4] See IV, iii n. (p. 88 below).   [5] See Gunnar Boklund, *op. cit.*, pp. 111–12.
[6] See I. ii, 280–82.

temporaries no less than among scholars and historians for hundreds
of years after her death.[1] In real life the opportunities for the inter-
ested public to judge her for themselves must have been rare; in his
play John Webster gave Vittoria a public trial, in fact throughout the
play, but especially in the great scene of her arraignment. It is in
this scene, supremely, that Vittoria defies analysis and challenges our
judgment, not only of herself, but of her accusers.

The facts that Vittoria is right in so many things while her judges
are wrong, and that she is able to handle her own defence so much
more efficiently than they can conduct a case against her provide
grounds for admiration, but not for judgment: for the judges are
in some senses right to bring her to trial, if wrong in their method
of procedure; and if Vittoria is an arrant whore, the Cardinal
Monticelso is an unchristianly arrogant churchman.[2]

In her trial, as throughout the play, Vittoria remains a white
devil,[3] a devil in crystal who at times appears to be a saint.[4] When she
is his mistress Brachiano distrusts her, calls her a whore; when she
is his wife and he is dying, he thinks of her as a good woman for
whom infinite worlds were too little; he denies himself a last kiss
from Vittoria lest he poison her. Her serving-maid is Zanche, dark-
skinned and treacherous, a black devil who offsets her mistress'
whiteness. It is in the attempted murder of Flamineo that Vittoria
is most devilish, her soul least white: but within a matter of minutes
she is brought face to face with her devilish murderers, in comparison with whose blackness she must again appear white.

All the major characters in the play can see the devil in human
form and feel the devil's power in human life. When Flamineo calls
his sister 'excellent devil' he does so in a tone of approval of her
cunning in instructing Brachiano how to be rid of Isabella and
Camillo. When, in the last scene, he exclaims that Vittoria and

---

[1] In the last hundred years Vittoria's life has been studied in D. Gnoli,
Vittoria Accoramboni (Florence, 1870), J. A. Symonds, *Italian Byways* (1883)
and Clifford Bax, *The Life of the White Devil* (1940).
[2] Charles Lamb's reference to Vittoria's 'innocence-resembling boldness'
(*Specimens of English Dramatic Poets*, . . . (1808), p. 229) provoked some
strong antipathy in other critics, but the ambivalence of Webster's attitude
to his heroine is now generally recognized: see F. L. Lucas, *Webster*, i, 96–97;
M. C. Bradbrook, *Themes and Conventions of Elizabethan Tragedy* (Cambridge, 1935), pp. 189–92; Ian Jack, 'The Case of John Webster', *Scrutiny*,
XVI (1949), 41–42; W. Farnham, *Shakespeare's Tragic Frontier* (Berkeley and
Los Angeles, 1950), pp. 29–30; Clifford Leech, *John Webster: A Critical
Study* (1951), pp. 38–44.
[3] The identification of the white devil with Vittoria may seem obvious, but
John Genest thought differently: 'the White Devil is Flamineo – he assists
Brachiano in debauching his sister Vittoria – kills Camillo and pretends
that he died by accident –' (*Some Account of the English Stage, from the
Restoration in 1660 to 1830* (Bath, 1832), i, 346).
[4] See IV. ii, 85 n. (p. 148 below).

Zanche are cunning devils, Flamineo is railing against their feigned
love of him which his mock death has proved to be real hatred.
Marcello describes Zanche as a devil who haunts Flamineo; Lodovico jokingly refers to her as an infernal. Monticelso sees Vittoria
as a devil in a good shape; Vittoria sees the Cardinal as a devil whom
she would like to have exposed at the day of judgment. Brachiano's
servant Flamineo, no less than his enemies and murderers Lodovico
and Gasparo, recognizes the devil in him. Distracted and dying,
Brachiano himself thinks he can see the devil indeed, wearing a rose
in his shoe to hide his cloven foot. In the last scene Vittoria speaks
of her brother as a most cursed devil;

> thy sins
> Do run before thee to fetch fire from hell,
> To light thee thither.   (V.vi, 137–9)

she exclaims, and her words personify those sins as devils. Similarly,
in the trial scene, Monticelso had spoken of the devil adultery and
the devil murder; and shortly afterwards he had described to
Francisco the many devils categorized in his 'black book'. Flamineo
perceives the power of the devil behind love of gold and lust for
women; Vittoria exclaims against the devil's ability to disguise sin
under sweetness. References to conjuration and exorcism suggest
that man may control the devil; but Brachiano's opening words in
the play

> Quite lost Flamineo

imply both that he has lost the battle against his desire for Vittoria
and that he is a lost soul. When the husband who loved her is dead,
Vittoria cries,

> O me! this place is hell.

This is a fitting description of the world of the play in which the
saintly Isabella and virtuous Marcello have been murdered, the good
old Cornelia has gone mad and the only surviving representative of
goodness at the end is the somewhat priggish child Giovanni. Thus
some critics have been led to assume that Webster's personal
philosophy was pessimistic. He has been accused of having in
general no profound hold on any system of moral values;[1] of revealing in *The White Devil* in particular a confusion of moral purpose, of
presenting us 'with admiration and horror fatally unrelated to each
other.'[2] The belief most obvious on the surface of the play may
indeed be *in unum Satanum*, but the patterns of drama and of
thought with which Webster organized his source material and his
characterization imply a strong belief *in unum Deum* which assures

[1] Ian Jack, *op. cit.*, pp. 38–43.
[2] T. B. Tomlinson, *A Study of Elizabethan and Jacobean Tragedy* (London
and Melbourne, 1964), p. 235.

us that there is a judgment for the White Devil as for others in the play. But the judgment belongs to God, not to the audience.

The dramatic form of the play is that of a tragedy of revenge for murder, a pattern dictated by the enormous success of Kyd's *The Spanish Tragedy*, probably written in the late 1580's, and other plays, including Shakespeare's *Hamlet*, which followed it. The incorporation of ghosts and scenes of real and feigned madness in the action and the use of disguise by Francisco and his accomplices in the pursuit of Brachiano and Vittoria suggest the stock ingredients of the Elizabethan revenge plays of the late 1590's. The revenge plot is organized by Francisco de Medici, Duke of Florence and brother to Brachiano's murdered Duchess. His chief accomplice, Count Lodovico, bears a grudge against the state which banished him at the beginning of the play. A professed secret love of Isabella gives Lodovico a personal motive for avenging her death. In resolving his action according to the pattern of the tragedy of revenge for murder Webster was able to utilize the traditional moral implications of that pattern. Thus the murders of Brachiano, Flamineo and Vittoria satisfy human desires for revenge and, at the same time, represent divinely ordained punishment for evil lives. None the less, the instruments of this divine vengeance are themselves evil. They are therefore sentenced to punishment by the young Duke Giovanni, the fount of justice and rightful executor of God's vengeance in his own dukedom.[1]

Francisco's plot provides a framework for a play which is chiefly concerned with Brachiano and Vittoria who, though indirectly responsible for evil and death, never stain their own hands with blood. Vittoria is a much more powerful figure than the Duke of Brachiano, yet Webster presents her almost impersonally. A mixture of sentiments—curses and considerations of religion—comes from her lips. Her interpretation on the stage must depend on the actress's performance. Vittoria could be characterized as an impudently immoral woman or as a girl bewildered at first by the force of her own beauty and its effect on a powerful Duke. She may be presented in a light which stresses her coldness, her ambition and her cruelty, or in one which gives prominence to her better qualities: her moments of consideration for her mother and her dying husband; her insistence on meting out justice to Flamineo, refusing to reward him for treachery and murder. An ideal performance might reconcile the

[1] A detailed examination of Webster's handling of this dramatic form will be found in Harold Jenkins, 'The Tragedy of Revenge in Shakespeare and Webster', *Shakespeare Survey 14* (Cambridge, 1961), pp. 45–55. For an exposition of the concept of divine vengeance operating through the Sovereign Magistrate as well as the local magistrate, see Hardin Craig, 'A Cutpurse of the Empire', *A Tribute to George Coffin Taylor* (Carolina, 1952), pp. 3–16.

conflicts of Vittoria's character by revealing her as a beautiful and
lively woman, responsive to love and to goodness, but unable to
resist the power of evil in the world around her.

The pattern of thought which Webster uses to organize facts concerned with horror and cruelty into an artistic unit is not single, but
multiple; its main purpose is to show what order lies behind a world
of evil. The play opens in an atmosphere of moral chaos as Lodovico,
the decayed Count, unjustly complains of his just banishment. He
admits, even scoffs at, the murders he has committed—' 'Las they
were flea-bitings'–and goes on to protest against the form of justice
which controls him while evil-doers who are great men, like the
Duke of Brachiano, are able to thrive. Thus, through Lodovico's
complaint, we are introduced to the love-story of Vittoria Corombona, a story that is referred to, not with words of romance, but with
those of blunt reality: 'close panderism', 'seeks to prostitute'. The
rest of the first act is our personal introduction to her. We meet her
cold and tedious husband, her disgustingly obscene brother, her
ineffectual old mother, her wealthy lover and the maid who has a
carpet and cushions ready to provide a comfortable setting for seduc-
tion. This household reflects the moral chaos of the state. Flamineo,
who should care for his sister's reputation, if not for her virtue, acts
as the Duke's pander to win Vittoria to adultery, and plots to get
her husband out of the way that it may be committed easily and soon.
Cornelia's advice and religious warnings, even curses, are disre-
garded with scorn. A great Duke promises only to spend such time
governing his dukedom as may be required to keep his mistress in
state. The picture of perversion and disorder revealed by the first
act is summed up in Flamineo's recognition of the devious paths
that lie ahead:

> We are engag'd to mischief and must on.
> As rivers to find out the ocean
> Flow with crook bendings beneath forced banks,
> Or as we see, to aspire some mountain's top
> The way ascends not straight, but imitates
> The subtle foldings of a winter's snake,
> So who knows policy and her true aspect,
> Shall find her ways winding and indirect.   (I.ii, 335–42)

In the multiple pattern of thought through which Webster brings
order to this chaotic and disturbed world the two most obvious
strands are a general commentary on life at court and a moral commentary which provides a basis for the whole play. Both are introduced in the first scene. Thus the conversation of the opening
minutes of the play fulfils more than the immediate purpose of providing an introduction to its personalities. The first of these com-
mentaries is epitomized in Lodovico's disgusted exclamation:

> Courtly reward,
> And punishment!

which performs the function of a motto to the following action. Yet it is not so much with Lodovico's own reward or punishment that we are to be concerned, but with Flamineo's. Flamineo's preferment in the service of the Duke of Brachiano depends solely on his success in prostituting his sister, Vittoria. When Brachiano is cast down at his lack of progress in the affair, suggesting that he might not be worthy of Vittoria, her brother cries:

> 'Bove merit! We may now talk freely: 'bove merit;
> what is't you doubt?   (I.ii, 17–18)

Vittoria is a commodity which Flamineo uses for his own profit. She is also Brachiano's reward, a reward of which Brachiano is to consider himself worthy. But what has Brachiano done to deserve any reward?

Having introduced this theme, Webster allows it to develop in the action alone for the rest of the first act. It features prominently in Flamineo's complaint to his mother: learning does not pay; sin does. Then, in Act II, Scene i, when Flamineo thinks he is on the road to prosperity, he gives an interestingly callous piece of advice to Doctor Julio:

> Remember this you slave; when knaves come to
> preferment they rise as gallowses are raised i'th'
> Low Countries: one upon another's shoulders.   (II.i, 317–19)

The greater his success, the harder does Flamineo become. When his younger brother Marcello, the only active advocate of virtue in their family, taxes him with acting as Brachiano's engine and stalking horse to undo their sister, Flamineo answers, casually:

> I made a kind of path
> To her and mine own preferment.
> MARCELLO   Your ruin.   (III.i, 35–36)

At first Flamineo taunts his virtuous brother with poverty, but he later links himself with Marcello in a general complaint against great men. Flamineo has not achieved the financial success he had sought:

> ... when we have even poured ourselves
> Into great fights, for their ambition
> Or idle spleen, how shall we find reward,
> But as we seldom find the mistletoe
> Sacred to physic on the builder oak
> Without a mandrake by it, so in our quest of gain.
> Alas the poorest of their forc'd dislikes
> At a limb proffers, but at heart it strikes: (III.i, 46–53)

After Vittoria's arraignment his discontent bursts forth in the rage of feigned distraction, tempered by sardonic humour:

Who shall do me right now? Is this the end of service?
I'd rather go weed garlic; travel through France, and
be mine own ostler; wear sheep-skin linings; or
shoes that stink of blacking; be ent'red into the list
of the forty thousand pedlars in Poland. (III.iii, 3–7)

As for Vittoria, she has been sent to the house of convertites where
she is left to consider how the Duke has fulfilled his promise to
advance her. This is the first time that this theme has been related to
Vittoria, for she has not been presented simply as a woman over-
come with gifts. The jewel which Brachiano offers her serves mainly
as something upon which her brother can make his lewd comments.
She is betrayed more by her own nature than by promises of wealth.
Nevertheless, when Brachiano accuses her of unfaithfulness to him,
womanly rage prompts her to cry out that all she has gained by him
is infamy; that the house she is in is no palace, but a house of penitent
whores.

For your gifts,
I will return them all; and I do wish
That I could make you full executor
To all my sins. (IV.ii, 119–22)

Lewdly coached in his lover's part by Flamineo, Brachiano wins
Vittoria's favour again and promises her a Duchess' title. Flamineo
immediately makes a bid for his own advancement by telling the
fable of the crocodile and the bird. Brachiano takes the hint; but
Flamineo pretends that he was addressing his sister. On the one hand,
he no longer has the courage to speak outright against his master;
on the other he may be looking – as a safety precaution – for more
than one source of income.

So far the theme of reward and punishment has been seen to
touch only the lives of the three central characters in the play. From
Act IV, Scene iii onwards the scope of its application is widened to
include others in the play and the rest of mankind. In this scene we
discover that not even the election of the Pope is free from the suspicion of bribery. Moreover, the person appointed by Francisco,
Duke of Florence to guard against this is none other than the murderer, Count Lodovico, the repeal of whose banishment was signed
by the late Pope on his death-bed. The new Pope is the former
Cardinal Monticelso who, though uncle to Vittoria's murdered
husband, warns Lodovico that persistence in the plan to avenge
Isabella's death is damnable. Yet, so low is Lodovico's estimate of
the new Pope's character that he easily believes that the thousand
ducats have been sent to him by the Pope, though it is Francisco
who has thus provided Lodovico with a subsidy for damnation.

The largest number of references to reward, preferment and
punishment is found in the last act of the play. Disguised as the

Moor, Mulinassar, the great Duke of Florence is promised a pension
from his enemy Brachiano. Flamineo warns him to get the promise
in writing. Zanche, Flamineo's Moorish mistress, is ready to betray
her lover's secrets to Francisco; she even tries to purchase Francisco's
love by promising to rob Vittoria. Marcello, whose death comes with
startling suddenness upon which we are not allowed to dwell, points
a moral in his dying words:

> There are some sins which heaven doth duly punish
> In a whole family. This it is to rise
> By all dishonest means. (V.ii, 20–22)

The fifth act had opened with Flamineo's joyful exclamation that
his sister's marriage had made him happy, and Hortensio agreed
that it was a good assurance, i.e. of prosperity. Yet within a short
time Flamineo has killed his own brother and sees his great master
lying poisoned. The dying Brachiano is oppressed by Flamineo's
importunity, and hints that his secretary has been secretly embezzling
the funds. Brachiano seems to see him dancing on a tightrope with
money bags to balance him. The image, conceived in a distracted
brain, is none the less a just estimate of Flamineo's dangerous career.
No sooner is the Duke dead than Flamineo utters a last disgusted
exclamation on courtly reward, which is parallel to Lodovico's at the
beginning of the play:

> Why here's an end of all my harvest, he has given me nothing.
> Court promises! Let wise men count them curs'd
> For while you live he that scores best pays worst.
>   (V.iii, 185–7)

It is his mother Cornelia who, in her distracted lament for Marcello,
gives the tenor of the play's moral in this theme:

> His wealth is summ'd, and this is all his store:
> This poor men get; and great men get no more.
>   (V.iv, 106–7)

This does not deflect her surviving son from the path of gain at all
costs. He has sold his sister's virtue; he would not hesitate to gain
by her death. So he sums up all the horror and distress of his situa-
tion–which he views in characteristically selfish terms–to steel his
resolution:

> ... All these
> Shall with Vittoria's bounty turn to good,
> Or I will drown this weapon in her blood. (V.iv, 144–6)

Vittoria's answer to Flamineo's demand is the same as Brachiano's
last offer to him: justice, not reward. All that Brachiano had ever
given him was a lease of his life, to be begged a day at a time, for the
murder of Marcello. All that Vittoria offers him is the portion of

Cain: the curse of God. Flamineo teases her, saying that he has jewels
which shall make him scorn her bounty. He fetches Brachiano's case
of pistols and in a sense brother and sister do fight for possession of
this wealth; for each would kill the other rather than be killed. After
the curious mock death, which deceives the audience as well as
Vittoria and Zanche, Flamineo rises only to encounter the disguised
revengers, Lodovico and Gasparo. The murderers do not hesitate to
reveal their identity, and it is Lodovico, who uttered the play's first
comment on courtly reward and punishment, who now makes the
last. Vittoria, asserting some dignity in the face of death, would be
killed by the great Duke of Florence himself. To this Lodovico
replies with contempt:

> Fool! Princes give rewards with their own hands,
> But death or punishment by the hands of others.
> (V.vi, 185–6)

For Vittoria and Flamineo there is no courtly reward; only courtly
punishment. Death may be–as Cornelia said–a reward for poor and
great alike; but even death is a reward that has to be earned. Flamineo
and Vittoria sought reward and preferment by means that could
only earn them the punishment of death.

The second strand in the multiple pattern of thought through
which Webster orders the chaotic world of the play is a moral commentary found in the group of poetic images concerned with blood.
Lodovico lightly dismisses the murders he has committed, though
Gasparo speaks of them as

> Bloody and full of horror.
> LODOVICO   'Las they were flea-bitings;
> Why took they not my head then?
> GASPARO   O my lord
> The law doth sometimes mediate, thinks it good
> Not ever to steep violent sins in blood;
> This gentle penance may both end your crimes,
> And in the example better these bad times. (I.i, 32–37)

Lodovico's life does not mend. His last murder, of which he boasts

> *I limb'd this night-piece and it was my best*

is punished by the state, through Duke Giovanni. What is important
to notice here is that murder is described as a sin first, then as a crime.
It is not the justice of the state that overtakes Vittoria, Brachiano and
Flamineo. It is the justice of heaven. Throughout the play blood and
sin are associated; and it is not always spilt blood that is intended.
Vittoria tells her mother of her yielding to Brachiano:

> I do protest if any chaste denial,
> If anything but blood could have allayed
> His long suit to me— (I.ii, 280–82)

It was accepted that all women, like Lucrece, should prefer death before dishonour. Vittoria valued her life–literally her blood–and would not sacrifice it. Later in the play (III.i, 37–44), Flamineo remarks to Marcello that not even bloodshed is rewarded in a great man's service. A voluntary expense of blood has no material reward. Vittoria is also proud of her blood in the sense of her family. So she cries to the Cardinal at her trial:

> You raise a blood as noble in this cheek
> As ever was your mother's. (III.ii, 54–55)

Yet quite a different view of it is expressed by Lodovico in the following scene. Flamineo has remarked that, for a pair like themselves, a saucer of congealed witch's blood would do to set their faces by in the mornings. So Lodovico suggests that Flamineo give him forty ounces of his sister's blood to water a mandrake. Such images as these contain an impression of a wanton misuse and disrespect of blood; and this impression recurs. Francisco, addressing Monticelso about the probability of Vittoria's responsibility for the murder of Camillo, declares:

> My lord there's great suspicion of the murder,
> But no sound proof who did it: for my part
> I do not think she hath a soul so black
> To act a deed so bloody; if she have,
> As in cold countries husbandmen plant vines,
> And with warm blood manure them, even so
> One summer she will bear unsavoury fruit,
> And ere next spring wither both branch and root.
> (III.ii, 179–86)

Much later Francisco comments on Monticelso's 'black book':

> See the corrupted use some make of books:
> Divinity, wrested by some factious blood,
> Draws swords, swells battles, and o'erthrows all good.
> (IV.i, 94–6)

This is a general comment on the way in which considerations of family quarrels might pervert religion; it does not apply particularly to Monticelso, though it could have been applied to the real Cardinal Montalto, later Pope Sixtus V, or to the Cardinal of Aragon, brother to the Duchess of Malfi, who laid aside his cardinal's robes to command an army and who used his ecclesiastical authority to persecute his sister, her husband and their children.

Among other images of blood may be included the description of Flamineo as a blood-hound, and it may be noted that, when the bird in Flamineo's fable has reminded the crocodile of the need for reward, it is captured in the crocodile's mouth and has to escape from a bloody prison. So Flamineo himself is trapped by his depen-

dence on Brachiano, and his prison is made bloody by the murders
of Camillo and Marcello.

The most important of this group of images are found in the last
scene which contains references to infected blood and blood stains
that will not wash off. The climax is reached in Vittoria's dying confession – or recognition – of the course of her life:

> O my greatest sin lay in my blood.
> Now my blood pays for't.

She had been proud of her blood in the sense of family, was betrayed
by her hot-blooded desires, and now pays for sin with her life blood.
The moral here contains an implicit echo of Gasparo's words to
Lodovico in the opening minutes of the play. The violent sins of
Flamineo and Vittoria are indeed steeped in blood, not by the law,
but through the operation of divine vengeance. In the scene of her
trial Vittoria had asserted:

> Sum up my faults I pray, and you shall find,
> That beauty and gay clothes, a merry heart,
> And a good stomach to a feast, are all,
> All the poor crimes that you can charge me with: . . .
>   (III.ii, 205–8)

She is right; she has committed no crime that men have a right to
judge. The sin she commits is, however, judged by God.

Among the other strands of the multiple pattern of Webster's
shaping thought in the play there is a continual comment on the
lives and deaths of princes. This is explicit in such statements as
Cornelia's

> The lives of princes should like dials move,
> Whose regular example is so strong,
> They make the times by them go right or wrong.
>   (I.ii, 276–8)

It is implicit in the action, in the lives of two great princes, Brachiano
and Francisco de Medici, and the only exemplary prince in the play,
the child Giovanni. Flamineo remarks that the deaths of princes are
solitary. Man's attitude to death is another strand of thought in the
play. The deaths of Isabella and Camillo are acted in dumb show,
making them impersonal, removing them beyond the reach of our
sympathy which is reserved for the group of people actually responsible for these murders: Brachiano, Vittoria and Flamineo.
Marcello's death is unexpected, but he has a moral comment ready
to meet it. Brachiano dies slowly of poison and goes mad before
Lodovico and Gasparo strangle him. Flamineo gives us a conven-
tional stage villain's attitude to death, describing its physical effects
in words which parody the dying speeches of villain heroes of early

revenge plays.[1] After his feigned death he meets his real end with
a satirical stoicism in which his own sardonic humour, displayed
throughout the play, reaches its climax. Vittoria faces her murderers
proudly, defiantly; refuses to let her servant die first, and declares:

> . . . I shall welcome death
> As princes do some great ambassadors;
> I'll meet thy weapon half way. (V.vi, 216–18)

Yet, as the blood flows from her wound she sees it as a payment for
sin. She feels that her soul is driven like a storm-tossed ship, and she
dies with an exclamation at the happiness of those

> that never saw the court,
> *Nor ever knew great man but by report.* (V.vi, 258–9)

Other major groups of images in the play which repay detailed
study are those associated with jewels, diamonds and glass; with
sickness, especially the palsy; and with poison, seen as a cure as well
as a means of death. A peculiar quality of the large groups of images
in *The White Devil* is that they complement the play's action. We see
blood spilt on the stage; we see Brachiano give Vittoria a jewel; we
witness the mental sickness of Cornelia, the death sickness of
Brachiano; Isabella and Brachiano are both poisoned before our
eyes. Though the action never moves far from the courts of princes–
the central scene is played in the ecclesiastical court of a Prince of the
Church–there are many hints of the world outside Italy, and re-
minders of the world of nature outside the confines of a palace. So
the lieger ambassadors attend Vittoria's arraignment and see her
lying dead; Lodovico turns pirate and marauds the sea coasts. The
world of nature is represented by imagery of the sea, ships and storms;
in a very large group of animal images in which we are repelled
by ill-scenting foxes or sense the terror of the screeching of an
owl, the howling of a wolf. The conflict between appearance and
reality, epitomized in the White Devil herself, is underlined by the
conspirators' use of disguise, particularly Francisco's disguise as
Mulinassar, which brings him into contact with Zanche. This conflict is echoed verbally in such phrases as 'painted devils', 'painted
meat', 'counterfeited coin', 'counterfeit jewels'. The interrelation of
images in the poetry of the play may be illustrated by a passage in
which several thematic images are finely woven together:

VITTORIA   You are deceived.
> For know that all your strict-combined heads,
> Which strike against this mine of diamonds,
> Shall prove but glassen hammers, they shall break;

---

[1] For example, Soliman in *Soliman and Perseda* cries that
> The poison is disperst through euerie vaine,
> And boyles like Etna in my frying guts.

Cf. Seneca, *Thyestes*, I, 197–8.

These are but feigned shadows of my evils.
Terrify babes, my lord, with painted devils,
I am past such needless palsy; for your names
Of whore and murd'ress, they proceed from you,
As if a man should spit against the wind,
The filth returns in's face. (III.ii, 140–49)

The last two lines remind us how often two other attributes of the White Devil–the beauty of whiteness or purity, and the ugliness of the devil–are juxtaposed in Webster's verse.

Themes and images communicate the qualities of Webster's thought primarily to the reader in his study. In the theatre Webster communicates chiefly through his characters and the dramatic action. Although the play's subtitle places the Duke of Brachiano before Vittoria, he is not very impressive. As a lover he is ruthless, easily moved to jealousy, as easily brought to fall again at his mistress' feet. Flamineo and Vittoria both know how to handle him. It has even been suggested that there is no evidence that Vittoria is in love with him.[1] Certainly this is much more a tragedy of a brother and sister than of a lover and mistress. Brachiano dies in the middle of the last act; Flamineo survives Vittoria, to hold the centre of the stage for his dying speeches.

Vittoria defies analysis and forbids judgment. Flamineo simply dares us–as once he dared Lodovico–to defy him. Viewed objectively, he excites disgust and arouses condemnation for his villainy; viewed subjectively he appears the most intelligent and amusing person in the play. He is the chief commentator on the action and on the world in general. Moreover, it must be admitted that what he has to say is not only true, but perceptive and, above all, witty, whether it be a comment on the service of great men, on the handling of women, or simply the description of a fool like Camillo or a rogue like Doctor Julio. Flamineo can relieve the tension of a long battle of others' wits by briefly–even clumsily–calling attention to himself, as he does at the end of Vittoria's arraignment:

MONTICELSO   . . . and your bawd—
FLAMINEO [aside]
     Who I?
MONTICELSO The Moor.
FLAMINEO   O I am a sound man again.
                         (III.ii, 262–3)

Doctor Julio remarks that Brachiano's secretary is merry, and it is obvious that people do enjoy Flamineo's wit. He knows all the news, and so the 'background story' for the disguise of Francisco, Lodovico and Gasparo comes naturally from Flamineo's lips as he tells Hortensio the latest court gossip. Above all, though he dies a villain

[1] Gunnar Boklund, op. cit., p. 163.

who has at last been rewarded for his villainy, Flamineo dies as he
lived: mocking life, mocking death, mocking himself; telling some
truth, but striking an attitude of defiance.

Lodovico, Gasparo and, when he is disguised as Mulinassar,
Francisco all echo and respond to Flamineo's satiric comments on
life. The great Duke of Florence seems to enjoy the part of Zanche's
lover, and we notice how his wooing of the maid echoes some aspects
of Brachiano's wooing of the mistress in the first act. Each lover is
told of a dream for which he can provide a ready response; but
whereas Brachiano sought to purchase Vittoria's love, it is Zanche
who tries to buy Francisco's.

Though there is a parallel between Zanche's love and Vittoria's
as there is between Julia's wooing of Bosola and the Duchess' wooing
of Antonio in *The Duchess of Malfi*, the heroines of Webster's two
great tragedies are seen almost in isolation from other women. In
moments of crisis and at the moment of death they are cruelly per-
secuted by men. Of the four chief women in *The White Devil*
Isabella, whom Vittoria never meets, is murdered in the second act,
and though Cornelia lives with Vittoria she would appear to be
deliberately excluded from her daughter's affairs. When Cornelia has
gone mad, Vittoria is left to face death, as she faced her trial, with
only an unreliable serving-maid beside her.[1] The speeches of the
play are full of man's adverse comments on women; its action shows
one woman hounded to death by men.

The White Devil is moving and disturbing, but it is difficult to act
out to a coherent conclusion. The characters of Vittoria and her
brother are complex, making considerable demands on the actors,
and their most difficult scene – that of Flamineo's mock-death – comes
so near the end of the play that faulty performances here can nullify
the effect of its last moments.[2] Despite some good examples of
dramatic economy,[3] despite the unifying force of Webster's thematic
imagery, the construction of *The White Devil* remains episodic. The

[1] Cariola is much more of a companion to the Duchess of Malfi than Zanche
is to Vittoria; but in fact Cariola is the only woman who is ever seen talking
to the Duchess.

[2] Similarly, the last act of *The Duchess of Malfi* presents the actor of Ferdinand's part with the problem of trying to characterize lycanthropy with the
correct balance of horror and seriousness: a feat which must have been
difficult in the seventeenth century and is almost impossible today when the
audience attaches no particular significance to this form of madness and is
dangerously ready to titter – partly to relieve the tension of the play's final
murders – at its representation on the stage.

[3] For example, it is necessary for the plot that Lodovico be one of Isabella's
avengers, and it is necessary for our belief in the world of the play that the
conjuror's powers be given credence. So the conjuror's statement that his
art reveals that Lodovico loved Isabella prepares us for the inclusion of
Lodovico among the avengers, while Lodovico's confession to Monticelso
that he loved Isabella confirms the conjuror's magic powers.

scene of the papal election provides colourful spectacle, but the amount of detail it includes is disproportionate to its relevance to the main plot. Brachiano and Vittoria are never seen alone together; rather they make a series of public appearances. Webster's great tragedies, like Shakespeare's, are rich in ideas as well as poetry. In Shakespeare's tragedies ideas and poetry are successfully fused with action; the plays communicate powerfully with a theatre audience. On the whole, *The White Devil* may offer as much to the reader as to the theatregoer.

Though disappointed at his play's first reception in the theatre, Webster asserts, in his address to the reader, that he had 'willingly, and not ignorantly' chosen to disregard classical example. Praising the work of his contemporaries, he wishes that what he writes 'may be read by their light.' Perhaps he did not intend us to take the verb 'read' literally; but one of the most interesting features of Webster's writing—his extensive borrowing from a wide range of reading—encourages us to do so. A study of this borrowing does not reveal an unimaginative mind, but an original one engaged in an unique method of poetic and dramatic composition.

Originality is the most obvious quality of John Webster's drama. None the less, the major surviving plays—*The White Devil, The Duchess of Malfi* and *The Devil's Law Case*—are so few, and the flaws in their construction so manifest that many critics have felt, and some yielded to, the temptation to classify him as a minor dramatist. Yet no adverse criticism can explain away the peculiar power of Webster's work which distinguishes it from the achievements of his contemporaries. It is not just that his plays make us more aware of human misery than human happiness; it is, rather, that Webster had the courage to face the fact that, though happiness and hope exist, they are indeed often less real than misery and death. His work reveals not only his originality; it reveals his integrity, too. In recognizing this quality in John Webster's mind and art we find the reason for his stature as a dramatist expressed in his own words:

> *Integrity of life is fame's best friend,*
> *Which nobly, beyond death, shall crown the end.*

NOTE ON THE TEXT

This edition of *The White Devil* is based on the text of the first quarto (British Museum copies: Ashley 2205; C.34. e.18 and 840. c.37), which has been collated with later quartos and the principal modern editions and emended where necessary. Q1 (1612), the most authoritative, is based on a manuscript that was prepared, possibly by Webster himself, for the printer rather than the actors.[1] The three

[1] See J. R. Brown, *The White Devil*, The Revels Plays (1960), Introduction, pp. lxiv–lxviii.

succeeding quartos all contain some emendations and introduce
some errors. Q2 (1631) is a page by page reprint of Q1; Q3 (1665)
reprints Q2, marking the beginnings of acts I, II, IV and V and
clearing up some ambiguities in the stage directions. Q4 (1672) reprints Q3, adds scene divisions and amplifies some stage directions.
A few mistakes in Q3 are corrected by reference to Q1 and the
spelling of some words introduces elision not present in Q1 (e.g.
poison'd and *she's* for *poisoned* and *she is*). This edition does not give
a complete collation of the quartos: only those variants which emend
or alter the Q1 text are considered. Major variants are recorded in
the page notes. Readings requiring some comment or fuller notes
are given in Textual Appendix–A, in which minor variants are also
recorded. Turned letters and minor variations in orthography, including the correction of Q1's *to* for *too* and the expansion of Q1's
& to *and* by later quartos, are not normally included.[1]

The text of Q1 is printed continuously without act or scene division, save for the marking of the arraignment of Vittoria. The act and
scene division accepted by most modern editors is that first proposed
by W. W. Greg in 'Webster's "White Devil": An Essay in Formal
Criticism', *Modern Language Quarterly*, III (London, 1900), 112–26.

In 'The Compositor of the Pied Bull *Lear*', *Studies in Bibliography*,
I (1948), 61–8, Philip Williams identified as A and B the two compositors employed by Nicholas Okes to set up the text of Q1, and
Dr. J. R. Brown has since been able to add to the number of dis-
tinguishing characteristics of these two workmen. A knowledge of
these characteristics, of which Dr. Brown makes full use in his
Revels edition of the play, is helpful in emending some orthographical
mistakes, and it is necessary in considering the correct placing of the
stage directions. Both compositors set the text in as small a space as
possible. Compositor B set some stage directions in the margins and,
for sheet L, at the end of the book, Compositor A did the same.
Since such directions have an obvious place in the text (perhaps
indicated by an asterisk, as in I. ii, 109) and their position in the
margin is sometimes inexact they have been removed from it.

Such errors as duplicate entries, omitted entries and some variation
in the names used in speech-prefixes and stage directions (e.g.
Zanche and *Moor*, *Francisco* and *Florence*) are corrected by regulariza-
tion of the speech-prefixes, which have all been expanded, and am-
plification of the stage-directions where necessary. All editorial
additions are enclosed in square brackets.

The elisions and contractions of the Q1 text, like those of the first
quarto of *The Duchess of Malfi* provide some guidance–which may

[1] Thus Q1 gentlewoman;   ; Q2 gentlewoman?; Q3 Gentlewoman?; Q4
Gentlewoman, (III. ii, 102) is collated as: gentlewoman? Q2, Q3 (Q1 gentlewoman; Q4 gentlewoman,).

have been Webster's own – in the scansion of the verse, e.g.:

CORNELIA   O that this fair garden,
Had with all poison'd herbs of Thessaly,
At first been planted, made a nursery
For witchcraft; . . . (I.ii, 263–6)

These elisions and contractions have been retained but not augmented or altered,[1] since the forty or fifty lines where additional
elisions could have been made are not difficult to scan if the reader
follows the guidance provided elsewhere by the text. Otherwise the
spelling of the Q1 text has been modernised. Where two or more forms
of spelling are found (e.g. *taine, ta'en* and *tane; a'* and *o'; ath', a'th'*
and *o'th'; ith'* and *i'th'*; — *t* and — *'d*) I have preferred one form (i.e.
tane, o', o'th', i'th' and — *'d*). Sententiæ, which in Q1 are marked by
the use of italics or by inverted commas, are here printed uni-
formly in italics.[2]

The punctuation of the play is light and requires much more
supplementation than that of *The Duchess of Malfi*. Many speeches
end with a comma, or without any punctuation mark. Where the
following line is an obvious interruption, a dash is added; otherwise
the line is punctuated in accordance with modern practice. Both
compositors used commas where one would today expect to find
colons, full stops or even question marks. The punctuation of Q1 has,
therefore, been augmented where this is necessary to help the modern
reader. Where such augmentation affects the sense of the passage, it
is recorded in the collation. A colon followed by a capital letter is
modernized as a full stop. Punctuation of the stage directions is
erratic. In accordance with the style of this series, single sentence
directions have been left without a full stop.

Q1 is printed in a way which indicates the division of the blank
verse. Lines divided between two speakers are printed continuously
across the page, e.g.

Then when shees hungry. GAS. You terme those enemies
Are men of Princely ranke. LOD. Oh I pray for them.
(I.i, 9–10)

None the less, the compositors' desire to save space led them to make
some mistakes in line division. All variant readings which affect the verse
structure of the play are grouped together in Textual Appendix–B.

Brief collations and notes on the text are given in the page notes.
Where a longer note is necessary, the reader is directed to Textual
Appendix–A or to the Additional Notes.

[1] Exceptions to this will be found at II. i, 153 and V. iv, 42. See also the note
on II. i, 365 in Textual Appendix—A.
[2] Though I have retained them, there are strong arguments for the omission
of the sententiæ markings altogether: see G. K. Hunter, 'The Marking of
Sententiæ in Elizabethan Printed Plays, Poems, and Romances', *The Library*,
5th Series, VI (1951), 171–88; J. R. Brown, *op. cit.*, p. lxx.

ABBREVIATIONS

In collations and notes the following abbreviations are used:

Q1—the edition of 1612 (British Museum copies: Ashley 2205; C.34. e.18. [the Garrick copy]; 840.c.37).

Q1a—uncorrected state of Q1.

Q1b—corrected state of Q1.

Q1c—second corrected state of Q1, found only in sheet M inner forme (in this edition V, vi, 205–78). Variant readings of Q1 are taken from the list given by Dr. J. R. Brown in 'The Printing of John Webster's Plays (II)', *Studies in Bibliography*, VIII (1956), 113–7.

Q2—the edition of 1631 (British Museum copy 644.a.7).

Q3—the edition of 1665 (British Museum copy 644.f.76).

Q4—the edition of 1672 (British Museum copy 644.f.77).

Qq—all four quarto editions.

Dodsley ii—R. Dodsley, *A Select Collection of Old Plays* (1780), vi.

Scott—Walter Scott, *Ancient British Drama* (1810), iii.

Dodsley iii—R. Dodsley, I. Reed, O. Gilchrist and J. P. Collier, *A Select Collection of Old Plays* (1825), vi.

Dyce—Alexander Dyce, *The Works of John Webster* (1857) [a revision of his edition of 1830].

Hazlitt—W. C. Hazlitt, *The Dramatic Works of John Webster* (1857), ii.

Sampson—Martin W. Sampson, *The White Devil* and *The Duchess of Malfi*, The Belles Lettres Series (1904).

Brereton—J. le Gay Brereton, 'Webster's Twin Masterpieces', *Elizabethan Drama: Notes and Studies* (Sydney, 1909) [an expanded version of his review, published in *Hermes* (1905), of Sampson's edition, with notes on readings and verse arrangement].

Wheeler—C. B. Wheeler, *Six Plays by Contemporaries of Shakespeare* (1915).

Lucas—F. L. Lucas, *The Complete Works of John Webster* (1927), i.

Harrison—G. B. Harrison, *The White Devil*, The Temple Dramatists (1933).

Brown—J. R. Brown, *The White Devil*, The Revels Plays (1960).

Dent—R. W. Dent, *John Webster's Borrowing* (Berkeley and Los Angeles, 1960).

FURTHER READING

The following books and articles have made valuable contributions to the study of John Webster and *The White Devil*:

Charles Lamb, *Specimens of English Dramatic Poets, who lived about the time of Shakespear: with notes* (1808).

William Hazlitt, *Lectures on the Dramatic Literature of the Age of Elizabeth* (1821).

John Addington Symonds, 'Vittoria Accoramboni, and the Tragedy of Webster', *Italian Byways* (1883), pp. 156–93.

W. W. Greg, 'Webster's "White Devil": An Essay in Formal Criticism', *Modern Language Quarterly*, III (1900), 112–26.

E. E. Stoll, *John Webster: The Periods of His Work as Determined by His Relations to the Drama of His Day* (Boston, Mass., 1905).

Rupert Brooke, *John Webster and the Elizabethan Drama* (1916).

P. Haworth, 'Prelude to the Study of Webster's Plays', *English Hymns and Ballads and Other Studies in Popular Literature*, (Oxford, 1927), pp. 71–148.

M. C. Bradbrook, *Themes and Conventions of Elizabethan Tragedy* (Cambridge, 1935).

Theodore Spencer, *Death and Elizabethan Tragedy* (Cambridge, Mass., 1936).

Una Ellis-Fermor, *The Jacobean Drama* (1936).

S. A. Tannenbaum, *Elizabethan Bibliographies: John Webster* (New York, 1941).

P. Williams, 'The Compositor of the Pied Bull *Lear*', *Studies in Bibliography*, I (1948), 61–68.

Clifford Leech, *John Webster: A Critical Study* (1951).

Gabriele Baldini, *John Webster e il linguaggio della tragedia* (Rome, 1953).

J. R. Brown, 'The Printing of John Webster's Plays'–3 parts: *Studies in Bibliography* VI (1954), 117–40; VIII (1956), 113–28; XV (1962), 57–69.

Travis Bogard, *The Tragic Satire of John Webster* (Berkeley and Los Angeles, 1955).

Hereward T. Price, 'The Function of Imagery in John Webster', *PMLA*, LXX (1955), 717–39.

Gunnar Boklund, *The Sources of 'The White Devil'* [*Essays and Studies in English Language and Literature, 17*] (Uppsala, 1957).

B. J. Layman, 'The Equilibrium of Opposites in *The White Devil*', *PMLA*, LXXIV (1959), 336–47.

J. R. Mulryne, ' "The White Devil" and "The Duchess of Malfi" ', *Stratford-upon-Avon Studies 1: Jacobean Theatre* (1960), pp. 201–25.

R. W. Dent, *John Webster's Borrowing* (Berkeley and Los Angeles, 1960).

H. Bruce Franklin, 'The Trial Scene of Webster's *The White Devil* examined in terms of Renaissance Rhetoric', *Studies in English Literature*, I, 2 (Houston, Texas, 1961), 35–51.

E. J. Benjamin, 'Patterns of Morality in *The White Devil*', *English Studies* XLVI (1965), 1–15.

Other books and articles, which throw light on particular passages of the play, are listed in the notes on the passages concerned.

THE
WHITE DIVEL,

O R,

The Tragedy of *Paulo Giordano*
Ursini, Duke of *Brachiano*,

With

The Life and Death of Vittoria
Corombona the famous
Venetian Curtizan.

Acted by the Queenes Maiesties Seruants.

Written by IOHN WEBSTER.

Non inferiora secutus.

LONDON,
Printed by *N.O.* for *Thomas Archer,* and are to be sold
at his Shop in Popes head Pallace, neere the
Royall Exchange. 1612.

the famous / Venetian Curtizan: see Additional Notes, p. 143.
non inferiora secutus 'Engaged in no less noble service' (Virgil, Æneid,
vi, 170): 'The words should perhaps be rendered - "following no ignoble
theme" or "a theme not less noble than my rivals or predecessors have
treated".' (Lucas, *Webster*, i, 194)

[DRAMATIS PERSONÆ]

[MONTICELSO, a Cardinal; afterwards Pope PAUL IV.

FRANCISCO DE MEDICIS, Duke of Florence; in the fifth act disguised for a Moor, under the name of MULINASSAR

BRACHIANO, otherwise PAULO GIORDANO URSINI, Duke of Brachiano; husband to Isabella and in love with Vittoria

GIOVANNI, his son, by Isabella

LODOVICO or LODOWICK, an Italian Count, but decayed

ANTONELLI }
GASPARO } his friends, and dependants of the Duke of Florence

CAMILLO, husband to Vittoria

HORTENSIO, one of Brachiano's officers

MARCELLO, an attendant of the Duke of Florence, and brother to Vittoria

FLAMINEO, his brother; secretary to Brachiano

CARDINAL OF ARRAGON

DOCTOR JULIO, a conjuror

*CHRISTOPHERO, his assistant

*GUID-ANTONIO

*FERNEZE

*JACQUES, a Moor, servant to Giovanni

ISABELLA, sister to Francisco de Medicis, and wife to Brachiano

VITTORIA COROMBONA, a Venetian Lady, first married to Camillo, afterwards to Brachiano

CORNELIA, mother to Vittoria, Flamineo and Marcello

ZANCHE, a Moor; servant to Vittoria

MATRONA of the House of Convertites

AMBASSADORS	PHYSICIANS
COURTIERS	LAWYERS
OFFICERS	ATTENDANTS
CHANCELLOR	REGISTER
PAGE	ARMOURER
CONJUROR	CONCLAVIST]

* non-speaking parts or 'ghost characters'

    [DRAMATIS PERSONÆ]: see Additional Notes, p. 143.

MONTICELSO. Some stage directions give the form 'Montcelso'. The real Cardinal Montalto, uncle of Vittoria's husband, Francesco Peretti, took the title of Sixtus V when he succeeded Pope Gregory XIII.

3

TO THE READER

IN publishing this tragedy, I do but challenge to myself that liberty, which other men have tane before me; not that I affect praise by it, for *nos haec novimus esse nihil*, only since it was acted, in so dull a time of winter, presented in so open and black a theatre, that it wanted (that which is the only grace and setting out of a tragedy) a full and understanding auditory: and that since that time I have noted, most of the people that come to that playhouse, resemble those ignorant asses (who visiting stationers' shops, their use is not to inquire for good books, but new books) I present it to the general view with this confidence: 5 10

> *Nec rhoncos metues, maligniorum,*
> *Nec scombris tunicas, dabis molestas.*

If it be objected this is no true dramatic poem, I shall easily confess it, – *non potes in nugas dicera plura meas: ipse ego quam dixi,* –willingly, and not ignorantly, in this kind have I faulted: for should a man present to such an auditory, the most sententious tragedy that ever was written, observing all the critical laws, as height of style, and gravity of person; enrich it with the sententious *Chorus*, and as it were lifen death, in the passionate and weighty *Nuntius:* yet after all this divine rapture, *O dura messorum ilia*, the breath that comes from the 15 20

1 *challenge* claim; demand as a right
3 *nos haec novimus esse nihil* 'we know these things are nothing' (Martial, XIII, 2)
4 *in so . . . presented* Q1 (Q2, Q3, Q4 [omit])
4–6 see Introduction, p. viii above.
6 *auditory* audience
15–16 'You are unable to say more against my trifles than I have said myself.' (Martial, XIII, 2)
16 *have I faulted* have I been deficient; come short of a desired standard
20 *lifen* ed. (Q1, Q2 life'n; Q3, Q4 enliven)
22 *O dura messorum ilia* 'O strong stomachs of harvesters!' (Horace, *Epodes*, III, 4)

12–13 'You [i.e. the poet's book] shall not fear the turned-up noses of the malicious
Nor give robes of torture to mackerel.' (Martial, IV, 86).
A *tunica molesta* was 'the inflammable garment smeared with pitch which was put on criminals destined to be burnt alive in the Amphitheatre or to illuminate the Imperial Gardens.' (Lucas). Brown renders these lines: 'You [the poet's book] will not fear the sneers of the malicious, nor be used for wrapping mackerel.'

5

uncapable multitude is able to poison it, and ere it be acted, let
the author resolve to fix to every scene, this of Horace,

     – – – – *Haec hodie porcis comedenda relinques.*   25

To those who report I was a long time in finishing this
tragedy, I confess I do not write with a goose-quill, winged
with two feathers, and if they will needs make it my fault, I
must answer them with that of Euripides to Alcestides, a
tragic writer: Alcestides objecting that Euripides had only in   30
three days composed three verses, whereas himself had written
three hundred: 'Thou tell'st truth', quoth he, 'but here's the
difference: thine shall only be read for three days, whereas
mine shall continue three ages.'

Detraction is the sworn friend to ignorance. For mine own   35
part I have ever truly cherish'd my good opinion of other
men's worthy labours, especially of that full and height'ned
style of Master Chapman, the labour'd and understanding
works of Master Jonson: the no less worthy composures of
the both worthily excellent Master Beaumont, and Master   40
Fletcher: and lastly (without wrong last to be named) the
right happy and copious industry of Master Shakespeare,
Master Dekker, and Master Heywood, wishing what I write
may be read by their light: protesting, that, in the strength of
mine own judgement, I know them so worthy, that though I   45
rest silent in my own work, yet to most of theirs I dare
(without flattery) fix that of Martial:

     – – – *non norunt, haec monumenta mori.*

25 'What you leave will go today to feed the pigs.' (Horace, *Epistles*,
     I.vii, 19)
31 *verses* i.e. lines
32 *hundred* Q2, Q3, Q4 (Q1 hundreth)
42–43 *Master* Q3 (Q1, Q2 M.; Q4 Mr.)
48 'These monuments do not know how to die.' (Martial, XII, 2.)

29–34 In the original version of this story, told by Valerius Maximus (*De
     Dictus*, III, 7) 'Alcestis' writes a hundred verses in three days. Erasmus,
     Manutius and Lycosthenes say '*Alcestidi glorianti quod ipse perfacile
     centum absoluisset uno die.*' Webster probably found the story, with the
     change of the poet's name to Alcestides (caused by the use of the dative
     form) and the reference to three hundred verses in three days, in
     Lodowick Lloyd's *Linceus Spectacles* (1607).
38–43 George Chapman (*c.* 1560–1634); Ben Jonson (1572–1637); Francis
     Beaumont (1584–1616) and John Fletcher (1575–1625); William
     Shakespeare (1564–1616) and Thomas Heywood (?1573–1641) had all
     written tragedies before 1611–12. Thomas Dekker (*c.* 1572–1632) col-
     laborated with Webster in the citizen comedies *Westward Ho!* and
     Northward Ho!. He is not now known as a tragic writer, but some of the
     lost collaborative plays, written during the period of his dramatic
     apprenticeship in the employment of Philip Henslowe (1598–1604)
     were tragedies.

THE TRAGEDY
OF PAVLO GIORDANO
Vrſini Duke of Brachiano, and Vittoria Corombona.

[Act I, Scene i]

Enter Count LODOVICO, ANTONELLI *and* GASPARO

LODOVICO
Banish'd?
ANTONELLI   It griev'd me much to hear the sentence.
LODOVICO
Ha, ha, O Democritus thy gods
That govern the whole world! Courtly reward,
And punishment! Fortune's a right whore.
If she gives ought, she deals it in small parcels,   5
That she may take away all at one swoop.
This 'tis to have great enemies, God quite them:
Your wolf no longer seems to be a wolf
Than when she's hungry.
GASPARO   You term those enemies
Are men of princely rank.   10
LODOVICO   Oh I pray for them.

5 *in small parcels* in small portions, piecemeal
6 *at one swoop* at one stroke or blow; *swoop* Q4 (Q1, Q2 swope; Q3 swop)
7 *quite* Q1 (Q2, Q3, Q4 quit) requite, reward
10 *rank.* Q1 (Q2, Q3, Q4 rank?)

Act I, Scene i. The action, up to the end of Act IV, takes place in Rome. An interesting and detailed analysis of the opening scene is given by James Smith in 'The Tragedy of Blood', *Scrutiny*, VIII (Cambridge, 1939), 266–72.

1 *Banish'd?* ed. (Qq Banisht?) W. W. Greg thought the scene could possibly be located in a gallery or anteroom to a judgement-hall. '. . . More probably, however, a street, since at the opening of the play the quartos read 'Banished?' (query, not exclamation), as if Lodovico had not heard his own sentence, but had just received the news from his friends.' 'Webster's "White Devil"', *Modern Language Quarterly*, III (London, 1900), 122–123.

2–3 In fact, Democritus did not hold these views, but they were attributed to him by Pliny and, specifically, in Webster's probable source for these lines, North's translation of Guevara's *Diall of Princes* (1557).

7

The violent thunder is adored by those
Are pash'd in pieces by it.
ANTONELLI   Come my lord,
You are justly doom'd; look but a little back
Into your former life: you have in three years
Ruin'd the noblest earldom—
GASPARO   Your followers   15
Have swallowed you like mummia, and being sick
With such unnatural and horrid physic
Vomit you up i'th' kennel—
ANTONELLI   All the damnable degrees
Of drinkings have you stagger'd through; one citizen
Is lord of two fair manors, call'd you master   20
Only for caviare.
GASPARO   Those noblemen
Which were invited to your prodigal feasts,
Wherein the phoenix scarce could scape your throats,
Laugh at your misery, as fore-deeming you
An idle meteor which drawn forth the earth   25
Would be soon lost i'th' air.
ANTONELLI   Jest upon you,
And say you were begotten in an earthquake,
You have ruin'd such fair lordships.

12 *pash'd* ed. (Q1, Q2 pasht; Q3, Q4 dasht) dashed.
16 *mummia* a medicinal preparation made from Egyptian mummies;
    cf. The Duchess of Malfi, IV.ii, 124.
18 *kennel* channel, i.e. gutter
19 *you* Q3, Q4 (Q1 you, you Q2 you,)
20 *call'd* ed. (Q1 cald; Q2, Q3, Q4 call)
20–21 i.e. 'he had sold his estates to purchase dainties' (Wheeler)
22 *prodigal* extravagant
24 *fore-deeming* prejudging

21 *caviare* was extremely rare in the early seventeenth century. The first
   use of the name recorded by *O.E.D.* is in Giles Fletcher's *Of the Russe
   Common Wealth* (1591).
23 *the phoenix*. This legendary bird was supposed to live about a hundred
   years. Only one bird, and that a male, lived at any time, and the young
   phoenix was said to rise from the ashes of the old bird, which died in a
   conflagration of its nest. Thus, if it were possible to have the phoenix
   as an edible delicacy, it would be the rarest dish in the world.
25 *meteor*. 'In Elizabethan cosmology . . . meteors belonged to the sub-
   lunary world of change and decay, and were transitory, of evil omen,
   and the result, or indication, of corruption . . .' N. W. Bawcutt, Ed.
   The Changeling (Revels Plays, 1958), p. 109.

LODOVICO   Very good,
This well goes with two buckets, I must tend
The pouring out of either.

GASPARO   Worse than these,   30
You have acted certain murders here in Rome,
Bloody and full of horror.

LODOVICO   'Las they were flea-bitings:
Why took they not my head then?

GASPARO   O my lord
The law doth sometimes mediate, thinks it good
Not ever to steep violent sins in blood;   35
This gentle penance may both end your crimes,
And in the example better these bad times.

LODOVICO
So; but I wonder then some great men scape
This banishment; there's Paulo Giordano Orsini,
The Duke of Brachiano, now lives in Rome,   40
And by close panderism seeks to prostitute
The honour of Vittoria Corombona:
Vittoria, she that might have got my pardon
For one kiss to the Duke.

ANTONELLI   Have a full man within you.
We see that trees bear no such pleasant fruit   45
There where they grew first, as where they are new set.
Perfumes the more they are chaf'd the more they render
Their pleasing scents, and so affliction
Expresseth virtue, fully, whether true,
Or else adulterate.

---

29 *This well goes with two buckets* i.e. 'the full content of this speech
   is shared between you two.'; *tend* attend, wait for
31 *acted* Q4 (Q1, Q2, Q3 acted,) brought about; performed
38 *scape* escape
39 *Orsini* Q1 (Q2 Vrsini; Q3, Q4 Ursini)
41 *close* secret, private
44 *Have a full man within you.* i.e. 'Be complete in yourself; self-
   reliant.'
45 *such* Q1b (Q1a sweet)
46 *they are* Q2, Q3, Q4 (Q1 the are)
47 *render* give out, emit, yield
49 *Expresseth* presses out

29–30 Cf. *The Duchess of Malfi*, I.ii, 213–49 where Ferdinand and the
   Cardinal use a similar technique in criticizing the Duchess.
43–44 These lines imply that Lodovico's banishment, decreed by the Pope,
   was at Duke Brachiano's instigation. Thus Lodovico is seen as an enemy
   of Brachiano from the start. See W. W. Greg, *op. cit.*, p. 115.

LODOVICO   Leave your painted comforts.   50
I'll make Italian cut-works in their guts
If ever I return.
GASPARO   O sir.
LODOVICO   I am patient.
I have seen some ready to be executed
Give pleasant looks, and money, and grown familiar
With the knave hangman; so do I, I thank them,   55
And would account them nobly merciful
Would they dispatch me quickly.
ANTONELLI   Fare you well,
We shall find time I doubt not, to repeal
Your banishment.   [*A sennet sounds.*]
LODOVICO   I am ever bound to you:
This is the world's alms; pray make use of it: 60
Great men sell sheep, thus to be cut in pieces,
When first they have shorn them bare and sold their fleeces.
                                              Exeunt

[Act I, Scene ii]

Enter BRACHIANO, CAMILLO, FLAMINEO, VITTORIA
COROMBONA [*and* ATTENDANTS]

BRACHIANO
Your best of rest.
VITTORIA   Unto my lord the Duke,
The best of welcome. More lights, attend the Duke.
                        [*Exeunt* VITTORIA *and* CAMILLO]

BRACHIANO
Flamineo.
FLAMINEO   My lord.
BRACHIANO   Quite lost Flamineo.

50 *painted* artificial, unreal
51 *Italian cut-works* a kind of open-work made by cutting out or
   stamping, worn in Italy in the late sixteenth and the seventeenth
   centuries.
54 *grown*: see Textual Appendix—A.
59 s.D.: see Textual Appendix—A.
60 *This* i.e. the following
61 *sell sheep, thus* Qq (Dodsley iii, Dyce, Wheeler and Harrison:
   sell sheep thus   ; Lucas: sell sheep thus,)
 1 *Your best of rest.* 'Apparently a normal idiom for "good night".'
   (Dent)

Act I, Scene ii. This scene would appear to take place in Camillo's house.
   As Brown points out (p. 11 n.) the sennet 'gives force to Monticelso's
   charge that Vittoria "did counterfeit a prince's court." '

FLAMINEO
    Pursue your noble wishes, I am prompt
    As lightning to your service, O my lord!   5
    (*whispers*) The fair Vittoria, my happy sister
    Shall give you present audience. Gentlemen
    Let the caroche go on, and 'tis his pleasure
    You put out all your torches and depart.
                                        [*Exeunt* ATTENDANTS]

BRACHIANO
    Are we so happy?
FLAMINEO   Can't be otherwise?   10
    Observ'd you not tonight my honour'd lord,
    Which way so e'er you went she threw her eyes?
    I have dealt already with her chamber-maid
    Zanche the Moor, and she is wondrous proud
    To be the agent for so high a spirit.   15

BRACHIANO
    We are happy above thought, because 'bove merit.

FLAMINEO
    'Bove merit! We may now talk freely: 'bove merit; what is't
    you doubt? her coyness? That's but the superficies of lust
    most women have; yet why should ladies blush to hear that
    nam'd, which they do not fear to handle? O they are politic!   20
    They know our desire is increas'd by the difficulty of
    enjoying; whereas satiety is a blunt, weary and drowsy
    passion; if the buttery-hatch at court stood continually
    open there would be nothing so passionate crowding, nor
    hot suit after the beverage, —   25

BRACHIANO
    O but her jealous husband.

FLAMINEO
    Hang him, a gilder that hath his brains perish'd with

6 (*whispers*) ed. (Q1 (*whisper* in the margin, opposite l. 7)
7 *present* immediate
8 *caroche* large coach
10 *Can't* can it
18 *superficies* outside covering
22 *whereas* ed. (Qq where a); *satiety* Q1b (Q1a sotiety)
23 *buttery-hatch* half-door over which provisions, especially, drinks
    are served from the buttery (the room where they are stored)

27–28 In gilding, through the application of heat, mercury was drawn off
    an object covered with mercury and gold. The mercury vapour was
    poisonous and thus gilders, by inhaling it, became subject to tremors
    and insanity.
27–33. For an analysis of these lines see J. R. Brown, *The White Devil*,
    Introduction, p. xlviii.

quicksilver is not more cold in the liver. The great barriers
moulted not more feathers than he hath shed hairs, by the
confession of his doctor. An Irish gamester that will play   30
himself naked, and then wage all downward, at hazard, is
not more venturous. So unable to please a woman that
like a Dutch doublet all his back is shrunk into his breeches.
Shroud you within this closet, good my lord;
Some trick now must be thought on to divide   35
My brother-in-law from his fair bed-fellow.

BRACHIANO

O should she fail to come, —

FLAMINEO

I must not have your lordship thus unwisely amorous; I
myself have loved a lady and pursued her with a great deal
of under-age protestation, whom some 3 or 4 gallants that   40
have enjoyed would with all their hearts have been glad to
have been rid of. 'Tis just like a summer bird-cage in a
garden: the birds that are without, despair to get in, and
the birds that are within despair and are in a consumption
for fear they shall never get out. Away, away my lord,   45

Enter CAMILLO

See, here he comes.

[*Exit* BRACHIANO; FLAMINEO *speaks aside*]
This fellow by his apparel
Some men would judge a politician,
But call his wit in question you shall find it
Merely an ass in's foot-cloth. [*To* CAMILLO] How now,
brother,

28 *the liver* the supposed seat of the passions; *great barriers* waist
    high barriers which prevented dangerous close fighting during
    duels which wcre performed for entertainment
29 *moulted* i.e. caused the plumes of the combatants' helmets to fall
31 *wage all downward* Q1 (Q2, Q3, Q4 wage all downwards): see
    Additional Notes, p. 143.
33 *Dutch doublet:* a Dutch doublet was close-fitting, its accompany-
    ing breeches were wide; *back* virility (*cf. The Duchess of Malfi,* II.
    iv, 53–56.)
40 *under-age protestation* immature wooing
44 *consumption* a wasting disease
47 *politician* crafty person   49 *in's* in his

29 *shed hairs.* F. L. Lucas says that this implies the shedding of hairs
    through the treatment of venereal disease (*Webster,* i, 202) but Brown
    thinks that possibly it here merely implies lack of virility (p. 13 n.).
49 *foot-cloth* an ornamental cloth which covered the horse's back and hung
    down to the ground. It was considered a sign of dignity. Thus Camillo's
    long gown, also worn as a sign of dignity, resembles the foot-cloth. His
    mind is like the dull ass under the dignified trappings.

What, travelling to bed to your kind wife?   50
CAMILLO
I assure you brother, no. My voyage lies
More northerly, in a far colder clime;
I do not well remember, I protest,
When I last lay with her.
FLAMINEO   Strange you should lose your count.
CAMILLO
We never lay together but ere morning   55
There grew a flaw between us.
FLAMINEO   'T had been your part
To have made up that flaw.
CAMILLO   True, but she loathes
I should be seen in't.
FLAMINEO   Why sir, what's the matter?
CAMILLO
The Duke your master visits me, I thank him,
And I perceive how like an earnest bowler   60
He very passionately leans that way,
He should have his bowl run.
FLAMINEO   I hope you do not think —
CAMILLO
That noblemen bowl booty? 'Faith his cheek
Hath a most excellent bias; it would fain
Jump with my mistress.
FLAMINEO   Will you be an ass   65
Despite your Aristotle or a cuckold
Contrary to your ephemerides

---

50 *travelling* Q3, Q4 (Q1, Q2 travailing). Webster may have intended
a pun on the two meanings implicit in the spelling of Q1: travelling; working hard.
54 *lose* Q4 (Q1, Q2, Q3 loose); *count* a double entendre
56–57 *flaw* storm, squall; crack, imperfection
61–62 *that way,* / *He* i.e. that way, that he . . .
66 *your* Q3, Q4 (Q1, Q2 you); *Despite your Aristotle* illogically
(Sampson); 'despite your knowledge of Aristotle' (Lucas)
67 *ephemerides* almanac or calendar containing astrological or
meteorological predictions for each day of a specific period

63–65 Camillo's quibbles refer to the game of bowls. In bowling booty two
players combined together against a third. 'Booty' also carries the usual
connotations of plunder. The 'cheek' is the round surface of the bowl;
the 'bias' is a weight in its side; the mistress is the 'jack' at which the
bowls are aimed. To 'jump with' is to run up against; also to lie with.

Which shows you under what a smiling planet
You were first swaddled?

CAMILLO   Pew wew, sir tell not me
Of planets nor of ephemerides.   70
A man may be made cuckold in the day-time
When the stars' eyes are out.

FLAMINEO   Sir God boy you,
I do commit you to your pitiful pillow
Stuff'd with horn-shavings.

CAMILLO   Brother?

FLAMINEO   God refuse me,
Might I advise you now your only course   75
Were to lock up your wife.

CAMILLO   'Twere very good.

FLAMINEO
Bar her the sight of revels.

CAMILLO   Excellent.

FLAMINEO
Let her not go to church, but like a hound
In leon at your heels.

CAMILLO   'Twere for her honour.

FLAMINEO
And so you should be certain in one fortnight,   80
Despite her chastity or innocence
To be cuckolded, which yet is in suspense:
This is my counsel and I ask no fee for't.

CAMILLO
Come, you know not where my nightcap wrings me.

FLAMINEO
Wear it o'th' old fashion, let your large ears come through,   85
it will be more easy; nay, I will be bitter: bar your wife of
her entertainment: women are more willingly and more
gloriously chaste, when they are least restrained of their
liberty. It seems you would be a fine capricious mathematically jealous coxcomb, take the height of your own   90

72 *God boy you* God buy you, i.e. 'God be with you'
74 *horn-shavings* shavings from the horns which were supposed to
   grow on the foreheads of men cuckolded by their wives' adultery;
   God refuse me 'May God cast me off' (an oath)
78 *but* except
79 *leon* leash: see Textual Appendix-A.
84 *wrings* pinches. (The nightcap would be tight if there were
   cuckold's horns on Camillo's forehead.)
89–90 *mathematically* with mathematical accuracy

horns with a Jacob's staff afore they are up. These politic
enclosures for paltry mutton makes more rebellion in the
flesh than all the provocative electuaries doctors have
uttered since last Jubilee.

CAMILLO

This does not physic me.   95

FLAMINEO

It seems you are jealous. I'll show you the error of it by a
familiar example: I have seen a pair of spectacles fashion'd
with such perspective art, that lay down but one twelve
pence o'th' board, 'twill appear as if there were twenty;
now should you wear a pair of these spectacles, and see   100
your wife tying her shoe, you would imagine twenty hands
were taking up of your wife's clothes, and this would put
you into a horrible causeless fury.

CAMILLO

The fault there sir is not in the eyesight—

FLAMINEO

True, but they that have the yellow jaundice, think all   105
objects they look on to be yellow. Jealousy is worser, her
fits present to a man, like so many bubbles in a basin of
water, twenty several crabbed faces; many times makes
his own shadow his cuckold-maker.

Enter [VITTORIA] COROMBONA

See she comes; what reason have you to be jealous of this   110
creature? What an ignorant ass or flattering knave might

91 *Jacob's staff* an instrument for measuring heights and distances;
   politic cunning
92 makes Q1, Q2, Q3 (Q4 make)
93 *provocative electuaries* aphrodisiacs which excite to lust
94 *uttered* put forth for sale; *last* Q1, Q2 (Q3, Q4 the last)
106 *worser* Q1 (Q2, Q3, Q4 worse)   107 *fits* Q3, Q4 (Q1, Q2 fit's)
108 *several* different

---

92 *mutton* ed. (Qq mutton,) loose women (slang). The passage also refers
   to the enclosure of land for sheepfarming by rich landowners. This
   caused great hardship and provoked minor peasants' risings in the early
   seventeenth century.
94 *Jubilee*. Since the institution of the year of Jubilee in 1300 by Pope
   Boniface VIII as a time when plenary indulgence could be obtained by
   certain acts of piety, the period between recurrances of the year had
   been reduced from a hundred years to fifty, and in 1450, to twenty-five
   years. The 'last Jubilee' before the performance of the play would
   therefore have been in 1600.
97–99: these spectacles were made from glass cut into facets by optical skill
   so that one image was made to seem a hundred.

he be counted, that should write sonnets to her eyes, or call
her brow the snow of Ida, or ivory of Corinth, or compare
her hair to the blackbird's bill, when 'tis liker the blackbird's feather. This is all. Be wise; I will make you friends   115
and you shall go to bed together; marry look you, it shall
not be your seeking, do you stand upon that by any means;
walk you aloof, I would not have you seen in't. Sister,
[*aside to* VITTORIA] my lord attends you in the banqueting-
house—your husband is wondrous discontented.   120

VITTORIA

I did nothing to displease him, I carved to him at supper-
time.

FLAMINEO [*aside to* VITTORIA]

You need not have carved him in faith, they say he is a capon
already. I must now seemingly fall out with you.—Shall a
gentleman so well descended as Camillo—a lousy slave that   125
within this twenty years rode with the black-guard in the
Duke's carriage 'mongst spits and dripping-pans,—

CAMILLO

Now he begins to tickle her.

FLAMINEO

An excellent scholar,—one that hath a head fill'd with
calves' brains without any sage in them,—come crouching   130
in the hams to you for a night's lodging—that hath an itch
in's hams, which like the fire at the glass-house hath not

---

117 *stand upon* be urgent or insistent about   118 *aloof* at a distance
119 *attends* waits for.
121 *carved* served at table; made advances to ('a sort of digitary ogle'
      Lucas)
123 *carved* castrated; *capon* a castrated cock.
126 *black-guard* meanest drudges; scullions and turnspits
127 *carriage* baggage train   128 *tickle* excite, arouse.
130 *calves' brains* usual meaning; fools' brains; *sage* the herb; wisdom
130–31 *crouching in the hams* squatting down in a position of humility
      or pleading
131 *itch* irritating desire; disease
132 *hams* thighs and buttocks; *glass-house* glass factory. There was a famous
      one near the Blackfriars theatre: *cf. The Duchess of Malfi*, II. ii, 6; IV.
      ii, 78.

---

113 *Ida* was the sacred mountain, rising above Troy. Brown thinks the
      reference here may be ironic, for Ida was usually associated with the
      green groves where Paris lived as a shepherd; or, possibly, Ida is the
      mountain in Crete.
113 *ivory of Corinth*. Corinth was a trading centre famous for its expensive
      wares, including marble and beautiful prostitutes. Perhaps Flamineo
      is thinking of the latter.
114–15: the blackbird's bill was yellow; his feathers black.

gone out this seven years.—Is he not a courtly gentleman?—
When he wears white satin one would take him by his black
muzzle to be no other creature than a maggot.—You are a   135
goodly foil, I confess, well set out—but cover'd with a false
stone yon counterfeit diamond.

CAMILLO
He will make her know what is in me.

FLAMINEO
Come, my lord attends you; thou shalt go to bed to my lord.

CAMILLO
Now he comes to't.   140

FLAMINEO
With a relish as curious as a vintner going to taste new wine.
[*To* CAMILLO] I am opening your case hard.

CAMILLO
A virtuous brother, o' my credit.

FLAMINEO
He will give thee a ring with a philosopher's stone in it.

CAMILLO
Indeed I am studying alchemy.   145

FLAMINEO
Thou shalt lie in a bed stuff'd with turtles' feathers, swoon
in perfumed linen like the fellow was smothered in roses;
so perfect shall be thy happiness, that as men at sea think
land and trees and ships go that way they go, so both heaven
and earth shall seem to go your voyage. Shalt meet him,   150
'tis fix'd, with nails of diamonds to inevitable necessity.

---

136 *foil* thin metal foil placed under a gem to enhance its brilliance;
   setting for a jewel; *cover'd* Q3, Q4 (Q1a couer; Q1b couerd; Q2
   couer'd): a double entendre
137 *yon* Q1b, Q3 (Q1a your; Q2, Q4 you)
139 Flamineo refers to Brachiano; Camillo thinks Flamineo speaks of
   him.
142 *case* usual (legal) meaning; a case of wine; also a double entendre.
146 *turtles'* i.e. turtle doves'; turtle doves were proverbially renowned
   for devotion to their mates.

---

144 The *philosopher's stone*, sought after by the experiments of the alchemist, would turn base metals to gold; prolong life; and cure disease.
   Flamineo uses the phrase as a double entendre.
147 *smothered in roses:* cf. *The Duchess of Malfi*, IV.ii, 213–14.
151 *nails of diamond.* Dent (p. 83) points out that Webster is here merely
   repeating an idea found in de Serres-Matthieu, *General Inventorie*,
   '. . . that which was yesterday voluntarie, is this day fastened with
   nayles of Diamonds to an ineuitable necessity.'

VITTORIA [*aside to* FLAMINEO]
How shall's rid him hence?

FLAMINEO
I will put breese in's tail, set him gadding presently. [*To*
CAMILLO] I have almost wrought her to it, I find her coming,
but might I advise you now for this night I would not lie   155
with her; I would cross her humour to make her more
humble.

CAMILLO
Shall I? Shall I?

FLAMINEO
It will show in you a supremacy of judgement.

CAMILLO
True, and a mind differing from the tumultuary opinion,   160
for *quae negata grata.*

FLAMINEO
Right: you are the adamant shall draw her to you, though
you keep distance off.

CAMILLO
A philosophical reason.

FLAMINEO
Walk by her o' the nobleman's fashion, and tell her you   165
will lie with her at the end of the progress.

CAMILLO
Vittoria, I cannot be induc'd or as a man would say incited —

VITTORIA
To do what sir?

CAMILLO
To lie with you tonight; your silkworm useth to fast every
third day, and the next following spins the better. Tomorrow   170
at night I am for you.

152 *shall's* shall us
153 *breese* gadflies; *presently* immediately
154 *coming* forward
156 *humour* mood, inclination
160 *tumultuary* irregular, hastily formed
161 *quae negata grata* 'what is denied is desired'
162 *adamant* loadstone, magnet and (by confused etymology) the
    hardest metal or stone
166 *progress* state journey
169 *useth to* is accustomed to

169–70 *every third day*. Brown notes that 'silkworms fast two days before they
spin, and then spin for not more than nine days consecutively without
food.' (p. 22 n.) There was considerable interest in the possibility of
founding a silk industry in England at this time.

VITTORIA

You'll spin a fair thread, trust to't.

FLAMINEO

But do you hear, I shall have you steal to her chamber
about midnight.

CAMILLO

Do you think so? Why look you brother, because you shall   175
not think I'll gull you, take the key, lock me into the chamber, and say you shall be sure of me.

FLAMINEO

In troth I will, I'll be your jailer once;
But have you ne'er a false door?

CAMILLO

A pox on't, as I am a Christian tell me tomorrow how   180
scurvily she takes my unkind parting.

FLAMINEO

I will.

CAMILLO

Didst thou not mark the jest of the silkworm?
Good night: in faith I will use this trick often, —

FLAMINEO

Do, do, do.   *Exit* CAMILLO   185
So now you are safe. Ha ha ha, thou entanglest thyself
in thine own work like a silkworm.   *Enter* BRACHIANO
Come sister, darkness hides your blush; women are like
curs'd dogs, civility keeps them tied all daytime, but they
are let loose at midnight; then they do most good or most   190
mischief. My lord, my lord.

BRACHIANO

Give credit: I could wish time would stand still
And never end this interview, this hour,
But all delight doth itself soon'st devour.

ZANCHE *brings out a carpet, spreads it and lays on it two fair*
cushions. Enter CORNELIA [*listening, behind*].

181 *scurvily* sourly
183 *mark* Q4 (Q1, Q2, Q3 make; Wheeler ?take)
189 *curs'd* fierce, savage; *civility* Q1 (Q2, Q3, Q4 cruelty) civil order

---

172 *You'll spin a fair thread.* This proverbial phrase was usually applied
ironically to a badly performed action. Brown calls attention to a close
parallel to Vittoria's usage in Sharpham's *Cupid's Whirligig* (1607):
'. . . haue not I spun a faire thred . . . to be a verry Baude, and arrant
wittall.' (p. 22 n.)
173-4 Flamineo is, perhaps, suggesting that Camillo set a wife trap, to
catch Vittoria with a lover; but Camillo thinks that he is advocating
spending the night with Vittoria after all.

Let me into your bosom happy lady,   195
Pour out instead of eloquence my vows;
Loose me not madam, for if you forgo me
I am lost eternally.
VITTORIA   Sir in the way of pity
I wish you heart-whole.
BRACHIANO   You are a sweet physician.
VITTORIA
Sure sir a loathed cruelty in ladies   200
Is as to doctors many funerals.
It takes away their credit.
BRACHIANO   Excellent creature.
We call the cruel fair, what name for you
That are so merciful?
                    [*Embraces her*]
ZANCHE   See now they close.
FLAMINEO
Most happy union.   205
CORNELIA [*aside*]
My fears are fall'n upon me, oh my heart!
My son the pander: now I find our house
Sinking to ruin. Earthquakes leave behind,
Where they have tyrannized, iron or lead, or stone,
But, woe to ruin! violent lust leaves none.   210
BRACHIANO
What value is this jewel?
VITTORIA   'Tis the ornament
Of a weak fortune.
BRACHIANO
In sooth I'll have it; nay I will but change
My jewel for your jewel.
FLAMINEO   Excellent,
His jewel for her jewel; well put in Duke.   215
BRACHIANO
Nay let me see you wear it.
VITTORIA   Here sir.
BRACHIANO
Nay lower, you shall wear my jewel lower.
FLAMINEO
That's better; she must wear his jewel lower.
VITTORIA
To pass away the time I'll tell your Grace

209 *or lead*, Q1 (Q2, Q3, Q4 lead,)
211–18: a series of double entendres connected with 'jewel'
216 *Here* Q2, Q3, Q4 (Q1 Heare)

A dream I had last night.
BRACHIANO   Most wishedly.   220
VITTORIA
A foolish idle dream:
Methought I walk'd about the mid of night,
Into a church-yard, where a goodly yew-tree
Spread her large root in ground; under that yew,
As I sat sadly leaning on a grave,   225
Checkered with cross-sticks, there came stealing in
Your Duchess and my husband; one of them
A pick-axe bore, th'other a rusty spade,
And in rough terms they gan to challenge me,
About this yew.
BRACHIANO   That tree.
VITTORIA   This harmless yew.   230
They told me my intent was to root up
That well-grown yew, and plant i'th' stead of it
A withered blackthorn, and for that they vow'd
To bury me alive: my husband straight
With pick-axe gan to dig, and your fell Duchess   235
With shovel, like a fury, voided out
The earth and scattered bones. Lord how methought
I trembled, and yet for all this terror
I could not pray.

223–30 In Q1 'yew' is written *Eu*, the italics emphasizing the punning
          meaning of Vittoria's words.
229 *gan* began
232 *stead of* Q3, Q4 (Q1, Q2 steed of) in the place of; in succession
          to (one who has died)
234 *straight* immediately
235 *fell* cruel, ruthless
236 *a fury* Q1 (Q2 a Furie; Q3, Q4 a Fury) see IV.iii, 125, 151 note;
          voided out emptied out; cleared out

221–39 For comments on and interpretations of Vittoria's dream see P.
          Haworth, *English Hymns and Ballads* . . . (Oxford, 1927), pp. 80–81;
          F. L. Lucas, *Webster*, i, 213; Lord David Cecil, *Poets and Storytellers*
          (1949), pp. 41–43; Gabriele Baldini, *John Webster e il linguaggio della
          tragedia* (Rome, 1953), pp. 79–80; Henri Fluchère, *Shakespeare and the
          Elizabethans* [translated by Guy Hamilton] (New York, 1956), pp.
          112–13; J. R. Brown ed. *The White Devil* (1960), p. 25; R. W. Dent,
          John Webster's Borrowing (Berkeley and Los Angeles, 1960), pp. 87–88;
          Harold Jenkins, '*The White Devil*, edited by J. R. Brown', *Review of
          English Studies*, N.S. XII (1961), 292–4.
226 *cross-sticks*. No satisfactory explanation has been given for this. The
          cross-sticks may be either wooden crosses stuck in a grave or osiers
          which are criss-crossed to protect or bind a grave together. Dent (p. 87)
          records a reference in Ben Jonson's *Masque of Queenes* to cross sticks
          as one of the devices used by witches to raise storm and tempest.

FLAMINEO   No the devil was in your dream.

VITTORIA
When to my rescue there arose methought   240
A whirlwind, which let fall a massy arm
From that strong plant,
And both were struck dead by that sacred yew
In that base shallow grave that was their due.

FLAMINEO
Excellent devil.   245
She hath taught him in a dream
To make away his Duchess and her husband.

BRACHIANO
Sweetly shall I interpret this your dream:
You are lodged within his arms who shall protect you,
From all the fevers of a jealous husband,   250
From the poor envy of our phlegmatic Duchess;
I'll seat you above law and above scandal,
Give to your thoughts the invention of delight
And the fruition; nor shall government
Divide me from you longer than a care   255
To keep you great: you shall to me at once
Be dukedom, health, wife, children friends and all.

CORNELIA [approaching them]
Woe to light hearts, they still forerun our fall.

FLAMINEO
What fury rais'd thee up? Away, away!   Exit ZANCHE

CORNELIA
What make you here my lord this dead of night?   260
Never dropp'd mildew on a flower here,
Till now.

FLAMINEO   I pray will you go to bed then,
Lest you be blasted?

251 *envy* usual meaning; ill-will, malice
252 *scandal*, see Textual Appendix–A.
254–6 i.e. 'Governing my dukedom shall keep me from you only as
      long as it takes to maintain your great position.'
259 *fury* see IV.iii, 125, 151 note.
263 *blasted* blighted; stricken by a supernatural agency; cursed

251 *phlegmatic*. Of the four humours, each characterized by its association
    with one of the four elements, the phlegmatic or watery humour was
    thought to be obvious in a cold temperament. Thus Brachiano may
    here refer to Isabella's 'cold' chastity as well as to her cold personality.
    In either sense she is obviously contrasted with Vittoria.
258ff: see Travis Bogard, *The Tragic Satire of John Webster*, pp. 103–4.

CORNELIA   O that this fair garden,
  Had with all poison'd herbs of Thessaly,
  At first been planted, made a nursery   265
  For witchcraft; rather than a burial plot
  For both your honours.
VITTORIA   Dearest mother hear me.
CORNELIA
  O thou dost make my brow bend to the earth,
  Sooner than nature; see the curse of children:
  In life they keep us frequently in tears,   270
  And in the cold grave leave us in pale fears.
BRACHIANO
  Come, come, I will not hear you.
VITTORIA   Dear my lord.
CORNELIA
  Where is thy Duchess now adulterous Duke?
  Thou little dream'd'st this night she is come to Rome.
FLAMINEO
  How? Come to Rome,—
VITTORIA   The Duchess,—
BRACHIANO   She had been better,— 275
CORNELIA
  The lives of princes should like dials move,
  Whose regular example is so strong,
  They make the times by them go right or wrong.
FLAMINEO
  So, have you done?
CORNELIA   Unfortunate Camillo.
VITTORIA
  I do protest if any chaste denial,   280
  If anything but blood could have allayed
  His long suit to me —
CORNELIA   I will join with thee,
  To the most woeful end e'er mother kneel'd,
  If thou dishonour thus thy husband's bed,
  Be thy life short as are the funeral tears   285
  In great men's.

264 *with all* Q3, Q4 (Q1, Q2 all)
266 *rather than* Q3, Q4 (Q1, Q2 rather)
270 *frequently* incessantly; repeatedly
271 *leave* Q4 (Q1, Q2, Q3 leaues)
276 *dials* sundials
281 *blood* life-blood; bloodshed; sensual desire: *cf.* V.vi, 237–8.
286 *In great men's.* i.e. 'In great men's lives': see Textual Appendix–A.

264 *herbs of Thessaly.* Thessaly, a district of Northern Greece, was renowned for poisonous herbs.

BRACHIANO   Fie, fie, the woman's mad.

CORNELIA
Be thy act Judas-like, betray in kissing;
May'st thou be envied during his short breath,
And pitied like a wretch after his death.

VITTORIA
O me accurs'd.   *Exit* VITTORIA   290

FLAMINEO
Are you out of your wits, my lord?
I'll fetch her back again.

BRACHIANO   No I'll to bed.
Send Doctor Julio to me presently.
Uncharitable woman, thy rash tongue
Hath rais'd a fearful and prodigious storm,   295
Be thou the cause of all ensuing harm.   *Exit* BRACHIANO

FLAMINEO
Now, you that stand so much upon your honour,
Is this a fitting time o' night think you,
To send a duke home without e'er a man?
I would fain know where lies the mass of wealth   300
Which you have hoarded for my maintenance,
That I may bear my beard out of the level
Of my lord's stirrup.

CORNELIA   What? Because we are poor
Shall we be vicious?

FLAMINEO   Pray what means have you
To keep me from the galleys, or the gallows?   305
My father prov'd himself a gentleman,
Sold all's land, and like a fortunate fellow,
Died ere the money was spent. You brought me up,
At Padua I confess, where, I protest,
For want of means, (the university judge me,)   310

289 *his death* Q2, Q3, Q4 (Q1 this death)
293 *presently* immediately
295 *prodigious* ominous; monstrous
302–303 i.e. 'that I may become one of his mounted attendants instead
       of one who has to walk on foot beside his horse.'
304 *means* methods; financial means
307 *all's* all his
308 *brought me up* educated me

282–9 For the significance of this curse, see M. C. Bradbrook, 'Two
       Notes upon Webster', *Modern Language Review*, XLII (1947), 282–3.
       Cornelia later prays for Brachiano's forgiveness: V.ii, 52–55.
298–9 In the real story, Vittoria's husband Francesco Peretti set out with
       only a single torchbearer to keep the assignation which proved to be
       for his death.

I have been fain to heel my tutor's stockings
At least seven years. Conspiring with a beard
Made me a graduate, then to this Duke's service;
I visited the court, whence I return'd —
More courteous, more lecherous by far,   315
But not a suit the richer; and shall I,
Having a path so open and so free
To my preferment, still retain your milk
In my pale forehead? No, this face of mine
I'll arm and fortify with lusty wine   320
'Gainst shame and blushing.

CORNELIA
O that I ne'er had borne thee, —
FLAMINEO   So would I.
I would the common'st courtezan in Rome
Had been my mother rather than thyself.
Nature is very pitiful to whores   325
To give them but few children, yet those children
Plurality of fathers; they are sure
They shall not want. Go, go,
Complain unto my great lord cardinal,
Yet may be he will justify the act.   330
Lycurgus wond'red much men would provide
Good stallions for their mares, and yet would suffer
Their fair wives to be barren, —
CORNELIA   Misery of miseries.

                                        Exit CORNELIA

FLAMINEO
The Duchess come to court? I like not that;
We are engag'd to mischief and must on.   335
As rivers to find out the ocean
Flow with crook bendings beneath forced banks,

---

315 *courteous* polite; like a courtier (i.e. in expensive habits)
325–7: see Additional Notes, p. 144.
330 *Yet may* Q1 (Q2, Q3, Q4 It may)
337 *crook* ed. (Q1, Q2 crooke; Q3, Q4 crookt) crooked; *forced*
    artificial

312–13 Flamineo may mean either that the passing of his youth towards
       maturity rather than academic study or attainment, made him a grad-
       uate; or that his degree was obtained by corrupt conspiracy with an
       older member of the university.
331–3 The source of these lines is Plutarch's *Lycurgus*, 15. Dent comments
       that 'the argument is highly appropriate to both speaker and dramatic
       situation. Flamineo has repeatedly stressed the impotence of Camillo,
       has frequently equated man with the beasts, and is now bitterly attempt-
       ing to "justifie" serving as pander.' (p. 89)

Or as we see, to aspire some mountain's top
The way ascends not straight, but imitates
The subtle foldings of a winter's snake,   340
So who knows policy and her true aspect,
Shall find her ways winding and indirect.   *Exit*

[Act II, Scene i]

Enter FRANCISCO DE MEDICI, *Cardinal* MONTICELSO,
MARCELLO, ISABELLA, *young* GIOVANNI, *with little* JAQUES
the Moor

FRANCISCO
Have you not seen your husband since you arrived?
ISABELLA
Not yet sir.
FRANCISCO   Surely he is wondrous kind.
If I had such a dove house as Camillo's
I would set fire on't, were't but to destroy
The pole-cats that haunt to't, – – – my sweet cousin.   5
GIOVANNI
Lord uncle you did promise me a horse
And armour.
FRANCISCO   That I did my pretty cousin.
Marcello see it fitted.
MARCELLO   My lord, the Duke is here.
FRANCISCO
Sister away, you must not yet be seen.
ISABELLA
I do beseech you   10
Entreat him mildly, let not your rough tongue
Set us at louder variance; all my wrongs
Are freely pardoned, and I do not doubt
As men to try the precious unicorn's horn
Make of the powder a preservative circle   15
And in it put a spider, so these arms

338 *aspire* attain to
340 *winter's snake* ed. (Q1, Q4 Winters snake; Q2, Q3 Winter snake)
S.D. MEDICI ed. (Qq *Medicis*); MONTICELSO Q4 (Q1, Q2 *Mountcelso*;
    Q3 Monu'celso); *little* JAQUES *the Moor* Qq.
2 *wondrous* Q1 (Q2 wonderfull; Q3, Q4 wonderful)
3 *such a* Q2, Q4 (Q1 a such; Q3 Iuch a)
5 *pole-cats* fetid smelling animals, like ferrets; prostitutes; *haunt to't*
    resort to it; *cousin* a term used generally of kinsfolk and often
    applied to nephew or niece

14–18 see Additional Notes, p. 144.

Shall charm his poison, force it to obeying
And keep him chaste from an infected straying.

FRANCISCO
I wish it may. Be gone.   *Exit* [ISABELLA]

Enter BRACHIANO *and* FLAMINEO

                    Void the chamber.
[*Exeunt* FLAMINEO, MARCELLO, GIOVANNI *and* JAQUES]
You are welcome, will you sit? I pray my lord   20
Be you my orator, my heart's too full;
I'll second you anon.

MONTICELSO   Ere I begin
Let me entreat your Grace forgo all passion
Which may be raised by my free discourse.

BRACHIANO
As silent as i'th' church – you may proceed.   25

MONTICELSO
It is a wonder to your noble friends,
That you that have as 'twere ent'red the world,
With a free sceptre in your able hand,
And have to th'use of nature well applied
High gifts of learning, should in your prime age   30
Neglect your awful throne, for the soft down
Of an insatiate bed. Oh my lord,
The drunkard after all his lavish cups,
Is dry, and then is sober; so at length,
When you awake from this lascivious dream,   35
Repentance then will follow; like the sting
Plac'd in the adder's tail: wretched are princes
When fortune blasteth but a petty flower
Of their unwieldy crowns; or ravisheth
But one pearl from their sceptre: but alas!   40
When they to wilful shipwreck loose good fame

---

18 *infected* poisoned; diseased; immoral
19 *Void* empty, clear
25 *church–you* Lucas, Brown (Q1, Q2, Q3, Sampson: church you;
   Q4 church, you)
27 *you that have* ed. (Q1 you have; Q2, Q3, Q4 you having): see
   Textual Appendix–A.
29 *And have to* Qq: see Textual Appendix–A.
29–30 i.e. 'And have [previously] well applied high gifts of learning
   to the ability to use your natural capacity . . .'
31 *awful* commanding profound respect

36–37 Adders were supposed to be able to sting with both mouth and tail.

All princely titles perish with their name.

BRACHIANO

You have said my lord, —

MONTICELSO   Enough to give you taste
How far I am from flattering your greatness?

BRACHIANO

Now you that are his second, what say you?   45
Do not like young hawks fetch a course about;
Your game flies fair and for you, —

FRANCISCO   Do not fear it:
I'll answer you in your own hawking phrase.
Some eagles that should gaze upon the sun
Seldom soar high, but take their lustful ease   50
Since they from dunghill birds their prey can seize.
You know Vittoria?

BRACHIANO   Yes.

FRANCISCO   You shift your shirt there
When you retire from tennis.

BRACHIANO   Happily.

FRANCISCO

Her husband is lord of a poor fortune
Yet she wears cloth of tissue, —

BRACHIANO   What of this?   55
Will you urge that my good lord cardinal
As part of her confession at next shrift,
And know from whence it sails?

FRANCISCO   She is your strumpet, —

BRACHIANO

Uncivil sir there's hemlock in thy breath
And that black slander; were she a whore of mine   60
All thy loud cannons, and thy borrowed Switzers
Thy galleys, nor thy sworn confederates
Durst not supplant her.

FRANCISCO   Let's not talk on thunder.

42 *name* i.e. good name, reputation
46 *fetch a course about* turn tail, refusing to fly to the mark; *about*;
   Q4 (Q1, Q2 about   ; Q3 about,)
52 *shift* change
53 *Happily* Q3 (Q1, Q2 Happely; Q4 Haply) haply, perhaps
54 *lord of* Qq: see Textual Appendix–A.
'55 *cloth of tissue* expensive material into which gold or silver was
   often woven
56 *urge* press by inquiry or statement   57 *shrift* confession
61 *Switzers* Swiss mercenary soldiers: *cf. The Duchess of Malfi*, II.
   ii, 35–58.
63 *supplant her* trip her up, cause her to fall from her position
   talk on Q1, Q2, Q3 (Q4 talk of) talk about

Thou hast a wife, our sister; would I had given
Both her white hands to death, bound and lock'd fast   65
In her last winding-sheet, when I gave thee
But one.
BRACHIANO Thou hadst given a soul to God then.
FRANCISCO   True:
Thy ghostly father with all's absolution,
Shall ne'er do so by thee.
BRACHIANO   Spit thy poison,—
FRANCISCO
I shall not need, lust carries her sharp whip   70
At her own girdle; look to't for our anger
Is making thunder-bolts.
BRACHIANO   Thunder? in faith,
They are but crackers.
FRANCISCO   We'll end this with the cannon.
BRACHIANO
Thou'lt get nought by it but iron in thy wounds,
And gunpowder in thy nostrils.
FRANCISCO   Better that   75
Than change perfumes for plasters,—
BRACHIANO   Pity on thee,
'Twere good you'ld show your slaves or men condemn'd
Your new-plough'd forehead. Defiance!—and I'll meet thee,
Even in a thicket of thy ablest men.
MONTICELSO
My lords, you shall not word it any further   80
Without a milder limit.
FRANCISCO   Willingly.
BRACHIANO
Have you proclaimed a triumph that you bait
A lion thus?

68 *ghostly* spiritual
73 *crackers* fireworks that explode with a sharp report; ?boasts or
   lies (Brown)
76 *change perfumes for plasters* change indulgence for its results:
   disease
78 : see Textual Appendix–A.
79 *thicket* closely packed group
80 *lords* Q1 (Q2, Q3, Q4 lord); *word it* talk excessively or violently

67 *Thou hadst given a soul to God then.* Lucas wondered if this were a
momentary admission of Isabella's goodness or a sneer at the saintliness
of one who would have made a fitter bride for Christ (i.e. as a nun) than
for Brachiano. In support of the latter suggestion Lucas compares the
sentiment with Gloucester's gibe at the expense of the dead Henry VI
in Shakespeare's *Richard III*, I.ii, 105. See Lucas, *Webster*, i, 215–16.

MONTICELSO   My lord.
BRACHIANO   I am tame, I am tame sir.
FRANCISCO
    We send unto the Duke for conference
    'Bout levies 'gainst the pirates; my lord Duke   85
    Is not at home; we come ourself in person,
    Still my lord Duke is busied; but we fear
    When Tiber to each prowling passenger
    Discovers flocks of wild ducks, then my lord
    ('Bout moulting time I mean,) we shall be certain   90
    To find you sure enough and speak with you.
BRACHIANO   Ha?
FRANCISCO
    A mere tale of a tub, my words are idle,
    But to express the sonnet by natural reason,
    When stags grow melancholic you'll find the season—

Enter GIOVANNI

MONTICELSO
    No more my lord; here comes a champion,   95
    Shall end the difference between you both,
    Your son the prince Giovanni. See my lords
    What hopes you store in him; this is a casket
    For both your crowns, and should be held like dear:
    Now is he apt for knowledge; therefore know   100
    It is a more direct and even way
    To train to virtue those of princely blood
    By examples than by precepts: if by examples
    Whom should he rather strive to imitate
    Than his own father? Be his pattern then,   105
    Leave him a stock of virtue that may last,
    Should fortune rend his sails, and split his mast.
BRACHIANO
    Your hand boy—growing to a soldier?

88 *prowling* ed. (Qq, Sampson, Lucas: proling; Dodsley ii, Scott: prouling)
89 *wild ducks* prostitutes (Lucas)
90 *moulting time* i.e. when the mating season is over; when hair is falling through disease: *cf*. I.ii, 29.
92 *tale of a tub* cock-and-bull story; a story that refers to the use of the sweating-tub in the treatment of venereal disease
93 Lucas suggests 'to give a commonsense explanation to my rhyme'
95 *champion* i.e. Giovanni, in his new suit of armour
101 *even* straightforward
106 *stock* line of ancestors (i.e. to be proud of); supply
108 *boy–growing . . . soldier?* Q3, Q4 (Q1, Q2 boy growing . . . soldier.) *a soldier* Q2, Q3, Q4 (Q1 soldier)

GIOVANNI
  Give me a pike.
FRANCISCO
  What, practising your pike so young, fair coz?   110
GIOVANNI
  Suppose me one of Homer's frogs, my lord,
  Tossing my bullrush thus. Pray sir tell me
  Might not a child of good discretion
  Be leader to an army?
FRANCISCO   Yes cousin, a young prince
  Of good discretion might.
GIOVANNI   Say you so?   115
  Indeed I have heard 'tis fit a general
  Should not endanger his own person oft,
  So that he make a noise, when he's a horseback
  Like a Dansk drummer. O 'tis excellent!
  He need not fight; methinks his horse as well   120
  Might lead an army for him; if I live
  I'll charge the French foe, in the very front
  Of all my troops, the foremost man.
FRANCISCO   What, what,—
GIOVANNI
  And will not bid my soldiers up and follow
  But bid them follow me.
BRACHIANO   Forward lapwing.   125
  He flies with the shell on's head.

113 *discretion* good judgement
115 *discretion* prudence; ability to distinguish what is advisable with
    regard to one's own conduct, i.e. when to lead the army and when
    to follow
119 *Dansk* ed. (Q1 danske; Q2 Danske; Q3 Dantzicke; Q4 Dantzick)
    Danish

---

110 Francisco's question is a double entendre. *Cf.* Eric Partridge, *Shakes-*
    peare's Bawdy (1947), p. 164.
111 *Homer's frogs.* Giovanni is here thinking of *The Battle of Frogs and Mice*
    which was a burlesque epic, attributed to Homer. Brown, p. 38 n.
    indicates that Webster's source seems to have been W. Fowldes' trans-
    lation of 1603 which mentions the tossing of the bulrush 'for a pike or
    spear.'
125 *lapwing* the type of precocity. In 'John Webster: Playwright and
    Naturalist', *Nineteenth Century*, CIII (January, 1928) E. W. Hendy
    pointed out that the lapwing's young are incapable of flying until some
    weeks after they are hatched. Horatio's comment on the lapwing that
    runs away with the shell on his head (*Hamlet*, V.ii, 177) shows Shakes-
    peare's greater ornithological accuracy. 'But Webster's phrase is the
    more telling because of its conscious exaggeration.' Such exaggeration
    was, in fact, part of the Elizabethan view of the precocity of the lapwing.

FRANCISCO   Pretty cousin.

GIOVANNI

  The first year uncle that I go to war
  All prisoners that I take I will set free
  Without their ransome.

FRANCISCO   Ha, without their ransome?
  How then will you reward your soldiers   130
  That took those prisoners for you?

GIOVANNI   Thus my lord:
  I'll marry them to all the wealthy widows
  That falls that year.

FRANCISCO   Why then the next year following
  You'll have no men to go with you to war.

GIOVANNI

  Why then I'll press the women to the war,   135
  And then the men will follow.

MONTICELSO   Witty prince.

FRANCISCO

  See a good habit makes a child a man,
  Whereas a bad one makes a man a beast:
  Come, you and I are friends.

BRACHIANO   Most wishedly;
  Like bones which broke in sunder and well set   140
  Knit the more strongly.

FRANCISCO [*calls offstage*] Call Camillo hither.
  You have received the rumour, how Count Lodowick
  Is turn'd a pirate?

BRACHIANO   Yes.

FRANCISCO   We are now preparing
  Some ships to fetch him in.

                         [*Enter* ISABELLA]

                         Behold your Duchess;
  We now will leave you and expect from you   145
  Nothing but kind entreaty.

BRACHIANO   You have charm'd me.

141 *Camillo* Q1, Q2, Q3 (Q4, Sampson: Isabella)
144 S.D. Q4 adds to end of 146 S.D.; (Q1, Q2, Q3 [omit])

142–3 Although the Italian coast was marauded by pirates at the time of the
    action of the play, none of the documents referring to Count Lodovico
    describe him as one. Before his execution at the age of thirty-four he is
    supposed to have admitted that he personally murdered forty people,
    but the exact details of his life between his banishment and his execution
    are unknown. See Gunnar Boklund, *The Sources of 'The White Devil'*,
    pp. 66–68; 79–80.

Exeunt FR[ANCISCO], MON[TICELSO], GIOV[ANNI]

You are in health we see.

ISABELLA   And above health
To see my lord well.

BRACHIANO   So I wonder much,
What amorous whirlwind hurried you to Rome—

ISABELLA
Devotion my lord.

BRACHIANO   Devotion?   150
Is your soul charg'd with any grievous sin?

ISABELLA
'Tis burdened with too many, and I think
The oft'ner that we cast our reck'nings up,
Our sleeps will be the sounder.

BRACHIANO   Take your chamber.

ISABELLA
Nay my dear lord, I will not have you angry;   155
Doth not my absence from you two months
Merit one kiss?

BRACHIANO   I do not use to kiss.
If that will dispossess your jealousy,
I'll swear it to you.

ISABELLA   O my loved lord,
I do not come to chide; my jealousy?   160
I am to learn what that Italian means;
You are as welcome to these longing arms,
As I to you a virgin.

                [*She tries to embrace him; he turns away*]

BRACHIANO   O your breath!
Out upon sweetmeats, and continued physic!
The plague is in them.

ISABELLA   You have oft for these two lips   165
Neglected cassia or the natural sweets
Of the spring violet; they are not yet much withered.
My lord I should be merry; these your frowns
Show in a helmet lovely, but on me,
In such a peaceful interview methinks   170
They are too too roughly knit.

156 *two* Q1, Q2 (Q3, Q4 *now* two): see Textual Appendix–A;
    months ed. (Qq moneths)
157 *I do not use to* I am not accustomed to
160 *jealousy?* Q2, Q3, Q4 (Q1 jealousy,)
161 *I am to learn* i.e. I am yet to learn; *am to* Q1b (Q1a come to);
    Italian i.e. because Italians were proverbially jealous
166 *cassia* a kind of cinnamon; but also used to refer to a fragrant or
    expensive perfume. *Cf. The Duchess of Malfi*, IV.ii, 212–214.

BRACHIANO   O dissemblance!
    Do you bandy factions 'gainst me? Have you learnt
    The trick of impudent baseness to complain
    Unto your kindred?
ISABELLA   Never my dear lord.
BRACHIANO
    Must I be haunted out, or was't your trick   175
    To meet some amorous gallant here in Rome
    That must supply our discontinuance?
ISABELLA
    I pray sir burst my heart, and in my death
    Turn to your ancient pity, though not love.
BRACHIANO
    Because your brother is the corpulent Duke,   180
    That is the great Duke,—'Sdeath I shall not shortly
    Racket away five hundred crowns at tennis,
    But it shall rest upon record. I scorn him
    Like a shav'd Polack; all his reverent wit
    Lies in his wardrobe; he's a discreet fellow   185
    When he's made up in his robes of state,—
    Your brother the great Duke, because h'as galleys,
    And now and then ransacks a Turkish fly-boat,
    (Now all the hellish Furies take his soul,)
    First made this match,—accursed be the priest   190
    That sang the wedding mass, and even my issue.
ISABELLA
    O too too far you have curs'd.
BRACHIANO   Your hand I'll kiss:

172 *bandy factions* form leagues (Lucas); *learnt* Q4 (Q1, Q2, Q3 learn't)
175 *was't* Q3, Q4 (Q1, Q2 wast)
177 *supply our discontinuance* make up for [my] absence
179 *ancient* former
181 *great Duke*: Francisco was Grand Duke of Tuscany; *'Sdeath* [By] God's death!
187 *h'as* he has
188 *fly-boat* a pinnace or small fast boat used in the coasting trade
189 *Furies* Q2, Q3, Q4 (Q1 furies): see IV.iii, 125, 151 note.

---

175 *haunted out* Q1, Q2, (Q4 hunted out). Brown points out (p. 42 n.) that though 'to haunt' could mean 'to frequent' or 'to visit' the closest parallel to the meaning here is not found earlier than *c.* 1679, according to *O.E.D.*: 'My ghost shall haunt thee out in every place.' Q4's 'hunted out' may be correct. 'Or, possibly, Webster intended to combine the meanings of both verbs.'
183–4 *I scorn ... Polack* I scorn him as worthless. In his *Itinerary* (1617) Fynes Moryson reported that the Poles shaved all their heads, except for the hair of the forehead, very close.

This is the latest ceremony of my love,
Henceforth I'll never lie with thee, by this,
This wedding ring: I'll ne'er more lie with thee.   195
And this divorce shall be as truly kept,
As if the judge had doom'd it: fare you well,
Our sleeps are sever'd.

ISABELLA   Forbid it the sweet union
Of all things blessed; why the saints in heaven
Will knit their brows at that.

BRACHIANO   Let not thy love   200
Make thee an unbeliever; this my vow
Shall never on my soul be satisfied
With my repentance: let thy brother rage
Beyond a horrid tempest or sea-fight,
My vow is fixed.

ISABELLA   O my winding sheet,   205
Now shall I need thee shortly. Dear my lord,
Let me hear once more what I would not hear:
Never?

BRACHIANO Never!

ISABELLA
O my unkind lord may your sins find mercy,
As I upon a woeful widowed bed   210
Shall pray for you, if not to turn your eyes
Upon your wretched wife, and hopeful son,
Yet that in time you'll fix them upon heaven.

BRACHIANO
No more; go, go, complain to the great Duke.

ISABELLA
No my dear lord, you shall have present witness   215
How I'll work peace between you; I will make
Myself the author of your cursed vow.
I have some cause to do it, you have none;
Conceal it I beseech you, for the weal
Of both your dukedoms, that you wrought the means   220
Of such a separation; let the fault
Remain with my supposed jealousy,
And think with what a piteous and rent heart
I shall perform this sad ensuing part.

        Enter FRANCISCO, FLAMINEO, MONTICELSO, MARCELLO

193 *latest* last, final
202–3 *satisfied / With* fully discharged by
204 *horrid* frightful   215 *present* immediate
224–5 S.D. MONTICELSO Q4 (Q1, Q2, Q3 *Montcelso*). Qq add *Camillo:*
     an unnecessary duplication.

BRACHIANO
　　Well, take your course; my honourable brother!　　225
FRANCISCO
　　Sister!–this is not well my lord,–why sister!
　　She merits not this welcome.
BRACHIANO　　　　　　　　　　Welcome, say?
　　She hath given a sharp welcome.
FRANCISCO　　　　　　　　　　Are you foolish?
　　Come dry your tears; is this a modest course?
　　To better what is nought, to rail, and weep?　　230
　　Grow to a reconcilement, or by heaven,
　　I'll ne'er more deal between you.
ISABELLA　　　　　　　　　　Sir you shall not,
　　No though Vittoria upon that condition
　　Would become honest.
FRANCISCO　　　　　　　Was your husband loud,
　　Since we departed?
ISABELLA　　　　　　　By my life sir no.　　235
　　I swear by that I do not care to lose.
　　Are all these ruins of my former beauty
　　Laid out for a whore's triumph?
FRANCISCO　　　　　　　　　　Do you hear?
　　Look upon other women, with what patience
　　They suffer these slight wrongs, with what justice　　240
　　They study to requite them; take that course.
ISABELLA
　　O that I were a man, or that I had power
　　To execute my apprehended wishes,
　　I would whip some with scorpions.
FRANCISCO　　　　　　　　　　What? turn'd fury?
ISABELLA
　　To dig the strumpet's eyes out, let her lie　　245

225 *course*; Q4 (Q1, Q2, Q3 course　)
227 *say?* say you?
229 *course?* Q2, Q3, Q4 (Q1 course.)
230 *weep?* ed. (Q1 weepe,　; Q2 weepe:　; Q3, Q4 weep:)
234 *honest* chaste, virtuous
236 *lose* Q4 (Q1, Q2, Q3 loose)
243 *my apprehended wishes* 'the desires of which I feel the force'
244 *fury* Q1 (Q2, Q3, Q4 Fury): see IV.iii, 225, 251 note.

---

244 *I would whip some with scorpions.* Isabella here echoes–with the kind of
　　slight variation that is typical of Webster's borrowing–the young men's
　　advice to Rehoboam in I Kings xii, 11: '. . . my father chastised you
　　with whips, but I will chastise you with scorpions.' Webster repeated
　　the idea in *The Duchess of Malfi*, II.v, 79–80.

Some twenty months a-dying, to cut off
Her nose and lips, pull out her rotten teeth,
Preserve her flesh like mummia, for trophies
Of my just anger. Hell to my affliction
Is mere snow-water: by your favour sir, —   250
Brother draw near, and my lord cardinal, —
Sir let me borrow of you but one kiss,
Henceforth I'll never lie with you, by this,
This wedding-ring.
FRANCISCO   How? ne'er more lie with him?
ISABELLA
And this divorce shall be as truly kept,   255
As if in thronged court, a thousand ears
Had heard it, and a thousand lawyers' hands
Seal'd to the separation.
BRACHIANO
Ne'er lie with me?
ISABELLA   Let not my former dotage
Make thee an unbeliever; this my vow   260
Shall never on my soul be satisfied
With my repentance: *manet alta mente repostum.*
FRANCISCO
Now by my birth you are a foolish, mad,
And jealous woman.
BRACHIANO   You see 'tis not my seeking.
FRANCISCO
Was this your circle of pure unicorn's horn,   265
You said should charm your lord? Now horns upon thee,
For jealousy deserves them; keep your vow,
And take your chamber.
ISABELLA
No sir I'll presently to Padua,
I will not stay a minute.
MONTICELSO   O good madam.   270

---

248 *mummia* Q1 (Q2 Mummie; Q3, Q4 Mummy): see I.i, 16 note.
253–63: see Additional Notes, p. 144.
262 *manet alta mente repostum* Q2, Q3, Q4 (Q1 *manet . . . repositum*):
       'It is treasured up deep in my mind'. Virgil, *Aeneid*, I, 26.

---

266 *horns* i.e. the horns supposedly acquired by the cuckold, the man whose
       wife is unfaithful. Although the cuckold's horns belong to the husband
       Francisco here wishes them on his sister, and thus expresses the hope
       that she may be cursed with the mental agony that they bring with
       them: the misery of jealousy.

BRACHIANO
  'Twere best to let her have her humour,
  Some half-day's journey will bring down her stomach,
  And then she'll turn in post.
FRANCISCO   To see her come
  To my lord cardinal for a dispensation
  Of her rash vow will beget excellent laughter.   275
ISABELLA
  Unkindness do thy office, poor heart break,
  Those are the killing griefs which dare not speak.   *Exit*

                          Enter CAMILLO

MARCELLO
  Camillo's come my lord.
FRANCISCO   Where's the commission?
MARCELLO
  'Tis here.   280
FRANCISCO   Give me the signet.
FLAMINEO [*to* BRACHIANO]
  My lord do you mark their whispering; I will compound a
  medicine out of their two heads, stronger than garlic, deadlier
  than stibium; the cantharides which are scarce seen to stick
  upon the flesh when they work to the heart, shall not do it   285
  with more silence or invisible cunning.

                       Enter Doctor [JULIO]

BRACHIANO
  About the murder.

271 *humour* strange disposition, unaccountable frame of mind
272 *bring down her stomach* reduce the swelling caused by hysterical
    passion (the mother): *cf. The Duchess of Malfi*, II.i, 119–20.
273 *turn in post* return in post-haste.
276–7: see Textual Appendix–A.
282 [*to* BRACHIANO] ed. i.e. Flamineo and Brachiano walk apart,
    claiming the audience's attention till II.i, 319; *do you mark* pay
    attention to; *whispering*; Q2, Q3 (Q1, Lucas: whispering,   ;
    Q4, Dyce, Sampson, Brown *et al.*: whispering?)
284 *stibium* metallic antimony, used especially as a poison;
    cantharides i.e. cantharis vesicatoria or Spanish fly: see Additional
    Notes, p. 145.

277: *Cf.* the words of Seneca's Phaedra in *Hippolytus*, 607: 'Curae leves
locuntur, ingentes stupent.' This was frequently repeated as a common
proverb in the sixteenth and seventeenth centuries.

FLAMINEO

They are sending him to Naples, but I'll send him to Candy;
here's another property too.

BRACHIANO

O the doctor, —   290

FLAMINEO

A poor quack-salving knave, my lord, one that should have
been lash'd for's lechery, but that he confess'd a judgement,
had an execution laid upon him, and so put the whip to a
non plus.

DOCTOR

And was cozen'd, my lord, by an arranter knave than myself,   295
and made pay all the colourable execution.

FLAMINEO

He will shoot pills into a man's guts, shall make them have
more ventages than a cornet or a lamprey; he will poison a
kiss, and was once minded, for his masterpiece, because
Ireland breeds no poison, to have prepared a deadly vapour   300
in a Spaniard's fart that should have poison'd all Dublin.

BRACHIANO

O Saint Anthony's fire!

DOCTOR

Your secretary is merry my lord.

FLAMINEO

O thou cursed antipathy to nature! Look his eye's bloodshed
like a needle a chirurgeon stitcheth a wound with. Let me   305
embrace thee toad, and love thee, O thou abhominable

---

288 *him* i.e. Camillo, commissioned to fight the pirates; *Candy* (literally) Crete; to his death
289 *here's* Q3, Q4 (Q1, Q2 her's); *property* tool; means to an end
291 *quack-salving knave* rascal acting like a quack doctor
295 *cozen'd* cheated; *arranter* more rascally; more good-for-nothing
296 *colourable* pretended, feigned
298 *cornet* musical instrument like an oboe; *lamprey* see Additional
Notes, p. 145.
299-301: see Additional Notes, p. 145.
303 *secretary*: this meant confidant as well as amanuensis.
304 *eye's* ed. (Qq eyes); *bloodshed* bloodshot   305 *chirurgeon* surgeon
306 *abhominable* Q1, Q2 (Q3, Q4 abominable): see Textual Appendix–A.

291-4 When convicted and sentenced to whipping for his lechery the doctor
pretended that he had already been sentenced for debt. He was taken
into custody, but though he escaped the whipping, another rogue,
pretending to be the creditor, made him pay according to the supposed
judgment.
302 *O Saint Anthony's fire!* Dent (p. 96) thinks that this may be slang for
breaking wind.

loathsome gargarism, that will fetch up lungs, lights, heart,
and liver by scruples.

BRACHIANO
No more; I must employ thee honest doctor,
You must to Padua and by the way,   310
Use some of your skill for us.

DOCTOR   Sir I shall.

BRACHIANO
But for Camillo?

FLAMINEO
He dies this night by such a politic strain,
Men shall suppose him by's own engine slain.
But for your Duchess' death?

DOCTOR   I'll make her sure.   315

BRACHIANO
Small mischiefs are by greater made secure.

FLAMINEO
Remember this you slave; when knaves come to preferment
they rise as gallowses are raised i'th' Low Countries: one
upon another's shoulders.

        Exeunt [BRACHIANO, FLAMINEO *and Doctor* JULIO]

MONTICELSO
Here is an emblem nephew, pray peruse it.   320
'Twas thrown in at your window,—

CAMILLO   At my window?
Here is a stag my lord hath shed his horns,
And for the loss of them the poor beast weeps.
The word *Inopem me copia fecit*.

MONTICELSO   That is:
Plenty of horns hath made him poor of horns.   325

---

307 *gargarism* gargle
308 *by scruples* in small quantities
311b Q1b (Q1a [omits])
313 *politic strain* cunning compulsion; spraining of a muscle
314 *by's own engine* by his own ingenuity, contrivance
318 *gallowses* gallows-birds
319 *another's* ed. (Q1, Q2 another; Q3, Q4 anothers)
320 *emblem* emblematic picture
324 *word* motto; *Inopem me copia fecit* 'Abundance has left me desti-
    tute': see Additional Notes, p. 145. *That is*: Q2, Q3 (Q1 That
    is. ; Q4 That is;)

318–19 *they rise . . . shoulders*. Flamineo refers here to improvised gallows
    made by 'placing the condemned man on the shoulders of another man,
    who then steps aside, leaving the person hanging.' (Sampson). *Cf. The
    Duchess of Malfi*, I.i, 66–68.

CAMILLO
  What should this mean?
MONTICELSO   I'll tell you: 'tis given out
  You are a cuckold.
CAMILLO   Is it given out so?
  I had rather such report as that my lord,
  Should keep within doors.
FRANCISCO   Have you any children?
CAMILLO
  None my lord.
FRANCISCO   You are the happier: 330
  I'll tell you a tale.
CAMILLO   Pray my lord.
FRANCISCO   An old tale.
  Upon a time Phoebus the god of light,
  Or him we call the sun, would need be married.
  The gods gave their consent, and Mercury
  Was sent to voice it to the general world.   335
  But what a piteous cry there straight arose
  Amongst smiths, and feltmakers, brewers and cooks,
  Reapers and butter-women, amongst fishmongers
  And thousand other trades, which are annoyed
  By his excessive heat; 'twas lamentable.   340
  They came to Jupiter all in a sweat
  And do forbid the bans; a great fat cook
  Was made their speaker, who entreats of Jove
  That Phoebus might be gelded, for if now
  When there was but one sun, so many men   345
  Were like to perish by his violent heat,
  What should they do if he were married
  And should beget more, and those children
  Make fireworks like their father? So say I,
  Only I will apply it to your wife: 350
  Her issue, should not providence prevent it,
  Would make both nature, time, and man repent it.
MONTICELSO
  Look you cousin,
  Go change the air for shame; see if your absence

327 *Is it* Q1 (Q2, Q3, Q4 It is); *given out* published abroad; sent forth
331 *Pray* i.e. pray do
335 *the general world* the whole world
342 *bans* i.e. of marriage, called in church
343 *speaker* spokesman
349 *fireworks* sparks of fire; created works (i.e. children) of fire
354 *Go change the air* go [and] leave this place

Will blast your cornucopia; Marcello   355
Is chosen with you joint commissioner
For the relieving our Italian coast
From pirates.
MARCELLO   I am much honour'd in't.
CAMILLO   But sir
Ere I return the stag's horns may be sprouted,
Greater than these are shed.
MONTICELSO   Do not fear it,   360
I'll be your ranger.
CAMILLO   You must watch i'th' nights,
Then's the most danger.
FRANCISCO   Farewell good Marcello.
All the best fortunes of a soldier's wish
Bring you o' ship-board.
CAMILLO
Were I not best now I am turn'd soldier,   365
Ere that I leave my wife, sell all she hath
And then take leave of her.
MONTICELSO   I expect good from you,
Your parting is so merry.
CAMILLO
Merry my lord, o'th' captain's humour right;
I am resolved to be drunk this night.   370
                    Exit [CAMILLO; *with* MARCELLO]
FRANCISCO
So, 'twas well fitted: now shall we discern
How his wish'd absence will give violent way
To Duke Brachiano's lust,—
MONTICELSO   Why that was it;
To what scorn'd purpose else should we make choice
Of him for a sea-captain, and besides,   375
Count Lodowick which was rumour'd for a pirate,
Is now in Padua.
FRANCISCO   Is't true?
MONTICELSO   Most certain.
I have letters from him, which are suppliant
To work his quick repeal from banishment;
He means to address himself for pension   380

355 *blast* blow on perniciously; destroy; *cornucopia* 'horn of plenty',
    i.e. the cuckold's horn: *cf.* II.i, 325.
360 *these are* Q1 (Q2, Q3, Q4 those are) i.e. these [that] are
361 *ranger* game-keeper
365 *turn'd* Qq: See Textual Appendix–A.
369 *lord,* ed. (Q1 Lord,   ; Q2, Q3, Q4 Lord?); *right* exactly

Unto our sister Duchess.
FRANCISCO   O 'twas well.
We shall not want his absence past six days;
I fain would have the Duke Brachiano run
Into notorious scandal, for there's nought
In such curs'd dotage, to repair his name,   385
Only the deep sense of some deathless shame.
MONTICELSO
It may be objected I am dishonourable,
To play thus with my kinsman, but I answer,
For my revenge I'd stake a brother's life,
That being wrong'd durst not avenge himself.   390
FRANCISCO
Come to observe this strumpet.
MONTICELSO   Curse of greatness,
Sure he'll not leave her.
FRANCISCO   There's small pity in't.
Like mistletoe on sere elms spent by weather,
Let him cleave to her and both rot together.   *Exeunt*

[Act II, Scene ii]

Enter BRACHIANO *with one in the habit of a Conjuror*

BRACHIANO
Now sir I claim your promise; 'tis dead midnight,
The time prefix'd to show me by your art
How the intended murder of Camillo,
And our loathed Duchess grow to action.
CONJUROR
You have won me by your bounty to a deed   5
I do not often practise; some there are,
Which by sophistic tricks, aspire that name

392 *pity* cause for pity (Brown)
  7 *sophistic* of the nature of sophistry or specious reasoning

381 *our sister Duchess*. In *Modern Language Quarterly*, III (1900), 115,
    W. W. Greg suggested that Webster had confused his Monticelso—the
    real Cardinal Montalto—with Isabella's brother, the Cardinal de Medici;
    but Lucas indicated that '*sister* need be no more than a courtesy title.'
    (*Webster*, i, 222)
383–6 The code of honour taught that, among gentlemen, honour was to
    be preferred before life. Public dishonour was the thing most feared by
    gentlemen of the sixteenth and seventeenth centuries. The sense that
    his dishonour was publicly known should, therefore, make Brachiano
    return to honourable behaviour and thus repair his reputation.
Act II, Scene ii. This scene takes place in Camillo's house.

Which I would gladly lose, of nigromancer;
As some that use to juggle upon cards,
Seeming to conjure, when indeed they cheat;   10
Others that raise up their confederate spirits,
'Bout windmills, and endanger their own necks,
For making of a squib; and some there are
Will keep a curtal to show juggling tricks
And give out 'tis a spirit: besides these   15
Such a whole ream of almanac-makers, figure-flingers,
Fellows indeed that only live by stealth,
Since they do merely lie about stol'n goods,
They'd make men think the devil were fast and loose,
With speaking fustian Latin. Pray sit down,   20
Put on this night-cap sir, 'tis charm'd, and now
I'll show you by my strong-commanding art
The circumstance that breaks your Duchess' heart.

A DUMB SHOW

Enter suspiciously, JULIO *and* CHRISTOPHERO; *they draw a curtain
where* BRACHIANO's *picture is, they put on spectacles of glass which
cover their eyes and noses, and then burn perfumes afore the
picture, and wash the lips of the picture; that done, quenching the
fire, and putting off their spectacles they depart laughing.*

  8 *lose* Q4 (Q1, Q2, Q3 loose) 12 *windmills* fanciful schemes or projects
 16 *ream* ream of paper; realm; *figure-flingers* those who cast figures or
      horoscopes
 20 *fustian* gibberish, bombastic: *cf.* III.ii, 46 note.
DUMB SHOW: see Additional Notes, p. 145; CHRISTOPHERO: See
      Textual Appendix–A; BRACHIANO's Q4 (Q1, Q2, Q3 Brachian's);
      spectacles of glass Q1b (Q1a *spectacles*); *cover* Q1b (Q1a *covers*);
      noses Q1b (Q1a *noses, of glass*)

---

  8 *nigromancer* necromancer, i.e. one who claims to foretell events by
    communicating with the dead; more generally, a wizard or conjuror.
    The spelling Webster uses here associates the word with the 'black art'
    (Latin *niger*).
 14 *curtal* a docked horse. This is a reference to Morocco, a docked bay
    gelding belonging to a travelling showman called Banks and exhibited
    by him from 1595 onwards. Banks had previously trained a white horse
    to perform tricks, but Morocco was famed for the variety of his,
    which ranged from dancing and counting money to showing appropriate
    reactions to the names of Queen Elizabeth and the King of Spain. It
    was commonly believed that Banks possessed magic powers and that
    Morocco was his familiar.
 18 On the casting of horoscopes to find stolen goods, see Johnstone Parr,
    *Tamburlaine's Malady and Other Essays on Astrology in Elizabethan
    Drama* (Alabama, 1953), pp. 101–6.
 19 Originally *fast and loose* was the name of a cheating game in which the
    person being gulled was invited to say whether a belt, handkerchief or
    string was knotted (i.e. fast) or loose. Either answer would be the
    wrong one.

Enter ISABELLA *in her nightgown as to bedward, with lights
after her, Count* LODOVICO, GIOVANNI, GUID-ANTONIO *and
others waiting on her; she kneels down as to prayers, then draws
the curtain of the picture, does three reverences to it, and kisses it
thrice, she faints and will not suffer them to come near it, dies;
sorrow express'd in* GIOVANNI *and in Count* LODOVICO; *she's
convey'd out solemnly.*

BRACHIANO
Excellent, then she's dead, —
CONJUROR   She's poisoned,
By the fum'd picture: 'twas her custom nightly,   25
Before she went to bed, to go and visit
Your picture, and to feed her eyes and lips
On the dead shadow; Doctor Julio
Observing this, infects it with an oil
And other poison'd stuff, which presently   30
Did suffocate her spirits.
BRACHIANO   Methought I saw
Count Lodowick there.
CONJUROR   He was, and by my art
I find he did most passionately dote
Upon your Duchess. Now turn another way,
And view Camillo's far more politic fate: 35
Strike louder music from this charmed ground,
To yield, as fits the act, a tragic sound.

THE SECOND DUMB SHOW

Enter FLAMINEO, MARCELLO, CAMILLO *with four more as Captains,
they drink healths and dance; a vaulting-horse is brought into the
room,* MARCELLO *and two more whisper'd out of the room, while*
FLAMINEO *and* CAMILLO *strip themselves into their shirts, as to
vault; compliment who shall begin, as* CAMILLO *is about to vault,*
FLAMINEO *pitcheth him upon his neck, and with the help of the*

      with lights Q1b (Q1a *lighs*); GUID-ANTONIO: see Textual Appen-
         dix–A.
   35 *politic* cunning, contrived; *fate* Q4 (Q1, Q2, Q3 face)
   SECOND DUMB SHOW: *whisper'd out of* signalled to leave, by whispers;
         compliment Q1 (Q2, Q3, Q4 *they compliment*)

DUMB SHOW: *sorrow express'd*. This 'probably meant that they tore their
   hair and wrung their hands'. (M. C. Bradbrook, *Themes and Conventions
   of Elizabethan Tragedy*, p. 28.)
SECOND DUMB SHOW: *a vaulting-horse*. In *John Webster e il linguaggio della
   tragedia* (Rome, 1953), pp. 291–2 Gabriele Baldini suggested that
   Webster might have misunderstood the original story and turned the
   place of Francesco Peretti's assassination, Montecavallo, into the means
   of his death. Brown points out that a 'curious and cumbersome means
   of murder was just what Webster required.' (p. 57 n.) He may have
   altered his source wittingly.

rest, writhes his neck about, seems to see if it be broke, and lays
him folded double as 'twere under the horse, makes shows to call
for help, MARCELLO *comes in, laments, sends for the Cardinal and*
Duke, who comes forth with armed men, wonder at the act;
commands the body to be carried home, apprehends FLAMINEO,
MARCELLO, *and the rest, and go as 'twere to apprehend* VITTORIA.

BRACHIANO
   'Twas quaintly done, but yet each circumstance
   I taste not fully.
CONJUROR   O 'twas most apparent,
   You saw them enter charged with their deep healths   40
   To their boon voyage, and to second that,
   Flamineo calls to have a vaulting-horse
   Maintain their sport. The virtuous Marcello
   Is innocently plotted forth the room,
   Whilst your eye saw the rest, and can inform you   45
   The engine of all.
BRACHIANO
   It seems Marcello, and Flamineo
   Are both committed.
CONJUROR   Yes, you saw them guarded,
   And now they are come with purpose to apprehend
   Your mistress, fair Vittoria; we are now   50
   Beneath her roof: 'twere fit we instantly
   Make out by some back postern.
BRACHIANO   Noble friend,
   You bind me ever to you; this shall stand
   As the firm seal annexed to my hand
   It shall enforce a payment.
CONJUROR   Sir I thank you. *Exit* BRACHIANO   55
   Both flowers and weeds spring when the sun is warm,
   As great men do great good, or else great harm.
                           Exit CONJUROR

SECOND DUMB SHOW: *shows* see Textual Appendix–A; *the Cardinal* i.e.
   Monticelso; *Duke* i.e. Francisco; *commands . . . go* i.e. Francisco
   commands and they go: see Textual Appendix–A.
38 *quaintly* ingeniously   40 *charged* loaded, filled
41 *boon voyage* 'bon voyage'   44 *plotted forth* sent out by contrivance
46 *engine* skill in contriving
47 speech-prefix: Q4 *Bra.* (Q1, Q2, Q3 *Mar.*)
53 *this* i.e. this that you have done
54 *annexed to my hand* attached to my signature
55 s.d. Q4 (Q1, Q2, Q3 *Exit Brac.* opposite 1.54)
57 s.d. Q4 (Q1, Q2, Q3 *Exit Con.*)

[Act III, Scene i]

Enter FRANCISCO, *and* MONTICELSO, *their* CHANCELLOR *and*
REGISTER

FRANCISCO

You have dealt discreetly to obtain the presence
Of all the grave lieger ambassadors
To hear Vittoria's trial.

MONTICELSO   'Twas not ill,
For sir you know we have nought but circumstances
To charge her with, about her husband's death;   5
Their approbation therefore to the proofs
Of her black lust, shall make her infamous
To all our neighbouring kingdoms. I wonder
If Brachiano will be here.

FRANCISCO   O fie,
'Twere impudence too palpable.   [*Exeunt*]   10

Enter FLAMINEO *and* MARCELLO *guarded, and a* LAWYER

LAWYER

What, are you in by the week? So–I will try now whether
thy wit be close prisoner: methinks none should sit upon
thy sister but old whore-masters,—

FLAMINEO

Or cuckolds, for your cuckold is your most terrible tickler
of lechery: whore-masters would serve, for none are judges   15
at tilting, but those that have been old tilters.

LAWYER

My lord Duke and she have been very private.

FLAMINEO

You are a dull ass; 'tis threat'ned they have been very
public.

2 *lieger ambassadors* 'resident ambassadors as contrasted with
  special envoys' (Lucas)
10 S.D. LAWYER: see Textual Appendix–A.
11 *in by the week?* thoroughly caught, ensnared; *week? So–* ed. (Q1
  week, so ; Q2, Q3 week, so, ; Q4 week? so,)
12 *sit upon* i.e. in judgement
14 *tickler* castigator; exciter
16 *tilting . . . tilters:* a double entendre
17 *private* intimate; secret
19 *public* unchaste; unconcealed

Act III, Scene i. This scene takes place in a court-room in Rome or in some
  room adjoining the papal consistory.

LAWYER

If it can be proved they have but kiss'd one another.   20

FLAMINEO

What then?

LAWYER

My lord cardinal will ferret them,—

FLAMINEO

A cardinal I hope will not catch conies.

LAWYER

For to sow kisses (mark what I say), to sow kisses, is to reap
lechery, and I am sure a woman that will endure kissing is   25
half won.

FLAMINEO

True, her upper part by that rule; if you will win her nether
part too, you know what follows.

LAWYER

Hark, the ambassadors are lighted,—

FLAMINEO [aside]

I do put on this feigned garb of mirth   30
To gull suspicion.

MARCELLO   O my unfortunate sister!
I would my dagger's point had cleft her heart
When she first saw Brachiano. You 'tis said,
Were made his engine, and his stalking-horse
To undo my sister.

FLAMINEO   I made a kind of path   35
To her and mine own preferment.

MARCELLO   Your ruin.

FLAMINEO

Hum! thou art a soldier,
Followest the great Duke, feedest his victories,
As witches do their serviceable spirits,
Even with thy prodigal blood; what hast got?   40

22 *ferret* (literally) to catch rabbits with ferrets; to hunt out; to
   question searchingly
23 *catch conies* (literally) catch rabbits; to cozen fools (usually of
   money)
29 *lighted* alighted from their carriages
31 *gull* Q1, Q4 (Q2, Q3 gall) cheat deceive
32 *dagger's point* ed. (Q1 daggers point; Q2, Q3, Q4 dagger-point).
34 *engine* tool, instrument; *stalking-horse* a person whose agency or
   participation in an action is made use of to prevent suspicion of
   its real design
35 *I made* Q1 (Q2, Q3, Q4 I am)
39 *serviceable* ministering
40 *prodigal* wastefully lavish

But, like the wealth of captains, a poor handful,
Which in thy palm thou bear'st, as men hold water;
Seeking to gripe it fast, the frail reward
Steals through thy fingers.
MARCELLO   Sir,—
FLAMINEO   Thou hast scarce maintenance
To keep thee in fresh chamois.
MARCELLO   Brother!
FLAMINEO   Hear me,—   45
And thus when we have even poured ourselves
Into great fights, for their ambition
Or idle spleen, how shall we find reward,
But as we seldom find the mistletoe
Sacred to physic on the builder oak   50
Without a mandrake by it, so in our quest of gain.
Alas the poorest of their forc'd dislikes
At a limb proffers, but at heart it strikes:
This is lamented doctrine.
MARCELLO   Come, come.
FLAMINEO
When age shall turn thee   55
White as a blooming hawthorn,—
MARCELLO   I'll interrupt you.
For love of virtue bear an honest heart,
And stride over every politic respect,
Which where they most advance they most infect.
Were I your father, as I am your brother,   60
I should not be ambitious to leave you
A better patrimony.

            Enter Savoy [Ambassador]

---

45 *chamois* i.e. the jerkins of chamois which were worn under
   armour
49–51: 'Good is often accompanied by evil, the beneficial mistletoe
   by the deadly mandrake; so too ambition finds poisonous flies in
   its ointment.'
50 *physic on* ed. See Textual Appendix–A; *builder* used for building
58 *politic respect* consideration of policy

---

49 *mistletoe*. According to Pliny, the Druids thought mistletoe would heal
   anything. (See Holland's translation of the *Natural History*, Book XVI,
   chapter xliv.)
51 *mandrake* a plant of the genus Mandragora. It has a forked root and thus
   resembles the human form. It was supposed to grow under the gallows,
   to feed on blood (*cf*. III.iii, 110–11) and to shriek when pulled from the
   ground (*cf*. V.vi, 65). Moreover, plucking it would lead to madness.
   (*Cf. The Duchess of Malfi*, II.v, 1–2.)

FLAMINEO   I'll think on't, —
The lord ambassadors.

Here there is a passage of the lieger Ambassadors over the stage
severally. Enter French Ambassador.

LAWYER
O my sprightly Frenchman, do you know him?
He's an admirable tilter.   65

FLAMINEO
I saw him at last tilting; he showed like a pewter candle-
stick fashioned like a man in armour, holding a tilting staff
in his hand, little bigger than a candle of twelve i'th' pound.

LAWYER
O but he's an excellent horseman.

FLAMINEO
A lame one in his lofty tricks; he sleeps o' horseback like a   70
poulter, —

Enter English and Spanish [Ambassadors]

LAWYER
Lo you my Spaniard.

FLAMINEO
He carries his face in's ruff, as I have seen a serving-man
carry glasses in a cypress hat-band, monstrous steady for
fear of breaking. He looks like the claw of a blackbird, first   75
salted and then broiled in a candle.   *Exeunt*

63 s.d. *French Ambassador* ed. (Q1, Q2 *French Embassadours;* Q3
   French Embassadors; Q4 *French Embassador*)
65 *tilter: cf.* III.i, 16 note.
66 *showed like* looked like
74 *cypress* cobweb fine lawn or crêpe
76 *broiled* grilled

---

71 *poulter* poulterer. Poulterers went to market so early that they often fell
asleep on horseback, leaning over the baskets which they carried in front
of them.

[Act III, Scene ii]

THE ARRAIGNMENT OF VITTORIA

Enter FRANCISCO, MONTICELSO, *the six lieger Ambassadors,*
BRACHIANO, VITTORIA, [ZANCHE, FLAMINEO, MARCELLO,]
LAWYER, *and a guard*

MONTICELSO
Forbear my lord, here is no place assign'd you,
The business by his holiness is left
To our examination.
BRACHIANO   May it thrive with you!
Lays a rich gown under him

FRANCISCO
A chair there for his lordship.

BRACHIANO
Forbear your kindness; an unbidden guest   5
Should travel as Dutch women go to church:
Bear their stools with them.
MONTICELSO   At your pleasure sir.
Stand to the table gentlewomen. Now signior
Fall to your plea.

LAWYER
Domine Judex converte oculos in hanc pestem mulierum   10
corruptissimam.

VITTORIA
What's he?
FRANCISCO   A lawyer, that pleads against you.

VITTORIA
Pray my lord, let him speak his usual tongue.
I'll make no answer else.
FRANCISCO   Why you understand Latin.

VITTORIA
I do sir, but amongst this auditory   15

S.D. MONTICELSO Q2, Q3, Q4 (Q1 *Montcelso*); VITTORIA, Q4 (Q1,
    Q2, Q3 *Vittoria, Isabella*)
1 *assign'd* Q3, Q4 (Q1, Q2 assing'd)   3 *our* Q1, Q4 (Q2, Q3 your)
6 *travel* Q3, Q4 (Q1, Q2 trauaile)
8 *gentlewomen* Q1, Q2, Q3 (Q4 gentlewoman) i.e. Vittoria and
    Zanche: see Textual Appendix–A.
10 speech-prefix: Q2, Q3, Q4 *Law.* (Q1 [omits])
10–11: 'Lord Judge, turn your eyes to this plague, the most corrupt
    of women.'

Act III, Scene ii: see Additional Notes, p. 146.

Which come to hear my cause, the half or more
May be ignorant in't.
MONTICELSO   Go on sir.
VITTORIA   By your favour,
I will not have my accusation clouded
In a strange tongue: all this assembly
Shall hear what you can charge me with.
FRANCISCO   Signior,   20
You need not stand on't much; pray change your language.
MONTICELSO
Oh for God sake: gentlewoman, your credit
Shall be more famous by it.
LAWYER   Well then have at you.
VITTORIA
I am at the mark sir, I'll give aim to you,
And tell you how near you shoot.   25
LAWYER
Most literated judges, please your lordships,
So to connive your judgements to the view
Of this debauch'd and diversivolent woman
Who such a black concatenation
Of mischief hath effected, that to extirp   30
The memory of't, must be the consummation
Of her and her projections—
VITTORIA   What's all this?—
LAWYER
Hold your peace.
Exorbitant sins must have exulceration.
VITTORIA
Surely my lords this lawyer here hath swallowed   35

18 *clouded* made obscure   21 *stand on't* insist on it
22 *credit* reputation
23 *have at you* 'here goes', an expression indicating desire to attack
24 *the mark* i.e. archery; *give aim to* to act as marker at the butts to
    signal where each shot strikes
26 *literated* learned
27 *connive your judgements:* 'This jargon, did it possess any meaning,
    would have exactly the wrong one—"shut your eyes towards".'
    (Lucas)
28 *diversivolent* desiring strife
29 *black concatenation* Q1 (Q2, Q3, Q4 concatenation)
30 *extirp* root out, exterminate
32 *projections* projects
34 *Exorbitant* anomalous, not coming within the intended scope of a
    law; *exulceration* (literally) ulceration; exasperation
35 *lawyer here* Q1 (Q2, Q3, Q4 lawyer)

Some pothecary's bills, or proclamations.
And now the hard and undigestible words
Come up like stones we use give hawks for physic.
Why this is Welsh to Latin.
LAWYER   My lords, the woman
Knows not her tropes nor figures, nor is perfect   40
In the academic derivation
Of grammatical elocution.
FRANCISCO   Sir your pains
Shall be well spared, and your deep eloquence
Be worthily applauded amongst those
Which understand you.
LAWYER   My good lord.
FRANCISCO *speaks this as in scorn*   Sir,   45
Put up your papers in your fustian bag,—
Cry mercy sir, 'tis buckram,—and accept
My notion of your learn'd verbosity.

LAWYER
I most graduatically thank your lordship.
I shall have use for them elsewhere.   50
                                              [*Exit*]

MONTICELSO
I shall be plainer with you, and paint out
Your follies in more natural red and white
Than that upon your cheek.
VITTORIA   O you mistake.
You raise a blood as noble in this cheek

36 *pothecary's* ed.: see Textual Appendix–A.
39 *to Latin* in comparison to Latin
40 *tropes nor figures* Q1 (Q2, Q3, Q4 tropes)
42 *elocution* expression
45 S.D. opposite 46–47 in Qq.
46 *fustian* coarse cloth; bombastic language
47 *Cry mercy* I cry you mercy; *buckram* ed. (Q1, Q2, Q3 buckeram;
    Q4 Buck'ram) coarse linen traditionally used for lawyers' bags
49 *graduatically* in the manner of a graduate

36 *Pothecaries' bills* or prescriptions were written in polysyllabic medical
   Latin; *proclamations* i.e. official notices, of which there were many in
   James I's reign, were also 'full of tortuous sentences and long unnecessary words.' (G. B. Harrison).
38 Gervase Markham's *Cheape and Good Husbandry* (1614) tells how to
   dose hawks with stones, 'seven to fifteen fine white pebbles from a
   river.' (Sampson).
40 In rhetoric, *tropes* are figures of speech in which words are used out of
   their literal meaning; *figures* are any of the various 'forms' of expression
   in which words are used out of their ordinary construction.

As ever was your mother's.   55
MONTICELSO
I must spare you till proof cry whore to that;
Observe this creature here my honoured lords,
A woman of a most prodigious spirit
In her effected.
VITTORIA   Honourable my lord,
It doth not suit a reverend cardinal   60
To play the lawyer thus—
MONTICELSO
Oh your trade instructs your language!
You see my lords what goodly fruit she seems,
Yet like those apples travellers report
To grow where Sodom and Gomorrah stood   65
I will but touch her and you straight shall see
She'll fall to soot and ashes.
VITTORIA   Your envenom'd
Pothecary should do't—
MONTICELSO   I am resolved
Were there a second paradise to lose
This devil would betray it.
VITTORIA   O poor charity!   70
Thou art seldom found in scarlet.
MONTICELSO
Who knows not how, when several night by night
Her gates were chok'd with coaches, and her rooms
Outbrav'd the stars with several kind of lights
When she did counterfeit a prince's court?   75

---

58 *prodigious* unnatural, monstrous
59 *In her effected* Q1, Q2 (Q3, Q4 [omit]); *Honourable my lord* Q1
   (Q2, Q3 My honourable lord; Q4 My honourable lords)
67–68 *envenom'd / Pothecary* i.e. the lawyer
68 *resolved* convinced
69 *lose* Q4 (Q1, Q2, Q3 loose)
71 *scarlet:* the colour both of the cardinal's vestments and of the
   lawyer's robes
75 *court?* ed.: see Textual Appendix–A.

---

59 *In her effected.* If this reading is correct, 'effected' must mean 'put into
   effect, fulfilled', though there is no evidence in *O.E.D.* to support this.
   If it is wrong, 'In her affected', as Brown points out (p. 68 n.) offers the
   simplest palaeographical explanation and, moreover, makes good sense
   in its meanings of 'desired' or 'cherished, beloved', which were common
   in the sixteenth and seventeenth centuries.
64–7 Sir John Mandeville was one traveller who elaborated this legend
   which is, apparently, based on Deuteronomy xxxii, 32: 'For their vine
   is of the vine of Sodom, and of the fields of Gomorrah: their grapes are
   grapes of gall, their clusters are bitter: . . .'

In music, banquets and most riotous surfeits
This whore, forsooth, was holy.
VITTORIA   Ha? whore? what's that?
MONTICELSO
    Shall I expound whore to you? Sure I shall;
    I'll give their perfect character. They are first
    Sweetmeats which rot the eater: in man's nostril   80
    Poison'd perfumes. They are coz'ning alchemy,
    Shipwracks in calmest weather! What are whores?
    Cold Russian winters, that appear so barren,
    As if that nature had forgot the spring.
    They are the true material fire of hell,   85
    Worse than those tributes i'th' Low Countries paid,
    Exactions upon meat, drink, garments, sleep;
    Ay even on man's perdition, his sin.
    They are those brittle evidences of law
    Which forfeit all a wretched man's estate   90
    For leaving out one syllable. What are whores?
    They are those flattering bells have all one tune,
    At weddings, and at funerals: your rich whores
    Are only treasuries by extortion fill'd,
    And emptied by curs'd riot. They are worse,   95
    Worse than dead bodies, which are begg'd at gallows
    And wrought upon by surgeons, to teach man
    Wherein he is imperfect. What's a whore?
    She's like the guilty counterfeited coin

77 *whore?* Q2, Q3, Q4 (Q1 whore   )
79 *character* character sketch: see Additional Notes, p. 146.
81 *coz'ning alchemy* see Additional Notes, p. 147.
82 *weather!* ed. (Q1, Q2, weather?; Q3 whether?; Q4 weather.)
85 *material fire* fire formed of matter: *cf. The Duchess of Malfi*, V.v, 2
88 *man's perdition* i.e. prostitution   89–91 see Additional Notes, p. 147.
96 *at gallows* Q1 (Q2, Q3, Q4 at th'gallows)
99 *guilty* Q1 (Q2, Q3, Q4 gilt): 'perhaps with a play on "gilt" '
    (Lucas)

---

77 *what's that?* Lucas (*Webster*, i, 230) supposes that Vittoria means 'what
    is a whore?', rather than 'what's that you say?', her question being 'an
    audacious climax of assumed innocence.' Dent (p. 103) thinks that
    'Vittoria may be shocked, or may be pretending to be shocked, that
    Monticelso actually dares call her "whore".'
86–88 At this time the taxes imposed on commodities 'for belly and back'
    in the Low Countries, and especially the tax on wine, either equalled or
    exceeded the original value of the commodity.
95–99 The reference here is to bodies used by surgeons for instructing
    students in anatomy. Lucas notes that 'the 1540 charter of the Barber-
    Surgeons allowed them four executed felons a year; but doubtless
    others were commonly begged for, by them or by private practitioners.'
    (*Webster*, i, 231)

Which whosoe'er first stamps it brings in trouble   100
All that receive it—
VITTORIA   This character scapes me.
MONTICELSO
You gentlewoman?
Take from all beasts, and from all minerals
Their deadly poison.
VITTORIA   Well what then?
MONTICELSO   I'll tell thee.
I'll find in thee a pothecary's shop   105
To sample them all.
FRENCH AMBASSADOR   She hath liv'd ill.
ENGLISH AMBASSADOR
True, but the cardinal's too bitter.
MONTICELSO
You know what whore is; next the devil, Adult'ry,
Enters the devil, Murder.
FRANCISCO   Your unhappy
Husband is dead.
VITTORIA   O he's a happy husband   110
Now he owes nature nothing.
FRANCISCO
And by a vaulting engine.
MONTICELSO   An active plot.
He jump'd into his grave.
FRANCISCO   What a prodigy was't,
That from some two yards' height a slender man
Should break his neck?
MONTICELSO   I'th'rushes.
FRANCISCO   And what's more,   115
Upon the instant lose all use of speech,
All vital motion, like a man had lain
Wound up three days. Now mark each circumstance.
MONTICELSO
And look upon this creature was his wife.

100 *brings* Q2, Q3, Q4 (Q1 bring)
101 *scapes* escapes, eludes
108–9: see Textual Appendix–A.
111: i.e. 'He has paid his debt to nature.'
112 *vaulting-engine* instrument for vaulting, i.e. vaulting-horse.
114 *height* Q1 (Q2, Q3, Q4 high)
116 *lose* Q4 (Q1, Q2, Q3 loose)
118 *Wound up* i.e. in his shroud

---

115 Monticelso's words imply that the rushes, commonly used as floor
covering at this time, must have been thickly strewn.

She comes not like a widow: she comes arm'd   120
With scorn and impudence. Is this a mourning habit?
VITTORIA
Had I foreknown his death as you suggest,
I would have bespoke my mourning.
MONTICELSO   O you are cunning.
VITTORIA
You shame your wit and judgement
To call it so. What, is my just defence   125
By him that is my judge call'd impudence?
Let me appeal then from this Christian court
To the uncivil Tartar.
MONTICELSO   See my lords,
She scandals our proceedings.
VITTORIA   Humbly thus,
Thus low, to the most worthy and respected   130
Lieger ambassadors, my modesty
And womanhood I tender; but withal
So entangled in a cursed accusation
That my defence of force like Perseus,
Must personate masculine virtue to the point.   135
Find me but guilty, sever head from body:
We'll part good friends: I scorn to hold my life
At yours or any man's entreaty, sir.
ENGLISH AMBASSADOR
She hath a brave spirit—
MONTICELSO   Well, well, such counterfeit jewels
Make true ones oft suspected.
VITTORIA   You are deceived.   140
For know that all your strict-combined heads,
Which strike against this mine of diamonds,
Shall prove but glassen hammers, they shall break;
These are but feigned shadows of my evils.

---

129 *scandals* disgraces
134 *of force* perforce, of necessity
135 *to the point* in every detail; see Textual Appendix–A.
141 *strict-combined* i.e. closely (possibly secretly) allied; *heads* military
    forces; hammer-heads (Brown)
143 *glassen* glazen; made of glass

---

128 *the uncivil Tartar.* For an account of the popular Elizabethan image of
    Tartars, see R. R. Cawley, *The Voyagers and Elizabethan Drama* (Boston
    and London, 1938), pp. 188–207.
134 *Perseus* Qq. (Hazlitt, Sampson, Wheeler: Portia's) In Jonson's *Masque
    of Queenes* (1609) Perseus was presented as expressing heroic and mas-
    culine virtue. There is no need to amend the reading of Qq.

Terrify babes, my lord, with painted devils,   145
I am past such needless palsy; for your names
Of whore and murd'ress, they proceed from you,
As if a man should spit against the wind,
The filth returns in's face.

MONTICELSO
Pray you mistress satisfy me one question: 150
Who lodg'd beneath your roof that fatal night
Your husband brake his neck?

BRACHIANO   That question
Enforceth me break silence: I was there.

MONTICELSO
Your business?

BRACHIANO   Why I came to comfort her,
And take some course for sett'ling her estate,   155
Because I heard her husband was in debt
To you my lord.

MONTICELSO   He was.

BRACHIANO   And 'twas strangely fear'd
That you would cozen her.

MONTICELSO   Who made you overseer?

BRACHIANO
Why my charity, my charity, which should flow
From every generous and noble spirit,   160
To orphans and to widows.

MONTICELSO   Your lust.

BRACHIANO
Cowardly dogs bark loudest. Sirrah priest,
I'll talk with you hereafter,——Do you hear?
The sword you frame of such an excellent temper,
I'll sheathe in your own bowels: 165
There are a number of thy coat resemble
Your common post-boys.

MONTICELSO   Ha?

BRACHIANO   Your mercenary post-boys;
Your letters carry truth, but 'tis your guise

146 *needless palsy* unnecessary, useless shaking
150 *satisfy me one question* answer one question fully for me
164 *sword* i.e. of justice; *temper* peculiar degree of hardness and
    elasticity or resiliency imparted to steel by tempering
166 *of thy coat* of thy profession
168 *guise* custom, habit

154–8. F. L. Lucas thinks Brachiano's accusation of Monticelso as de-
    frauding Vittoria and her husband 'is clearly an echo of the grievances
    of the Accoramboni family over her portion.' (*Webster*, i, 87.) *Cf.*
    III.ii, 171–2.

To fill your mouths with gross and impudent lies.

[He makes for the door]

SERVANT
My lord your gown.

BRACHIANO   Thou liest, 'twas my stool.   170
Bestow't upon thy master that will challenge
The rest o'th' household stuff; for Brachiano
Was ne'er so beggarly, to take a stool
Out of another's lodging: let him make
Valence for his bed on't, or a demi-foot-cloth,   175
For his most reverent moil; Monticelso,
Nemo me impune lacessit.   *Exit* BRACHIANO

MONTICELSO
Your champion's gone.

VITTORIA   The wolf may prey the better.

FRANCISCO
My lord there's great suspicion of the murder,
But no sound proof who did it: for my part   180
I do not think she hath a soul so black
To act a deed so bloody; if she have,
As in cold countries husbandmen plant vines,
And with warm blood manure them, even so
One summer she will bear unsavoury fruit,   185
And ere next spring wither both branch and root.
The act of blood let pass, only descend
To matter of incontinence.

VITTORIA   I discern poison
Under your gilded pills.

MONTICELSO
Now the Duke's gone, I will produce a letter,   190
Wherein 'twas plotted he and you should meet,
At an apothecary's summer-house,

171 *challenge* lay claim to
175 *valence* bed curtains; drapes around the canopy; *demi-foot-cloth*
   half-length covering for a horse: *cf.* I.ii, 49 note.
176 *moil* mule
177: 'No one injures me with impunity.'; *lacessit* Q2, Q3, Q4 (Q1
   lacescit)
178 *prey*: 'perhaps with a pun on "pray" ' (Lucas)
189 *gilded*: 'the ordinary medical term, not a metaphor' (Dent); but
   cf. The Duchess of Malfi, IV.i, 19–20.
191 *he* Q3, Q4 (Q1, Q2 *her*)
192 *summer-house* garden house; arbour

183–5 Lucas compared these lines with John Marston's *Sophonisba* (1606),
   II. iii, 35–36:
         Through the rotten'st dung best plants both sprout and live;
         By blood vines grow.   (*Webster*, i, 232.)

Down by the river Tiber:—view't my lords:—
Where after wanton bathing and the heat
Of a lascivious banquet.—I pray read it,   195
I shame to speak the rest.
VITTORIA   Grant I was tempted,
Temptation to lust proves not the act,
Casta est quam nemo rogavit,
You read his hot love to me, but you want
My frosty answer.
MONTICELSO   Frost i'th' dog-days! strange!   200
VITTORIA
Condemn you me for that the Duke did love me?
So may you blame some fair and crystal river
For that some melancholic distracted man,
Hath drown'd himself in't.
MONTICELSO   Truly drown'd indeed.
VITTORIA
Sum up my faults I pray, and you shall find,   205
That beauty and gay clothes, a merry heart,
And a good stomach to a feast, are all,
All the poor crimes that you can charge me with:
In faith my lord you might go pistol flies,
The sport would be more noble.
MONTICELSO   Very good.   210
VITTORIA
But take you your course, it seems you have beggar'd me
                                                        first
And now would fain undo me; I have houses,
Jewels, and a poor remnant of crusadoes,
Would those would make you charitable.
MONTICELSO   If the devil
Did ever take good shape behold his picture.   215
VITTORIA
You have one virtue left,
You will not flatter me.
FRANCISCO   Who brought this letter?
VITTORIA
I am not compell'd to tell you.

198: 'She is chaste whom no one has solicited.'
207 *a feast* ed. (Qq feast)
211 *you your* Qq: see Textual Appendix–A.
213 *crusadoes* gold or silver Portuguese coins

200 *dog-days* evil or unhealthy times, associated with hot weather when
   Sirius, the dog-star, is high in the sky. They were also traditionally
   associated with lust.

MONTICELSO
  My lord Duke sent to you a thousand ducats,
  The twelfth of August.
VITTORIA   'Twas to keep your cousin   220
  From prison; I paid use for't.
MONTICELSO   I rather think
  'Twas interest for his lust.
VITTORIA
  Who says so but yourself? If you be my accuser
  Pray cease to be my judge, come from the bench,
  Give in your evidence 'gainst me, and let these   225
  Be moderators. My lord cardinal,
  Were your intelligencing ears as long
  As to my thoughts, had you an honest tongue
  I would not care though you proclaim'd them all.
MONTICELSO
  Go to, go to.   230
  After your goodly and vain-glorious banquet,
  I'll give you a choke-pear.
VITTORIA   O' your own grafting?
MONTICELSO
  You were born in Venice, honourably descended
  From the Vitelli; 'twas my cousin's fate,—
  Ill may I name the hour–to marry you;   235
  He bought you of your father.
VITTORIA   Ha?
MONTICELSO
  He spent there in six months

220 *cousin* kinsman, i.e. nephew
221 *use* interest
226 *moderators* arbitrators, judges
227 *intelligencing* for finding out secret information; *long* ed. (Qq
    loving): see Textual Appendix–A.
228 *As to* i.e. as to reach to
230 *Go to, go to.* i.e. 'Come on, come on.'
232 *choke-pear* rough and unpalatable kind of pear; something diffi-
    cult to swallow; *grafting*: a double entendre; *cf. The Duchess of
    Malfi*, II.i, 148–9.

223–9 'The fact that Vittoria is given speeches of the wronged Agrippina
    and of Silius is perhaps an indication of Webster's attitude to her at this
    point.' (M. C. Bradbrook, *Themes and Conventions of Elizabethan
    Tragedy*, p. 93). The borrowings are from *Sejanus*, III, 200–201 and II,
    453–7.
233–4. The Vitelli were a famous Roman family, having no connection with
    the Accoramboni. Lucas suggested that, since Lodovico Orsini was
    banished for the murder of Vincenzo Vitelli, Webster may have remem-
    bered the name from that. (*Webster*, i, 80, 233)

Twelve thousand ducats, and to my acquaintance
Receiv'd in dowry with you not one julio:
'Twas a hard penny-worth, the ware being so light.   240
I yet but draw the curtain, now to your picture:
You came from thence a most notorious strumpet,
And so you have continued.
VITTORIA   My lord.
MONTICELSO   Nay hear me,
You shall have time to prate. My lord Brachiano,—
Alas I make but repetition,   245
Of what is ordinary and Rialto talk,
And ballated, and would be play'd o'th' stage,
But that vice many times finds such loud friends
That preachers are charm'd silent.
You gentlemen Flamineo and Marcello,   250
The court hath nothing now to charge you with,
Only you must remain upon your sureties
For your appearance.
FRANCISCO   I stand for Marcello.
FLAMINEO
And my lord Duke for me.
MONTICELSO
For you Vittoria, your public fault,   255
Join'd to th' condition of the present time,
Takes from you all the fruits of noble pity.
Such a corrupted trial have you made
Both of your life and beauty, and been styl'd
No less in ominous fate than blazing stars   260
To princes; here's your sentence: you are confin'd

238 *acquaintance* Q1, Q2 (Q3, Q4 knowledge)
239 *julio* coin of Pope Julius II (1503–13), worth about sixpence
240 *light* usual meaning; unchaste
246 *Rialto talk* common gossip
247 *ballated* balladed
252-3 *remain . . . appearance* remain pledged to appear (your sponsors
        being liable in the event of your non-appearance)
255 *public* cf. III.i, 19 note.
260 *in* Q1 (Q2, Q3, Q4 an)
261 *To princes; here's*: see Textual Appendix–A.

247 *play'd o'th' stage*. *The Late Murder of the Son upon the Mother, or Keep
     the Widow Waking* written by Webster, Dekker, Ford and Rowley, which
     was performed at the Red Bull theatre in September, 1624 presented on
     the stage a notorious murder and the story of fortune-hunters in pursuit
     of an intemperate and wealthy old widow. In the second plot actual
     incidents which had taken place were repeated on the stage. See C. J.
     Sisson, *Lost Plays of Shakespeare's Age* (Cambridge, 1936), pp. 80–124.

Unto a house of convertites and your bawd—
FLAMINEO [*aside*]
Who I?
MONTICELSO The Moor.
FLAMINEO [*aside*]   O I am a sound man again.
VITTORIA
A house of convertites, what's that?
MONTICELSO   A house
Of penitent whores.
VITTORIA   Do the noblemen in Rome   265
Erect it for their wives, that I am sent
To lodge there?
FRANCISCO
You must have patience.
VITTORIA   I must first have vengeance.
I fain would know if you have your salvation
By patent, that you proceed thus.
MONTICELSO   Away with her.   270
Take her hence.
VITTORIA
A rape, a rape!
MONTICELSO   How?
VITTORIA   Yes, you have ravish'd justice,
Forc'd her to do your pleasure.
MONTICELSO   Fie, she's mad—
VITTORIA
Die with those pills in your most cursed maw,
Should bring you health, or while you sit o'th' bench,   275
Let your own spittle choke you.
MONTICELSO   She's turn'd fury.
VITTORIA
That the last day of judgement may so find you,
And leave you the same devil you were before.
Instruct me some good horse-leech to speak treason,
For since you cannot take my life for deeds,   280

262 *Unto a* Q3, Q4 (Q1, Q2 VIT. Unto a); *convertites* Q1 (Q2, Q3,
    Q4 converts); *bawd—* ed. (Q1a, Q2, Q3 baud. ; Q1b baud ; Q4
    bawd.)
264 *convertites* Q1b (Q1a couertites; Q2, Q3, Q4 converts) reformed
    prostitutes
270 *patent* special licence, or title (Brown)
274 *those* Q4 (Q1, Q2, Q3 these); *maw* Q3, Q4 (Q1 mawes; Q2 mawe)
276 *fury* Q1 (Q2, Q3, Q4 Fury)
279 *horse-leech* blood-sucker

267: another borrowing from *Sejanus* (IV. i, 1–2.)

Take it for words. O woman's poor revenge
Which dwells but in the tongue! I will not weep,
No I do scorn to call up one poor tear
To fawn on your injustice; bear me hence,
Unto this house of—what's your mitigating title? 285
MONTICELSO
Of convertites.
VITTORIA
It shall not be a house of convertites.
My mind shall make it honester to me
Than the Pope's palace, and more peaceable
Than thy soul, though thou art a cardinal, 290
Know this, and let it somewhat raise your spite,
Through darkness diamonds spread their richest light.

Exit VITTORIA [*with* ZANCHE, *guarded*]

Enter BRACHIANO

BRACHIANO
Now you and I are friends sir, we'll shake hands,
In a friend's grave, together: a fit place,
Being the emblem of soft peace t'atone our hatred. 295
FRANCISCO
Sir, what's the matter?
BRACHIANO
I will not chase more blood from that lov'd cheek,
You have lost too much already; fare you well.

[*Exit*]

FRANCISCO
How strange these words sound? What's the interpretation?
FLAMINEO [*aside*]
Good, this is a preface to the discovery of the Duchess' 300
death. He carries it well. Because now I cannot counterfeit
a whining passion for the death of my lady, I will feign a
mad humour for the disgrace of my sister, and that will
keep off idle questions. Treason's tongue hath a villainous
palsy in't; I will talk to any man, hear no man, and for a 305
time appear a politic madman.

[*Exit*]

Enter GIOVANNI, *Count* LODOVICO

286;287: *convertites* Q1 (Q2, Q3, Q4 converts)
295 *atone* reconcile   304 *hath a* Q1 (Q2, Q3, Q4 with a)
305 *palsy* nervous disease, sometimes characterized by involuntary tremors
306 *politic* cunning

FRANCISCO
How now my noble cousin; what, in black?

GIOVANNI
Yes uncle, I was taught to imitate you
In virtue, and you must imitate me
In colours for your garments; my sweet mother   310
Is, —

FRANCISCO How? Where?

GIOVANNI
Is there, no yonder; indeed sir I'll not tell you,
For I shall make you weep.

FRANCISCO
Is dead.

GIOVANNI Do not blame me now,   315
I did not tell you so.

LODOVICO   She's dead my lord.

FRANCISCO
Dead?

MONTICELSO
Blessed lady; thou art now above thy woes.
Wilt please your lordships to withdraw a little?

                                [*Exeunt* AMBASSADORS]

GIOVANNI
What do the dead do, uncle? Do they eat,   320
Hear music, go a-hunting, and be merry,
As we that live?

FRANCISCO
No coz; they sleep.

GIOVANNI   Lord, Lord, that I were dead, —
I have not slept these six nights. When do they wake?

FRANCISCO
When God shall please.

GIOVANNI   Good God let her sleep ever.   325
For I have known her wake an hundred nights,
When all the pillow, where she laid her head,
Was brine-wet with her tears. I am to complain to you sir.
I'll tell you how they have used her now she's dead:
They wrapp'd her in a cruel fold of lead,   330
And would not let me kiss her.

FRANCISCO   Thou didst love her.

325 speech-prefix: Q3, Q4 (Q1, Q2 [misplace at 326])
326 *hundred* Q4 (Q1, Q2, Q3 hundreth)
330 *fold* wrapping; layer
331 *love her.* Qq (Lucas: love her?)

GIOVANNI

I have often heard her say she gave me suck,
And it should seem by that she dearly lov'd me,
Since princes seldom do it.

FRANCISCO

O, all of my poor sister that remains!   335
Take him away for God's sake.

                                        [*Exit* GIOVANNI, *attended*]
MONTICELSO   How now my lord?
FRANCISCO

Believe me I am nothing but her grave,
And I shall keep her blessed memory
Longer than thousand epitaphs.

                                                  [*Exeunt*]

[Act III, Scene iii]

Enter FLAMINEO *as distracted* [, MARCELLO *and* LODOVICO]

FLAMINEO

We endure the strokes like anvils or hard steel,
Till pain itself make us no pain to feel.
Who shall do me right now? Is this the end of service?
I'd rather go weed garlic; travel through France, and
be mine own ostler; wear sheep-skin linings; or shoes that   5
stink of blacking; be ent'red into the list of the forty
thousand pedlars in Poland.   *Enter Savoy* [*Ambassador*]
Would I had rotted in some surgeon's house at Venice,
built upon the pox as well as on piles, ere I had serv'd
Brachiano.   10

SAVOY AMBASSADOR

You must have comfort.

FLAMINEO

Your comfortable words are like honey. They relish well in
your mouth that's whole; but in mine that's wounded they

III, iii: see Textual Appendix—A.
   4 *travel* Q3, Q4 (Q1, Q2 trauaile)
   5 *linings* drawers; leather breeches; *shoes* Q4 (Q1, Q2, Q3 shoos)
   6 *list* roll
   9 *built upon the pox* financially established on fees taken for curing
      venereal disease; *piles* wooden supports; haemorrhoids

---

Act III, Scene iii. This scene is located in the ante-chamber of the Pope's
palace, adjoining the court room.
   7 *pedlars in Poland.* In the seventeenth century the Poles were, apparently,
      proverbially poor and there were many pedlars in the country.

go down as if the sting of the bee were in them. Oh they
have wrought their purpose cunningly, as if they would not   15
seem to do it of malice. In this a politician imitates the
devil, as the devil imitates a cannon. Wheresoever he comes
to do mischief, he comes with his backside towards you.

Enter the French [Ambassador]

FRENCH AMBASSADOR
The proofs are evident.

FLAMINEO
Proof! 'twas corruption. O gold, what a god art thou! and   20
O man, what a devil art thou to be tempted by that cursed
mineral! Yon diversivolent lawyer; mark him; knaves turn
informers, as maggots turn to flies; you may catch gudgeons
with either. A cardinal;–I would he would hear me,–there's
nothing so holy but money will corrupt and putrify it, like   25
victual under the line.   *Enter English Ambassador*
You are happy in England, my lord; here they sell justice
with those weights they press men to death with. O horrible
salary!

ENGLISH AMBASSADOR
Fie, fie, Flamineo.   30

FLAMINEO
Bells ne'er ring well, till they are at their full pitch, and I
hope yon cardinal shall never have the grace to pray well,
till he come to the scaffold.   *[Exeunt Ambassadors]*
If they were rack'd now to know the confederacy! But your
noblemen are privileged from the rack; and well may. For   35
a little thing would pull some of them a' pieces afore they
came to their arraignment. Religion; oh how it is commeddled with policy. The first bloodshed in the world
happened about religion. Would I were a Jew.

16 *politician* crafty and intriguing schemer
22 *Yon* ed.: see Textual Appendix–A; *diversivolent cf.* III.ii, 28 and
    note.
23 *gudgeons* small fish; simpletons
26 *victual* ed. (Q1 vittell; Q2, Q3, Q4 victuals); *under the line* at the
    equator
28 see Additional Notes, p. 147.
29 *salary* recompense; reward for services rendered
31 *pitch* height; *and* ed. (Qq And)   32 *grace* God's help
33 s.d. see Textual Appendix–A.
35 *well may* i.e. well they may (should) be
36 *pull . . . a' pieces* i.e. on the rack; in argument
37–38 *commeddled* mixed or mingled together; *policy* intrigue; dissimu-
    lation

38–39 *bloodshed . . . religion* i.e. Cain's murder of Abel: see Genesis iv, 3–8.

MARCELLO

O, there are too many.   40

FLAMINEO

You are deceiv'd. There are not Jews enough; priests
enough, nor gentlemen enough.

MARCELLO

How?

FLAMINEO

I'll prove it. For if there were Jews enough, so many
Christians would not turn usurers; if priests enough, one   45
should not have six benefices; and if gentlemen enough, so
many early mushrooms, whose best growth sprang from a
dunghill, should not aspire to gentility. Farewell. Let
others live by begging. Be thou one of them; practise the
art of Wolner in England to swallow all's given thee; and   50
let one purgation make thee as hungry again as fellows that
work in a sawpit. I'll go hear the screech-owl.   *Exit*

LODOVICO [*aside*]

This was Brachiano's pander, and 'tis strange
That in such open and apparent guilt
Of his adulterous sister, he dare utter   55
So scandalous a passion. I must wind him.

Enter FLAMINEO

FLAMINEO [*aside*]

How dares this banish'd count return to Rome,
His pardon not yet purchas'd? I have heard
The deceas'd Duchess gave him pension,
And that he came along from Padua   60
I'th' train of the young prince. There's somewhat in't.
Physicians, that cure poisons, still do work
With counterpoisons.

MARCELLO   Mark this strange encounter.

---

47 *mushrooms* upstarts
52 *in a* Q2, Q3, Q4 (Q1 in)
56 *wind him* i.e. get wind of his purposes
58 *purchas'd* obtained (not necessarily 'bought')

---

50 *Wolner*, a singing-man of Windsor, was a famous Elizabethan glutton,
   renowned for his ability to digest iron, glass, oyster-shells, raw meat and
   raw fish, who nevertheless died from eating a raw eel.
51–2 *as hungry again . . . sawpit*. I have been unable to trace the origin of
   this phrase; it is not recorded in Tilley's *A Dictionary of the Proverbs in
   England in the Sixteenth and Seventeenth Centuries*.

FLAMINEO
The god of melancholy turn thy gall to poison,
And let the stigmatic wrinkles in thy face,   65
Like to the boisterous waves in a rough tide
One still overtake another.
LODOVICO   I do thank thee
And I do wish ingeniously for thy sake
The dog-days all year long.
FLAMINEO   How croaks the raven?
Is our good Duchess dead?
LODOVICO   Dead.
FLAMINEO   O fate!   70
Misfortune comes like the crowner's business,
Huddle upon huddle.
LODOVICO
Shalt thou and I join housekeeping?
FLAMINEO   Yes, content.
Let's be unsociably sociable.
LODOVICO
Sit some three days together, and discourse.   75
FLAMINEO
Only with making faces;
Lie in our clothes.
LODOVICO
With faggots for our pillows.
FLAMINEO   And be lousy.
LODOVICO
In taffeta linings; that's gentle melancholy;
Sleep all day.
FLAMINEO   Yes: and like your melancholic hare   80
Feed after midnight.

Enter ANTONELLI [*and* GASPARO, *laughing*]

We are observed: see how yon couple grieve.
LODOVICO
What a strange creature is a laughing fool,
As if a man were created to no use
But only to show his teeth.

65 *stigmatic* marked with a 'stigma' or brand; deformed; ill-favoured
68 *ingeniously* usual meaning; also, ingenuously: thus equivocal here.
68–70: i.e. I wish thee 'an eternal season of heat and lust, best
    weather for panders.' (Dent); *cf*. III.ii, 200; *raven* bird of ill omen
72 *Huddle upon huddle* in heaps, piling up
79 *taffata linings* drawers or underclothes made of taffeta, which was
    supposed to be louse-proof

FLAMINEO   I'll tell thee what,   85
It would do well instead of looking-glasses
To set one's face each morning by a saucer
Of a witch's congealed blood.
LODOVICO   Precious girn, rogue.
We'll never part.
FLAMINEO   Never: till the beggary of courtiers,
The discontent of churchmen, want of soldiers,   90
And all the creatures that hang manacled,
Worse than strappado'd, on the lowest felly
Of Fortune's wheel be taught in our two lives
To scorn that world which life of means deprives.

ANTONELLI
My lord I bring good news. The Pope on's death-bed,   95
At th'earnest suit of the great Duke of Florence,
Hath sign'd your pardon, and restor'd unto you—
LODOVICO
I thank you for your news. Look up again
Flamineo, see my pardon.
FLAMINEO   Why do you laugh?
There was no such condition in our covenant.
LODOVICO   Why?   100
FLAMINEO
You shall not seem a happier man than I;
You know our vow sir, if you will be merry,
Do it i'th' like posture, as if some great man
Sat while his enemy were executed:
Though it be very lechery unto thee,   105
Do't with a crabbed politician's face.
LODOVICO
Your sister is a damnable whore.
FLAMINEO   Ha?
LODOVICO
Look you; I spake that laughing.

---

87 *saucer* a technical term in surgery (Lucas)
88 *girn, rogue* ed: see Textual Appendix-A; *girn* a snarl, growl,
   the act of showing the teeth in a disagreeable way (Wright, *English
   Dialect Dictionary*)
92 *strappado'd* hung up by the hands, which have been tied across
   the back; *felly* felloe or section of the rim of a wheel
106 *crabbed* Q1 (Q2, Q3, Q4 sabby)

---

93 *Fortune's wheel.* The goddess Fortune was supposed to turn a wheel
   upon which men would be raised to the highest 'felly' and then allowed
   to sink again to the lowest. Flamineo here also refers to the torturing
   wheel: *cf.* V.vi, 292.

FLAMINEO
  Dost ever think to speak again?
LODOVICO   Do you hear?
  Wilt sell me forty ounces of her blood,   110
  To water a mandrake?
FLAMINEO   Poor lord, you did vow
  To live a lousy creature.
LODOVICO   Yes;—
FLAMINEO   Like one
  That had for ever forfeited the daylight,
  By being in debt,—
LODOVICO   Ha, ha!
FLAMINEO
  I do not greatly wonder you do break: 115
  Your lordship learn't long since. But I'll tell you,—
LODOVICO
  What?
FLAMINEO And't shall stick by you.
LODOVICO   I long for it.
FLAMINEO
  This laughter scurvily becomes your face;
  If you will not be melancholy, be angry.   *Strikes him*
  See, now I laugh too.   120
MARCELLO
  You are to blame, I'll force you hence.
LODOVICO   Unhand me.

                        Exit MAR[CELLO] & FLAM[INEO]
  That e'er I should be forc'd to right myself,
  Upon a pander!
ANTONELLI   My lord.
LODOVICO
  H'had been as good meet with his fist a thunderbolt.
GASPARO
  How this shows!
LODOVICO   Ud's death, how did my sword miss him?   125
  These rogues that are most weary of their lives,
  Still scape the greatest dangers.
  A pox upon him: all his reputation;—
  Nay all the goodness of his family;—
  Is not worth half this earthquake.   130

111 *mandrake: cf.* III.i, 51 note.
115 *break* break your oath; go bankrupt
116 *learn't* Q1, Q2, Q3 (Q4 learnt) i.e. learnt it
124 *H'had* he had
127 *dangers.* Q2, Q3, Q4 (Q1 dangers,)

I learnt it of no fencer to shake thus;
Come, I'll forget him, and go drink some wine.   *Exeunt*

[Act IV, Scene i]

Enter FRANCISCO *and* MONTICELSO

MONTICELSO
Come, come my lord, untie your folded thoughts,
And let them dangle loose as a bride's hair.
Your sister's poisoned.
FRANCISCO   Far be it from my thoughts
To seek revenge.
MONTICELSO   What, are you turn'd all marble?
FRANCISCO
Shall I defy him, and impose a war   5
Most burthensome on my poor subjects' necks,
Which at my will I have not power to end?
You know; for all the murders, rapes, and thefts,
Committed in the horrid lust of war,
He that unjustly caus'd it first proceed,   10
Shall find it in his grave and in his seed.
MONTICELSO
That's not the course I'd wish you: pray, observe me.
We see that undermining more prevails
Than doth the cannon. Bear your wrongs conceal'd,
And, patient as the tortoise, let this camel   15
Stalk o'er your back unbruis'd: sleep with the lion,
And let this brood of secure foolish mice
Play with your nostrils; till the time be ripe
For th' bloody audit, and the fatal gripe:
Aim like a cunning fowler, close one eye,   20
That you the better may your game espy.
FRANCISCO
Free me my innocence, from treacherous acts:
I know there's thunder yonder: and I'll stand,
Like a safe valley, which low bends the knee
To some aspiring mountain: since I know   25

131 *learnt* Q1, Q4 (Q2, Q3 learn't)
  2 Jacobean brides wore their hair loose.
12 *observe me* Q1, Q2 (Q3, Q4 observe)
16 *your back unbruis'd* i.e. 'your back being unbruised'
19 *audit* day when accounts are presented for inspection
20 *fowler* one who hunts birds, especially for food

Act IV, Scene i. The scene takes place in another room of the pope's palace.

Treason, like spiders weaving nets for flies,
By her foul work is found, and in it dies.
To pass away these thoughts, my honour'd lord,
It is reported you possess a book
Wherein you have quoted, by intelligence,   30
The names of all notorious offenders
Lurking about the city.
MONTICELSO   Sir I do;
And some there are which call it my black book:
Well may the title hold: for though it teach not
The art of conjuring, yet in it lurk   35
The names of many devils.
FRANCISCO   Pray let's see it.
MONTICELSO
I'll fetch it to your lordship.   *Exit* MONTICELSO
FRANCISCO   Monticelso,
I will not trust thee, but in all my plots
I'll rest as jealous as a town besieg'd.
Thou canst not reach what I intend to act;   40
Your flax soon kindles, soon is out again,
But gold slow heats, and long will hot remain.

    Enter MONT[ICELSO,] *presents* FRAN[CISCO] *with a book*

MONTICELSO
'Tis here my lord.
FRANCISCO
First your intelligencers, pray let's see.
MONTICELSO
Their number rises strangely,   45
And some of them
You'd take for honest men.
Next are panders.
These are your pirates: and these following leaves,
For base rogues that undo young gentlemen   50
By taking up commodities: for politic bankrupts:
For fellows that are bawds to their own wives,
Only to put off horses and slight jewels,
Clocks, defac'd plate, and such commodities,

30 *by intelligence* by secret information
33 *black book:* originally the term for certain black-bound official
    registers, this came to mean a list of rogues and villians.
35 *The art of conjuring* i.e. the black art: *cf.* II, ii, 8 note.
39 *jealous* vigilant; apprehensive of evil
40 *reach* i.e. mentally
53 *put off* sell away fraudulently

    At birth of their first children.

FRANCISCO   Are there such?   55

MONTICELSO

    These are for impudent bawds,

    That go in men's apparel; for usurers

    That share with scriveners for their good reportage:

    For lawyers that will antedate their writs:

    And some divines you might find folded there,   60

    But that I slip them o'er for conscience' sake.

    Here is a general catalogue of knaves.

    A man might study all the prisons o'er,

    Yet never attain this knowledge.

FRANCISCO   Murderers.

    Fold down the leaf I pray.   65

    Good my lord let me borrow this strange doctrine.

MONTICELSO

    Pray us't my lord.

FRANCISCO   I do assure your lordship,

    You are a worthy member of the state,

    And have done infinite good in your discovery

    Of these offenders.

MONTICELSO   Somewhat sir.

FRANCISCO   O God!   70

    Better than tribute of wolves paid in England,

    'Twill hang their skins o'th' hedge.

MONTICELSO   I must make bold

---

57 *go in* go about in

58 *reportage* repute; recommendation

59 *writs* Q1, Q2 (Q3, Q4 Deeds)

60 *folded* included in the fold; the allusion is to divines as themselves
    spiritual shepherds of the fold

66 *doctrine* collection of information (with punning reference to the
    cardinal's doctrine in the sense of 'religious tenets')

50–55. By *taking up commodities* swindlers would demand a cash repayment
    for goods which they had given the young gentlemen who had asked for
    the loan of money, the goods being grossly exaggerated in value in the
    first instance; *politic bankrupts* were men who cunningly hid their assets
    and then absconded, thus making money out of their pretended 'bank-
    ruptcy'; the third kind of swindlers mentioned would act as bawds to
    their own wives, giving goods – again their value being exaggerated – in
    return for the high price really paid for their services and their silence
    when their wives had borne bastards.

57–58. These usurers would pay scriveners to recommend them to the
    clients who would probably have to borrow money to pay the scriveners
    for writing out lengthy and complicated legal documents.

To leave your lordship.

FRANCISCO   Dearly sir, I thank you;
If any ask for me at court, report
You have left me in the company of knaves.   75

Exit MONT[ICELSO]

I gather now by this, some cunning fellow
That's my lord's officer, one that lately skipp'd
From a clerk's desk up to a justice' chair,
Hath made this knavish summons; and intends,
As th'Irish rebels wont were to sell heads,   80
So to make prize of these. And thus it happens,
Your poor rogues pay for't, which have not the means
To present bribe in fist: the rest o'th' band
Are raz'd out of the knaves' record; or else
My lord he winks at them with easy will,   85
His man grows rich, the knaves are the knaves still.
But to the use I'll make of it; it shall serve
To point me out a list of murderers,
Agents for any villainy. Did I want
Ten leash of courtezans, it would furnish me;   90
Nay laundress three armies. That in so little paper
Should lie th'undoing of so many men!
'Tis not so big as twenty declarations.
See the corrupted use some make of books:
Divinity, wrested by some factious blood,   95
Draws swords, swells battles, and o'erthrows all good.
To fashion my revenge more seriously,

77 *one* Q1b (Q1a and)
80 *wont were* Q1 (Q2, Q3, Q4 were wont)
81–82: i.e. 'Thus it happens [that] your poor . . .'
82 *the means* Q1 (Q2, Q3, Q4 means)
88 *list* Q1b (Q1a life)
90 *leash* sporting term for a set of three; *furnish* supply
91 *Nay* Q1, Q2 (Q3, Q4 [omit]); *laundress* supply with laundresses,
   who were reputedly of easy virtue; *in so* Q2, Q3, Q4 (Q1a so;
   Q1b so in)
92 *lie* Q1b (Q1a be)
93 *declarations* official proclamations

---

71 *tribute of wolves.* King Edgar (944–975) is supposed to have exacted
   from the Welsh a tribute of three hundred wolves a year to rid the
   land of ravenous animals. Webster may have found the story in Drayton's
   Polyolbion (1612). The *Dictionary of National Biography* thinks it is
   highly improbable that such a tribute was exacted, but gives its supposed
   date as ?968.
80. On 9th April, 1600 Mountjoy wrote to Cecil: 'I have heard you complain that you could not hear of one head brought in for all the Queen's
   money; but I assure you now the kennels of the streets are full of them.'
   (Quoted by Lucas, *Webster*, i, 238.)

Let me remember my dead sister's face:
Call for her picture: no; I'll close mine eyes,
And in a melancholic thought I'll frame   100

Enter ISABEL[L]A's *Ghost*

Her figure 'fore me. Now I ha't – – – how strong
Imagination works! How she can frame
Things which are not! Methinks she stands afore me;
And by the quick idea of my mind,
Were my skill pregnant, I could draw her picture.   105
Thought, as a subtle juggler, makes us deem
Things supernatural, which have cause
Common as sickness. 'Tis my melancholy.
How cam'st thou by thy death?——How idle am I
To question my own idleness – – – Did ever   110
Man dream awake till now? – – – Remove this object,
Out of my brain with't: what have I to do
With tombs, or death-beds, funerals, or tears,
That have to meditate upon revenge?

                                        [*Exit Ghost*]

So now 'tis ended, like an old wives' story.   115
Statesmen think often they see stranger sights
Than madmen. Come, to this weighty business.
My tragedy must have some idle mirth in't,
Else it will never pass. I am in love,
In love with Corombona, and my suit   120
Thus halts to her in verse.—   *He writes.*
I have done it rarely: O the fate of princes!
I am so us'd to frequent flattery,

99 *Call* Q1b (Q1a Looke)
101 *I ha't* – – – ed: see Textual Appendix–A.
104 *quick* living; active; *idea* mental image
105 *pregnant* resourceful, inventive
106 *juggler* magician
107 *which* Q1, Q2 (Q3, Q4 which yet): see Textual Appendix–A.
121 *halts* limps; S.D. opposite 123 in Q1.

---

108 *melancholy.* Francisco treats the apparition as an hallucination, which
was one of the recognised symptoms of melancholy. See Burton's
Anatomy of Melancholy (Oxford, 1621), Part I, Section III, Member 3,
Subsection I, where 'hearing and seeing strange noyses, visions' are
included in a list of symptoms of melancholy which are expounded on
later in the same subsection. See also J. B. Bamborough, *The Little
World of Man* (1952), pp. 99–100.
117ff. See J. R. Mulryne, '*The White Devil* and *The Duchess of Malfi*',
Stratford-upon-Avon Studies: I: Jacobean Theatre (1960), p. 211.

That being alone I now flatter myself;
But it will serve; 'tis seal'd. [*calls offstage*] Bear this   125

Enter SERVANT

To th'house of convertites; and watch your leisure
To give it to the hands of Corombona,
Or to the matron, when some followers
Of Brachiano may be by. Away!   *Exit* SERVANT
He that deals all by strength, his wit is shallow: 130
When a man's head goes through, each limb will follow.
The engine for my business, bold Count Lodowick;
'Tis gold must such an instrument procure,
With empty fist no man doth falcons lure.
Brachiano, I am now fit for thy encounter.   135
Like the wild Irish I'll ne'er think thee dead,
Till I can play at football with thy head.
Flectere si nequeo superos, Acheronta movebo.   *Exit*

[Act IV, Scene ii]

Enter the MATRON, *and* FLAMINEO

MATRON
    Should it be known the Duke hath such recourse
    To your imprison'd sister, I were like
    T'incur much damage by it.
FLAMINEO   Not a scruple.
    The Pope lies on his death-bed, and their heads

126 *convertites* Q1 (Q2, Q3, Q4 converts)
132 *engine* tool, instrument
134 *man doth* Q1, Q4 (Q2, Q3 man do)
    3 *damage* discredit; disapprobation; *scruple* a minute quantity
    4 Gregory XIII died on 10th April, 1585.

---

131 This was a proverbial phrase, consistently applied to politic villians,
    though the image usually involved the head of a fox or snake rather
    than that of a man. (Dent, p. 121.)
134 The *lure* was a bunch of feathers or some other object resembling their
    prey with which falcons were recalled to the falconer. As a verb, *lure*
    came to mean, figuratively, 'to entice, tempt'.
136–7 It was commonly reported of the 'wild Irish' of Webster's day that
    they would not believe an enemy dead till they had cut off his head.
    The practice of playing football with heads or skulls was not uncommon.
    See Dent, pp. 121–2.
138 'If I cannot prevail upon the gods above, I will move the gods of the
    infernal regions.' (Virgil, *Æneid*, VII, 312). This 'was perhaps the most
    standard tag of all for villians. . . . Though often used soberly by in-
    dignant authors, it had become popular even within comic contexts.'
    (Dent, p. 122)
Act IV, Scene ii. This scene is set in the house of convertites, in Rome.

Are troubled now with other business   5
Than guarding of a lady.   *Enter* SERVANT
SERVANT [*aside*]
  Yonder's Flamineo in conference
With the Matrona. [*To the* MATRON] Let me speak with you.
I would entreat you to deliver for me
This letter to the fair Vittoria.   10
MATRON
  I shall sir.

Enter BRACHIANO

SERVANT   With all care and secrecy;
Hereafter you shall know me, and receive
Thanks for this courtesy.

                           [*Exit*]
FLAMINEO   How now? What's that?
MATRON
  A letter.
FLAMINEO To my sister: I'll see't delivered.

                       [*Exit* MATRON]
BRACHIANO
  What's that you read Flamineo?
FLAMINEO   Look.   15
BRACHIANO
  Ha? [*reads*] *To the most unfortunate his best respected*
  Vittoria—
Who was the messenger?
FLAMINEO   I know not.
BRACHIANO
  No! Who sent it?
FLAMINEO   Ud's foot you speak, as if a man
Should know what fowl is coffin'd in a bak'd meat   20
Afore you cut it up.
BRACHIANO
  I'll open't, were't her heart. What's here subscribed—
Florence? This juggling is gross and palpable.
I have found out the conveyance; read it, read it.

16–17; 23: Italics are used here to conform with the printing of other
    quotations from the letter.
20 *coffin'd* enclosed in a coffin i.e. pie-crust (*cf. Titus Andronicus*, V.
    ii, 189)
24 *conveyance* means of communication: *cf. The Duchess of Malfi*, II.v,
    8–11. There is also a play on the legal sense of a document by
    which property (i.e. Vittoria) is transferred from one person to
    another: *cf.* V.vi, 12.

FLAMINEO (*Reads the letter*)
  Your tears I'll turn to triumphs, be but mine.   25
  Your prop is fall'n; I pity that a vine
  Which princes heretofore have long'd to gather,
  Wanting supporters, now should fade and wither.
  Wine i'faith, my lord, with lees would serve his turn.
  Your sad imprisonment I'll soon uncharm,   30
  And with a princely uncontrolled arm
  Lead you to Florence, where my love and care
  Shall hang your wishes in my silver hair.
  A halter on his strange equivocation.
  Nor for my years return me the sad willow: 35
  Who prefer blossoms before fruit that's mellow?
  Rotten on my knowledge with lying too long i'th' bed-straw.
  And all the lines of age this line convinces:
  The gods never wax old, no more do princes.
  A pox on't, tear it, let's have no more atheists for God's
                                           sake.   40

BRACHIANO
  Ud's death, I'll cut her into atomies
  And let th'irregular north-wind sweep her up
  And blow her int' his nostrils. Where's this whore?
FLAMINEO
  That—? what do you call her?
BRACHIANO   O, I could be mad,
  Prevent the curs'd disease she'll bring me to,   45

---

25 s.d. opposite 25–26 in Q1; brackets ed.
29 *lees* sediment deposited at the bottom of wine; dregs
34 *equivocation* use of words with double meaning with intent to deceive; Flamineo puns on the equivocation of 'hang' with his reference to 'halter' i.e. noose.
35 *willow* sign of a rejected lover
37 *bed-straw* was used instead of mattresses; straw was used to help ripen fruit
40 *atheists* unbelievers (here referring to the confusion of gods and princes); wicked or infamous people
41 *atomies* Q1 (Q2 Atomes; Q3, Q4 Atoms) pieces as small as motes of dust   42 *irregular* wild, uncontrolled
44 *That—? what do* ed: see Textual Appendix–A.
45 *prevent* act in anticipation of
45–46: see notes on I, ii, 29; II. i, 90.

25–40. Webster repeats the device of a characters commenting on the equivocations of a letter in *The Duchess of Malfi*, III.v, 26–40.
38 *convinces* overcomes; demonstrates or proves any quality: 'a quibble: this maxim (1) "confutes all old maxims to the contrary", and (2) "is of more force than the wrinkles which suggest old age".' (Brown, p. 101 n.)

And tear my hair off. Where's this changeable stuff?

FLAMINEO

O'er head and ears in water, I assure you,
She is not for your wearing.

BRACHIANO   In you pander!

FLAMINEO

What me, my lord, am I your dog?

BRACHIANO

A blood-hound: do you brave? do you stand me?   50

FLAMINEO

Stand you? Let those that have diseases run;
I need no plasters.

BRACHIANO   Would you be kick'd?

FLAMINEO

Would you have your neck broke?
I tell you Duke, I am not in Russia;
My shins must be kept whole.

BRACHIANO   Do you know me?   55

FLAMINEO

O my lord! methodically.
As in this world there are degrees of evils:
So in this world there are degrees of devils.
You're a great Duke; I your poor secretary.
I look now for a Spanish fig, or an Italian sallet daily.   60

BRACHIANO

Pander, ply your convoy, and leave your prating.

FLAMINEO

All your kindness to me is like that miserable courtesy of
Polyphemus to Ulysses; you reserve me to be devour'd
last; you would dig turves out of my grave to feed your
larks: that would be music to you. Come, I'll lead you to her.   65

---

46 *changeable stuff* material that shows different colours under
different aspects (e.g. shot or watered silk); fickle women
48 *In you* Q1b (Q1a No you; Q2 ee'n you; Q3, Q4 You!)
50 *brave* defy; *stand* withstand
51 *run* is used here with reference to a 'running' sore
52 *plasters* ed. (Q1 plaisters; Q2, Q3, Q4 plaister)
54–55 see Additional Notes, p. 148.
56 *methodically* with scientific accuracy
60 *a Spanish fig, or an Italian sallet* i.e. poisoned food. A Spanish
fig was also an expression of contempt, accompanied by an in-
decent gesture.
61 *ply your convoy* get on with [the conduct of] your business, i.e.
bring us together
63 *Polyphemus* one of the Cyclops: see *Odyssey*, IX, 369–70.

BRACHIANO
  Do you face me?
FLAMINEO
  O sir I would not go before a politic enemy with my back
  towards him, though there were behind me a whirlpool.

  Enter VITTORIA *to* BRACHIANO *and* FLAMINEO

BRACHIANO
  Can you read mistress? Look upon that letter;
  There are no characters nor hieroglyphics.   70
  You need no comment, I am grown your receiver;
  God's precious, you shall be a brave great lady,
  A stately and advanced whore.
VITTORIA   Say sir?
BRACHIANO
  Come, come, let's see your cabinet, discover
  Your treasury of love-letters. Death and furies,   75
  I'll see them all.
VITTORIA   Sir, upon my soul,
  I have not any. Whence was this directed?
BRACHIANO
  Confusion on your politic ignorance!
                  [*Gives her the letter*]
  You are reclaimed, are you? I'll give you the bells
  And let you fly to the devil.
FLAMINEO   Ware hawk, my lord.   80

67 *O sir* Q1b (Q1a Sir)   69–70: see Textual Appendix–A.
70 *characters* emblematic signs; ciphers
71 *comment* commentary, exposition; *receiver* pimp who receives
   love-letters
72 *God's precious* i.e. blood or body
73 *sir?* ed. (Q1 Sir. ; Q2 Sir, ; Q3, Q4 S Sir?); *cf.* II.i, 227 note.
74 *cabinet* often a piece of furniture fitted with compartments for
   jewels, letters etc.; a case for valuables
75 *furies* Q1 (Q2, Q3, Q4 Furies)   78 *politic* cunning, scheming
79 *reclaimed* reformed; called back or tamed (a technical term in
   falconry); *bells* i.e. those worn by the hawk to direct one to her
   and her quarry and to frighten the prey

69–70. Hazlitt marked Scene ii here; Sampson Scene iii. Lucas points out
   that a scene division here destroys the tension. He suggests that Flamineo
   merely draws the traverse to reveal Vittoria in her room. (*Webster*, i,
   240)
80 *hawk* the bird; slang for swindler. *Ware hawk, my lord.* Vittoria is the
   hawk, or swindler and cheat. In the first sense, which is related to
   Brachiano's use of the terms of falconry in the previous lines, 'It is not
   clear whether Flamineo is being cynical and means "Let her fly to feast
   on her prey", or is warning Brachiano against ungenerous impatience.'
   (Dent, p. 125)

VITTORIA [*reads*]
    Florence! This is some treacherous plot, my lord.
    To me, he ne'er was lovely I protest,
    So much as in my sleep.
BRACHIANO   Right: they are plots.
    Your beauty! O, ten thousand curses on't.
    How long have I beheld the devil in crystal?   85
    Thou hast led me, like an heathen sacrifice,
    With music, and with fatal yokes of flowers
    To my eternal ruin. Woman to man
    Is either a god or a wolf.
VITTORIA   My lord.
BRACHIANO   Away.
    We'll be as differing as two adamants;   90
    The one shall shun the other. What? dost weep?
    Procure but ten of thy dissembling trade,
    Ye'ld furnish all the Irish funerals
    With howling, past wild Irish.
FLAMINEO   Fie, my lord.
BRACHIANO
    That hand, that cursed hand, which I have wearied   95
    With doting kisses! O my sweetest Duchess
    How lovely art thou now! [*to* VITTORIA] Thy loose thoughts
    Scatter like quicksilver; I was bewitch'd;
    For all the world speaks ill of thee.
VITTORIA   No matter.
    I'll live so now I'll make that world recant   100
    And change her speeches. You did name your Duchess.
BRACHIANO
    Whose death God pardon.
VITTORIA   Whose death God revenge
    On thee most godless Duke.
FLAMINEO   Now for two whirlwinds.

---

81 *Florence:* Q4 italics; Q1, Q2, Q3 roman type
82 *lovely* Q1b (Q1a thought on)
90 *adamants* loadstones
93 *Ye'ld* ed. (Q1a ee'ld; Q1b Yee'ld; Q2 Wee'l; Q3 Weel; Q4 We'l)
97 *Thy* Q1, Q2, Q3 (Q4, Sampson My); *loose* unconfined; unchaste
103 *two* ed. (Q1a ten; Q1b tow; Q2, Q3, Q4 the)

---

85 *the devil in crystal*: see Additional Notes, p. 148.
93–4 Webster here refers to the 'keening' lamentation still heard, as in the sixteenth century, particularly from women who lament at wakes and funerals in Ireland. Brown notes that Barnabe Riche's *A New Description* (1610) relates how, for the wealthy dead, women were hired who 'will furnish the cry, with greater shriking & howling, then those that are grieued indeede, . . .' (p. 105 n.)

VITTORIA
    What have I gain'd by thee but infamy?
    Thou hast stain'd the spotless honour of my house,   105
    And frighted thence noble society:
    Like those, which sick o'th' palsy, and retain
    Ill-scenting foxes 'bout them, are still shunn'd
    By those of choicer nostrils. What do you call this house?
    Is this your palace? Did not the judge style it   110
    A house of penitent whores? Who sent me to it?
    Who hath the honour to advance Vittoria
    To this incontinent college? Is't not you?
    Is't not your high preferment? Go, go brag
    How many ladies you have undone, like me.   115
    Fare you well sir; let me hear no more of you.
    I had a limb corrupted to an ulcer,
    But I have cut it off: and now I'll go
    Weeping to heaven on crutches. For your gifts,
    I will return them all; and I do wish   120
    That I could make you full executor
    To all my sins. O that I could toss myself
    Into a grave as quickly: for all thou art worth
    I'll not shed one tear more;——I'll burst first.
            She throws herself upon a bed

BRACHIANO
    I have drunk Lethe. Vittoria?   125
    My dearest happiness! Vittoria!
    What do you ail my love? Why do you weep?

VITTORIA
    Yes, I now weep poniards, do you see.

BRACHIANO
    Are not those matchless eyes mine?

107 *sick* are sick
114 *preferment* advancement or promotion in condition, status or
    position in life; often used with reference to the raising of social
    status through marriage   125 *Lethe* waters of oblivion

107–8 Lucas (*Webster*, i, 242) states that the use of the fox in the treatment
    of paralysis, or the palsy, seems to have been quite regular. Ben Jonson
    used one, which had been sent to him as a present, when he was stricken
    with the palsy in 1628.
119–20. *Cf.* St. Mark ix, 45: 'And if thy foot offend thee, cut it off: it is
    better for thee to enter halt into life, than having two feet to be cast into
    hell, into the fire that never shall be quenched:' One wonders if, per-
    haps, the words 'a limb corrupted to an ulcer' might imply, on Webster's
    part, not only a reference to the malignant ulcer on the real Duke of
    Bracciano's leg, but the idea that this physical corruption was a reflec-
    tion of spiritual corruption also.

VITTORIA   I had rather
They were not matches.
BRACHIANO   Is not this lip mine?   130
VITTORIA
Yes: thus to bite it off, rather than give it thee.
FLAMINEO
Turn to my lord, good sister.
VITTORIA   Hence you pander.
FLAMINEO
Pander! Am I the author of your sin?
VITTORIA
Yes. He's a base thief that a thief lets in.
FLAMINEO
We're blown up, my lord,—
BRACHIANO   Wilt thou hear me?   135
Once to be jealous of thee is t'express
That I will love thee everlastingly,
And never more be jealous.
VITTORIA   O thou fool,
Whose greatness hath by much o'ergrown thy wit!
What dar'st thou do, that I not dare to suffer,   140
Excepting to be still thy whore? For that,
In the sea's bottom sooner thou shalt make
A bonfire.
FLAMINEO   O, no oaths for God's sake.
BRACHIANO
Will you hear me?
VITTORIA   Never.
FLAMINEO
What a damn'd imposthume is a woman's will?   145
Can nothing break it? [*to* BRACHIANO, *aside*] Fie, fie, my
                                             lord.
Women are caught as you take tortoises,
She must be turn'd on her back.—Sister, by this hand
I am on your side.—Come, come, you have wrong'd her.
What a strange credulous man were you, my lord,   150
To think the Duke of Florence would love her?
Will any mercer take another's ware
When once 'tis tows'd and sullied? And, yet sister,

129–30 i.e. 'I had rather that they were ugly, or squinted.'
130 *matches* Q1 (Q2 matchles; Q3, Q4 matchless)
135 *blown up* i.e. by a mine   142 *sea's* ed. (Qq seas)
145 *imposthume* ulcer   151 *would* Q1b (Q1a could)
153 *tows'd* toused, dishevelled; also used of a woman who has been
     pulled about indelicately

How scurvily this frowardness becomes you!
Young leverets stand not long; and women's anger　　155
Should, like their flight, procure a little sport;
A full cry for a quarter of an hour;
And then be put to th' dead quat.
BRACHIANO　　　　　　　　　Shall these eyes,
Which have so long time dwelt upon your face,
Be now put out?
FLAMINEO　　　　No cruel landlady i'th' world,　　160
Which lends forth groats to broom-men, and takes use for
　　　　　　　　　　　　　　　　them
Would do't.
Hand her, my lord, and kiss her: be not like
A ferret to let go your hold with blowing.
BRACHIANO
Let us renew right hands.
VITTORIA　　　　　　　Hence.　　165
BRACHIANO
Never shall rage, or the forgetful wine,
Make me commit like fault.
FLAMINEO
Now you are i'th' way on't, follow't hard.
BRACHIANO
Be thou at peace with me; let all the world
Threaten the cannon.
FLAMINEO　　　　Mark his penitence.　　170
Best natures do commit the grossest faults,
When they're giv'n o'er to jealousy; as best wine
Dying makes strongest vinegar. I'll tell you;

---

154 *frowardness* perversity
155 *leverets* young hares; *stand* hunting term, usually 'stand up',
　　meaning hold out
156 *their* i.e. the leverets'
157 *full cry* full pursuit; full weeping
158 *quat* squat (a hunting term)
161 *broom-men* street-sweepers; *use* usury, interest
163 *hand* grasp, fondle
170 *Threaten the cannon* Q1, Q2 (Q3, Q4 Threaten, I care not) i.e.
　　'Threaten us with their cannon.'

163-4 It is apparently a superstition, not a fact, that blowing on a ferret will
　　make it let go of something in which its teeth are fixed. (Lucas, *Webster*,
　　i, 242-3)
166 *the forgetful wine.* Though in fact referring to the oblivion induced by
　　alcohol, Brachiano may also be echoing his sentiment of IV.ii, 125:
　　'I have drunk Lethe.'

The sea's more rough and raging than calm rivers,
But nor so sweet nor wholesome. A quiet woman   175
Is a still water under a great bridge.
A man may shoot her safely.

VITTORIA
O ye dissembling men!

FLAMINEO   We suck'd that, sister,
From women's breasts, in our first infancy.

VITTORIA
To add misery to misery.

BRACHIANO   Sweetest.   180

VITTORIA
Am I not low enough?
Ay, ay, your good heart gathers like a snowball
Now your affection's cold.

BRACHIANO   Ud's foot, it shall melt
To a heart again, or all the wine in Rome
Shall run o'th' lees for't.   185

VITTORIA
Your hawk or dog should be rewarded better
Than I have been. I'll speak not one word more.

FLAMINEO
Stop her mouth,
With a sweet kiss, my lord.
So now the tide's turn'd the vessel's come about.   190
He's a sweet armful. O we curl'd-hair'd men
Are still most kind to women. This is well.

BRACHIANO
That you should chide thus!

FLAMINEO   O, sir, your little chimneys
Do ever cast most smoke. I sweat for you.
Couple together with as deep a silence   195
As did the Grecians in their wooden horse.
My lord, supply your promises with deeds.
You know that painted meat no hunger feeds.

BRACHIANO
Stay—ingrateful Rome!

---

175 *But nor* Q1 (Q2, Q3, Q4 But not)
176 *a great bridge* Q1, Q2 (Q3, Q4 *London-Bridge*)
186 *rewarded:* a technical term for giving part of the hunting prey to
    dogs or hounds who have helped to bring it down; *cf. The Duchess
    of Malfi,* I.i, 58–59.
190 *come about* returned to port
192 *still* always
199 *Stay—ingrateful Rome* ed.: see Textual Appendix–A.

FLAMINEO   Rome! it deserves
  To be call'd Barbary, for our villainous usage.   200

BRACHIANO
  Soft; the same project which the Duke of Florence,
  (Whether in love or gullery I know not)
  Laid down for her escape, will I pursue.

FLAMINEO
  And no time fitter than this night, my lord;
  The Pope being dead; and all the cardinals ent'red   205
  The conclave for th'electing a new Pope;
  The city in a great confusion;
  We may attire her in a page's suit,
  Lay her post-horse, take shipping, and amain
  For Padua.   210

BRACHIANO
  I'll instantly steal forth the Prince Giovanni,
  And make for Padua. You two with your old mother
  And young Marcello that attends on Florence,
  If you can work him to it, follow me.
  I will advance you all: for you Vittoria,   215
  Think of a duchess' title.

FLAMINEO   Lo you sister.
  Stay, my lord; I'll tell you a tale. The crocodile, which lives
  in the river Nilus, hath a worm breeds i'th' teeth of't, which
  puts it to extreme anguish: a little bird, no bigger than a
  wren, is barber-surgeon to this crocodile; flies into the   220
  jaws of't; picks out the worm; and brings present remedy.
  The fish, glad of ease but ingrateful to her that did it, that

202 *gullery* trickery, deception
209 *Lay her post-horse* provide her with relays of post-horses;
     amain at main (i.e. full) speed; without delay
211 *I'll instantly* Q1 (Q2, Q3, Q4 Instantly)

---

200 *Barbary* literally 'was a term of convenience as used by the Elizabethans
     because it could be made to cover practically the whole of Africa's north
     coast west of Egypt.' Barbary pirates were 'a sore spot in the side of
     English traders.' (R. R. Cawley, *The Voyagers and Elizabethan Drama*,
     pp. 92; 93.) The reference here could be to pirates, but probably to the
     country of the Barbarians, i.e. cruel savages. From 1564 onwards
     (according to *O.E.D.*) Barbary was a term used to equal 'barbarity,
     barbarism' and 'barbarousness'.
217–29 This fable is not one of Webster's inventions. For notes on Webster's
     probable sources, e.g. Topsell's *Historie of Serpents* (1608) see Dent,
     pp. 129–30 and Brown, p. 112 n. For comment on its dramatic sig-
     nificance see: F. L. Lucas, *Webster*, i, 244–5; Clifford Leech, *John
     Webster: A Critical Study* (1951), p. 115 and Travis Bogard, *The
     Tragic Satire of John Webster* (Berkeley and Los Angeles, 1955), p.
     104.

the bird may not talk largely of her abroad for non-payment,
closeth her chaps intending to swallow her, and so put her
to perpetual silence. But nature loathing such ingratitude,   225
hath arm'd this bird with a quill or prick on the head, top
o'th' which wounds the crocodile i'th' mouth; forceth her
open her bloody prison; and away flies the pretty tooth-
picker from her cruel patient.

BRACHIANO

Your application is, I have not rewarded   230
The service you have done me.

FLAMINEO   No my lord;
You sister are the crocodile: you are blemish'd in your
fame, my lord cures it. And though the comparison hold
not in every particle; yet observe, remember, what good
the bird with the prick i'th' head hath done you; and   235
scorn ingratitude.
[aside] It may appear to some ridiculous
Thus to talk knave and madman; and sometimes
Come in with a dried sentence, stuff'd with sage.
But this allows my varying of shapes,   240
Knaves do grow great by being great men's apes.   *Exeunt*

[Act IV, Scene iii]

Enter LODOVICO, GASPARO, *and six Ambassadors.*
At another door [FRANCISCO] *the Duke of Florence.*

FRANCISCO

So, my lord, I commend your diligence.
Guard well the conclave, and, as the order is,
Let none have conference with the cardinals.

LODOVICO

I shall, my lord. Room for the ambassadors!

GASPARO

They're wondrous brave today: why do they wear   5
These several habits?

224 *chaps* jaws
239 *sentence* aphorism; maxim; *sage* the herb; wisdom (*cf.* I.ii, 130)
  5 *brave* finely or splendidly dressed
  6 and 15 *several* various, diverse

Act IV, Scene iii. The action of this scene takes place near the Sistine chapel,
outside the pope's palace. For Webster's use of sources in the scene, see:
J. R. Brown, 'The Papal Election in John Webster's "The White Devil"'
(1612), *Notes and Queries*, N.S. IV (1957), 490–94; Gunnar Boklund,
The Sources of 'The White Devil', pp. 30–32; Dent, pp. 130–33.

LODOVICO   O sir, they're knights
  Of several orders.
  That lord i'th' black cloak with the silver cross
  Is Knight of Rhodes; the next Knight of S. Michael;
  That of the Golden Fleece; the Frenchman there   10
  Knight of the Holy Ghost; my lord of Savoy
  Knight of th'Annunciation; the Englishman
  Is Knight of th'honoured Garter, dedicated
  Unto their saint, S. George. I could describe to you
  Their several institutions, with the laws   15
  Annexed to their orders; but that time
  Permits not such discovery.
FRANCISCO   Where's Count Lodowick?
LODOVICO
  Here my lord.
FRANCISCO   'Tis o'th' point of dinner time;
  Marshal the cardinals' service.
LODOVICO   Sir, I shall.

Enter SERVANTS *with several dishes covered*

  Stand, let me search your dish; who's this for?   20
SERVANT
  For my lord Cardinal Monticelso.
LODOVICO
  Who's this?
SERVANT   For my Lord Cardinal of Bourbon.
FRENCH AMBASSADOR
  Why doth he search the dishes? to observe
  What meat is dress'd?
ENGLISH AMBASSADOR   No sir, but to prevent
  Lest any letters should be convey'd in   25
  To bribe or to solicit the advancement

---

18 *Here* Q1, Q2 (Q3, Q4 [omit])
22 *Who's* ed. (Qq *Whose*): see Textual Appendix–A.
24 *dress'd* prepared

9–14 The *Knight of Rhodes* belongs to the order of the Knights of St. John
of Jerusalem which moved first from Jerusalem to Rhodes. The order
was founded during the First Crusade. Malta was granted to them by
the Emperor Charles V in 1530. The order of *St. Michael* was founded
in 1469 by Louis XI. The order of the *Golden Fleece* was founded by
Philip the Good, Duke of Burgundy in 1430. Henri III founded the
order of the *Holy Ghost* in 1578. The order of the *Annunciation*, the
highest order of Knights in Italy, was founded in 1362 by Amadeus VI
of Savoy. The order of the *Garter*, the highest order in England, was
apparently founded 1346–8. Its origin is obscure.

Of any cardinal. When first they enter
'Tis lawful for the ambassadors of princes
To enter with them, and to make their suit
For any man their prince affecteth best;   30
But after, till a general election,
No man may speak with them.

LODOVICO
You that attend on the lord cardinals
Open the window, and receive their viands.

A CARDINAL
You must return the service; the lord cardinals   35
Are busied 'bout electing of the Pope;
They have given o'er scrutiny, and are fallen
To admiration.

LODOVICO   Away, away.
                              [*Exeunt* SERVANTS *with dishes*]

FRANCISCO
I'll lay a thousand ducats you hear news
Of a Pope presently. Hark; sure he's elected,—   40

            [*The*] *Cardinal* [*of* ARRAGON *appears*] *on the terrace*

Behold! my lord of Arragon appears
On the church battlements.

ARRAGON
Denuntio vobis gaudium magnum. Reverendissimus Cardinalis
LORENZO *de* MONTICELSO *electus est in sedem apostolicam, et*
eligit sibi nomen PAULUM *quartum.*   45

OMNES
Vivat Sanctus Pater Paulus Quartus.

                              [*Enter* SERVANT]

35 *the service* the dishes   37 *scrutiny* counting the votes
39 *ducats* were worth 4/8d in 1608.
40 s.d. Brown (Qq *A Cardinal on the Tarras.*)
43 *Denuntio* Q1 (Q2, Q3, Q4 *Annuntio*)
43–45: 'I announce to you tidings of great joy. The Most Reverend
   Cardinal Lorenzo di Monticelso has been elected to the Apostolic
   See, and has chosen for himself the name of Paul IV.'
46 *Everybody.* 'Long live the Holy Father, Paul IV.'
46 s.d. Q4 (Q1, Q2, Q3 [omit])

---

38 *admiration.* The technical term 'adoration', which Webster should have
   used, described the method of electing a pope, an alternative to voting
   (i.e. scrutiny), whereby a pope was elected if two-thirds of the cardinals
   present turned towards and made reverence to the one whom they
   wished to be made pope.
43–45. The historical Cardinal Montalto became Pope Sixtus V.

SERVANT
  Vittoria my lord—
FRANCISCO   Well: what of her?
SERVANT
  Is fled the city—
FRANCISCO   Ha?
SERVANT   With Duke Brachiano.
FRANCISCO
  Fled? Where's the Prince Giovanni?
SERVANT   Gone with his father.
FRANCISCO
  Let the Matrona of the convertites   50
  Be apprehended. Fled? O damnable!

                                        [*Exit* SERVANT]

  [*aside*] How fortunate are my wishes. Why? 'Twas this
  I only labour'd. I did send the letter
  T'instruct him what to do. Thy fame, fond Duke,
  I first have poison'd; directed thee the way   55
  To marry a whore; what can be worse? This follows:
  The hand must act to drown the passionate tongue,
  I scorn to wear a sword and prate of wrong.

                Enter MONTICELSO *in state*

MONTICELSO
  Concedimus vobis apostolicam benedictionem et remissionem
  peccatorum.   60
                [FRANCISCO *whispers to him*]
  My lord reports Vittoria Corombona
  Is stol'n from forth the house of convertites
  By Brachiano, and they're fled the city.
  Now, though this be the first day of our seat,
  We cannot better please the divine power,   65
  That to sequester from the holy church
  These cursed persons. Make it therefore known,

---

50 *Matrona* Q1 (Q2, Q3 Matrone; Q4 Matron); *convertites* Q1 (Q2,
    Q3, Q4 converts)
51 *Fled?* Q4 (Q1 fled   ; Q2, Q3, fled?)
54 *fond* foolish
59–60: Q1b (Q1a [omits]) 'We grant you the apostolic blessing and
    remission of sins.'; *et* ed. (Qq &); *peccatorum* Q2, Q3, Q4 (Q1b
    peccatorem)
62 *convertites* Q1 (Q2, Q3, Q4 converts)
64 *seat* Q3, Q4 (Q1b, Q2 seate; Q1a state): 'the technical term for
    the throne or office of a Pope' (Brown)

We do denounce excommunication
Against them both: all that are theirs in Rome
We likewise banish. Set on.   70

Exeunt [all except FRANCISCO *and* LODOVICO]

FRANCISCO
Come dear Lodovico
You have tane the sacrament to prosecute
Th'intended murder.

LODOVICO   With all constancy.
But, sir, I wonder you'll engage yourself
In person, being a great prince.

FRANCISCO   Divert me not.   75
Most of this court are of my faction,
And some are of my counsel. Noble friend,
Our danger shall be 'like in this design;
Give leave, part of the glory may be mine.

Exit FRAN[CISCO]   *Enter* MONTICELSO

MONTICELSO
Why did the Duke of Florence with such care   80
Labour your pardon? Say.

LODOVICO
Italian beggars will resolve you that
Who, begging of an alms, bid those they beg of
Do good for their own sakes; or't may be
He spreads his bounty with a sowing hand,   85
Like kings, who many times give out of measure;
Not for desert so much as for their pleasure.

MONTICELSO
I know you're cunning. Come, what devil was that
That you were raising?

LODOVICO   Devil, my lord?

MONTICELSO   I ask you
How doth the Duke employ you, that his bonnet   90
Fell with such compliment unto his knee,
When he departed from you?

LODOVICO   Why, my lord,
He told me of a resty Barbary horse

---

78 *'like* Q1 (Q2, Q3, Q4 like) alike   79 s.d. Q1b (Q1a [omits])
80 speech-prefix: Q1b MON. (Q1a [omits])
81 *Labour* labour for
86 *out of measure* excessively
88 *was that* Q1, Q2 (Q3, Q4 is that)
93 *resty* restive; *Barbary horse* a small, swift and hot-tempered
   horse from Barbary (*cf.* IV.ii, 200 note.)

Which he would fain have brought to the career,
The 'sault, and the ring-galliard. Now, my lord,   95
I have a rare French rider.
MONTICELSO   Take you heed:
Lest the jade break your neck. Do you put me off
With your wild horse-tricks? Sirrah you do lie.
O, thou'rt a foul black cloud, and thou dost threat
A violent storm.
LODOVICO   Storms are i'th' air, my lord;   100
I am too low to storm.
MONTICELSO   Wretched creature!
I know that thou art fashion'd for all ill,
Like dogs, that once get blood, they'll ever kill.
About some murder? Was't not?
LODOVICO   I'll not tell you;
And yet I care not greatly if I do;   105
Marry with this preparation. Holy Father,
I come not to you as an intelligencer,
But as a penitent sinner. What I utter
Is in confession merely; which you know
Must never be reveal'd.
MONTICELSO   You have o'ertane me.   110
LODOVICO
Sir I did love Brachiano's Duchess dearly;
Or rather I pursued her with hot lust,
Though she ne'er knew on't. She was poison'd;
Upon my soul she was: for which I have sworn
T'avenge her murder.
MONTICELSO   To the Duke of Florence?   115

97 *jade* horse; woman (i.e. Vittoria)
98 *horse-tricks* tricks taught to horses; horse-play; *you do* Q1, Q2
   (Q3, Q4 you)
104 *murder* Q1, Q2 (Q3, Q4 murther)
107 *intelligencer* spy, informer
110 *o'ertane* overreached

94-95 *the career / The 'sault and the ring-galliard:* technical terms for the
   different exercises in the 'manage' of a horse. The *career* consisted in
   running a horse at full speed and then making him stop quickly and
   firmly; *the 'sault* was the name given to various leaps which the horse
   was trained to do; *the ring-galliard* was 'a mixture of bounding forward,
   curvetting, and yerking' i.e. lashing out with the heels. (Lucas, *Webster*,
   i, 247)
96 *French rider.* The French were famous for their horsemanship: *cf. The
   Duchess of Malfi* I.ii, 60-63.
111-15 P. Haworth comments: 'The illicit passion of Vittoria and Brachiano
   is thus punished by means of an equally criminal lust.' (*English Hymns
   and Ballads* . . . p. 92)

LODOVICO
  To him I have.
MONTICELSO   Miserable creature!
  If thou persist in this, 'tis damnable.
  Dost thou imagine thou canst slide on blood
  And not be tainted with a shameful fall?
  Or, like the black and melancholic yew-tree,   120
  Dost think to root thyself in dead men's graves,
  And yet to prosper? Instruction to thee
  Comes like sweet showers to over-hard'ned ground:
  They wet, but pierce not deep. And so I leave thee
  With all the Furies hanging 'bout thy neck,   125
  Till by thy penitence thou remove this evil,
  In conjuring from thy breast that cruel devil.
                                   Exit MON[TICELSO]
LODOVICO
  I'll give it o'er. He says 'tis damnable:
  Besides I did expect his suffrage,
  By reason of Camillo's death.   130
                   Enter SERVANT *and* FRANCISCO
FRANCISCO
  Do you know that count?
SERVANT   Yes, my lord.
FRANCISCO
  Bear him these thousand ducats to his lodging;
  Tell him the Pope hath sent them. Happily
  That will confirm more than all the rest.   [*Exit*]
SERVANT   Sir.
       [SERVANT *delivers purse of money to* LODOVICO]

128 *give it o'er* give it up
129 *suffrage* support, assistance
133 *Happily* Q1, Q2, Q3 (Q4 *Haply*) haply, perhaps
134 *confirm* Qq: see Textual Appendix–A

125; 151: *Furies:* the three avenging goddesses, with snakes in their hair–
        Tisiphone, Megæra and Alecto–who were sent from Tartarus to avenge
        wrong and punish crime. Reference to them was a common feature of
        Senecan revenge plays in the 1590's. For example, in George Peele's
        Battle of Alcazar (1594), written *circa* 1588–89
             Alecto with her brand and bloudie torch
             Megæra with her whip and snakie haire,
             Tysiphone with her fatall murthering yron   (Sig. B₃)
        are described as conspiring to avenge the wrongs and murders committed
        by the villain hero, Muly Mahamet. By transference *fury* was used for
        likening anyone–but especially a ferociously angry or malignant woman
        –to an infernal spirit or minister of vengeance. In transcribing *Fury* of
        Q1 I have distinguished between *Fury*–a direct reference to one of the
        goddesses–and *fury*–the metaphorical use of the word–by the use of
        the capital. In each case the collation is given.

LODOVICO
  To me sir?   135
SERVANT
  His Holiness hath sent you a thousand crowns,
  And wills you, if you travel, to make him
  Your patron for intelligence.
LODOVICO   His creature
  Ever to be commanded.   [*Exit* SERVANT]
  Why now 'tis come about. He rail'd upon me;   140
  And yet these crowns were told out and laid ready,
  Before he knew my voyage. O the art,
  The modest form of greatness! that do sit
  Like brides at wedding dinners, with their looks turn'd
  From the least wanton jests, their puling stomach   145
  Sick of the modesty, when their thoughts are loose,
  Even acting of those hot and lustful sports
  Are to ensue about midnight: such his cunning!
  He sounds my depth thus with a golden plummet;
  I am doubly arm'd now. Now to th'act of blood;   150
  There's but three Furies found in spacious hell;
  But in a great man's breast three thousand dwell.

                                 [*Exit*]

[Act V, Scene i]

A passage over the stage of BRACHIANO, FLAMINEO, MARCELLO,
HORTENSIO, [VITTORIA] COROMBONA, CORNELIA, ZANCHE
                 and others

      [*Enter* FLAMINEO *and* HORTENSIO]

137 *wills* Q3, Q4 (Q1 will; Q2 wils); *travel* Q4 (Q1, Q2 trauaile;
    Q3 travail)
138 *intelligence* supplying with secret information
141 *told out* counted out
145 *jests* Q1 (Q2, Q3, Q4 jest); *puling* sickly, weak
150 *arm'd now. Now* Qq: see Textual Appendix–A.

---

136 *crowns.* Since a ducat was worth 4/8d (see IV.iii, 39 note) the term
    crown–i.e. 5/––used here is rather a translation of the sum into English
    than a mistake or confusion between the names of coins.
Act V, Scene i et seq. The whole of the fifth act takes place in Brachiano's
    palace in Padua.
S.D. *and others.* Brown (p. 123 n.) comments that these probably include the
    ambassadors whose 'mere presence on the stage would enforce Webster's
    often-repeated comments on the power of great men and the sycophancy
    of court society.' Moreover, since there would hardly have been time
    for the actors to change their costumes, they would still be dressed in
    the habits of their various orders, worn at the papal election, 'tokens of
    holiness, virtue, and honour–an ironical display for the marriage of a
    proclaimed whore and an excommunicate duke.'

FLAMINEO

In all the weary minutes of my life,
Day ne'er broke up till now. This marriage
Confirms me happy.

HORTENSIO   'Tis a good assurance.
Saw you not yet the Moor that's come to court?

FLAMINEO

Yes, and conferr'd with him i'th' Duke's closet;   5
I have not seen a goodlier personage,
Nor ever talk'd with man better experienc'd
In state affairs or rudiments of war.
He hath by report serv'd the Venetian
In Candy these twice seven years, and been chief   10
In many a bold design.

HORTENSIO   What are those two
That bear him company?

FLAMINEO

Two noblemen of Hungary, that living in the emperor's
service as commanders, eight years since, contrary to the
expectation of all the court ent'red into religion, into the   15
strict order of Capuchins: but being not well settled in
their undertaking they left their order and returned to
court: for which being after troubled in conscience, they
vowed their service against the enemies of Christ; went to
Malta; were there knighted; and in their return back, at   20
this great solemnity, they are resolved for ever to forsake
the world, and settle themselves here in a house of Capuchins
in Padua.

HORTENSIO

'Tis strange.

FLAMINEO

One thing makes it so. They have vowed for ever to wear   25
next their bare bodies those coats of mail they served in.

HORTENSIO

Hard penance. Is the Moor a Christian?

---

8 *rudiments* principles (*not* fundamentals)
10 *Candy* Crete
20 *knighted* i.e. in the order of St. John of Jerusalem

1–3 With the dramatic irony of these confident lines of Flamineo's Dent
    (pp. 135–6) compares Jonson's *Sejanus*, V, 3–4.
16 *Capuchins*. This order had originally separated itself from the main body
    of the Franciscans about 1528 so that it might return to the strict
    austerity of St. Francis. It was not established as an independent order
    till 1619.

FLAMINEO
　He is.
HORTENSIO
　Why proffers he his service to our Duke?
FLAMINEO
　Because he understands there's like to grow　　　　30
　Some wars between us and the Duke of Florence,
　In which he hopes employment.
　I never saw one in a stern bold look
　Wear more command, nor in a lofty phrase
　Express more knowing, or more deep contempt　　　35
　Of our slight airy courtiers. He talks
　As if he had travell'd all the princes' courts
　Of Christendom; in all things strives t'express
　That all that should dispute with him may know,
　Glories, like glow-worms, afar off shine bright　　　40
　But look'd to near, have neither heat nor light.
　The Duke!

Enter BRACHIANO, [FRANCISCO, *Duke of*] *Florence disguised
like Mulinassar;* LODOVICO, ANTONELLI, GASPARO, FERNESE
having their swords and helmets.

BRACHIANO
　You are nobly welcome. We have heard at full
　Your honourable service 'gainst the Turk.
　To you, brave Mulinassar, we assign　　　　45
　A competent pension: and are inly sorrow,
　The vows of those two worthy gentlemen
　Make them incapable of our proffer'd bounty.
　Your wish is you may leave your warlike swords
　For monuments in our chapel. I accept it　　　　50
　As a great honour done me, and must crave
　Your leave to furnish out our Duchess' revels.

32 Q1, Q2 have duplicate entry for Brachiano here.
37 *travell'd* Q4 (Q1, Q2 trauail'd; Q3 travail'd)
42 *The Duke!* ed. (Q1, Q2, Q3 The Duke. ; Q4 *The Duke.*—)
42 s.d. LODOVICO, i.e. disguised as Carlo; GASPARO Q4 (Q1, Q2,
　Q3 *Gaspar*) i.e. disguised as Pedro; FARNESE *bearing* Q1 (Q2
　Farnese, bearing; Q3, Q4 *bearing*): see V.vi, 164 s.d. note p. 149.
46 *competent* sufficient in means for comfortable living; *sorrow* Q1
　(Q2 *sorrie;* Q3, Q4 *sorry*) sorry
48 *incapable of* i.e. incapable of accepting
50 *monuments* evidence, or tokens [of the fact of a change in a man's
　way of life]
52 *leave* permission for absence

40–41 Webster repeated these lines in *The Duchess of Malfi,* IV.ii, 141–2.

Only one thing, as the last vanity
You e'er shall view, deny me not to stay
To see a barriers prepar'd tonight;   55
You shall have private standings. It hath pleas'd
The great ambassadors of several princes
In their return from Rome to their own countries
To grace our marriage, and to honour me
With such a kind of sport.
FRANCISCO   I shall persuade them   60
To stay, my lord.
BRACHIANO   Set on there to the presence.
            Exeunt BRACHIANO, FLAMINEO *and* [HORTENSIO]
LODOVICO
Noble my lord, most fortunately welcome,
                              The conspirators here embrace
You have our vows seal'd with the sacrament
To second your attempts.
GASPARO   And all things ready.
He could not have invented his own ruin,   65
Had he despair'd, with more propriety.
LODOVICO
You would not take my way.
FRANCISCO   'Tis better ordered.
LODOVICO
T'have poison'd his prayer book, or a pair of beads,
The pommel of his saddle, his looking-glass,
Or th'handle of his racket. O that, that!   70
That while he had been bandying at tennis,
He might have sworn himself to hell, and struck
His soul into the hazard! O my lord!
I would have our plot be ingenious,
And have it hereafter recorded for example   75

55 *barriers*: cf. I.ii, 28 note.   56 *standings* standing-places
61 speech-prefix: Dyce *et al.* (Qq continue as Francisco's speech);
   presence presence or audience chamber
61 S.D. [HORTENSIO] ed. (Qq *Marcello*): see Textual Appendix–A.
62 speech-prefix: Q3, Q4 *Lod.* (Q1, Q2 *Car.*); *Noble my* Q1, Q2 (Q3,
   Q4 *My noble*); S.D. opposite 62–64 in Q1.
64 speech-prefix: Q3, Q4 *Gas.* (Q1, Q2 *Ped.*)
66 *propriety* Q1, Q2 (Q3, Q4 dexterity)
68 *pair of beads* set or string of beads
59 *our* Q1, Q4 (Q2 ,Q3 your)
68–70; 71–73: See Additional Notes, p. 148.
71 *bandying* knocking the ball about

68–76 This speech brands Lodovico as a real Machiavellian villain, comparable with Marlowe's Guise or Barabas.

Rather than borrow example.

FRANCISCO   There's no way
More speeding than this thought on.

LODOVICO   On then.

FRANCISCO
And yet methinks that this revenge is poor,
Because it steals upon him like a thief;
To have tane him by the cask in a pitch'd field,   80
Led him to Florence!

LODOVICO   It had been rare.—And there
Have crown'd him with a wreath of stinking garlic,
T'have shown the sharpness of his government,
And rankness of his lust. Flamineo comes.

                Exeunt LODOVICO, ANTONELLI [*and* GASPARO]

            Enter FLAMINEO, MARCELLO *and* ZANCHE

MARCELLO
Why doth this devil haunt you? Say.

FLAMINEO   I know not.   85
For by this light I do not conjure for her.
'Tis not so great a cunning as men think
To raise the devil: for here's one up already;
The greatest cunning were to lay him down.

MARCELLO
She is your shame.

FLAMINEO   I prithee pardon her.   90
In faith you see, women are like to burs;
Where their affection throws them, there they'll stick.

ZANCHE
That is my countryman, a goodly person;
When he's at leisure I'll discourse with him
In our own language.

FLAMINEO   I beseech you do.   *Exit* ZANCHE   95

---

76 *example* Q1, Q2 (Q3, Q4 from it)
77 *speeding* effective, decisive
80 *cask* casque, i.e. helmet or head-piece
84 (Q1, Q2 divide: *lust. / Flamineo;* Q3, Q4 *lust—But, peace: /
   Flamineo*)
87 *cunning* magical knowledge or skill

---

85 *this devil* i.e. Zanche, because she is dark-skinned
88-89 Lucas thinks that this is a double entendre comparable with *Romeo
   and Juliet*, II.i, 23-9, but Dent (p. 137) says that this seems far-fetched
   and comments that 'Flamineo is simply complaining that he cannot now
   get rid of his old mistress Zanche.'

How is't brave soldier? O that I had seen
Some of your iron days! I pray relate
Some of your service to us.

FRANCISCO

'Tis a ridiculous thing for a man to be his own chronicle;
I did never wash my mouth with mine own praise for fear of   100
getting a stinking breath.

MARCELLO

You're too stoical. The Duke will expect other discourse
from you.

FRANCISCO

I shall never flatter him, I have studied man too much to do
that. What difference is between the Duke and I? No more   105
than between two bricks; all made of one clay. Only 't may
be one is plac'd on the top of a turret; the other in the
bottom of a well by mere chance; if I were plac'd as high
as the Duke, I should stick as fast; make as fair a show;
and bear out weather equally.   110

FLAMINEO

If this soldier had a patent to beg in churches, then he
would tell them stories.

MARCELLO

I have been a soldier too.

FRANCISCO

How have you thriv'd?

MARCELLO

Faith, poorly.   115

FRANCISCO

That's the misery of peace. Only outsides are then respected.
As ships seem very great upon the river, which show very
little upon the seas: so some men i'th' court seem Colossuses
in a chamber, who if they came into the field would appear
pitiful pigmies.   120

FLAMINEO

Give me a fair room yet hung with arras, and some great

98 *service* military operations
109 *fair*. 'There may be a quibbling allusion to his disguise as the
   dark-skinned Mulinassar.' (Brown)
111 *patent* licence, obtained from a justice of the peace, without which
   beggars were not allowed to beg, on pain of whipping
118 *Colossuses* enormous statues (from the Colossus at Rhodes, a
   bronze statue of the sun-god Helios: one of the seven wonders of
   the ancient world)
121 *arras* a tapestry, often suspended a little distance from the walls:
   thus a spy could hide behind it. *Cf. Hamlet*, II.ii, 161–2; III.iv,
   1–33.

cardinal to lug me by th'ears as his endeared minion.

FRANCISCO

And thou may'st do,—the devil knows what villainy.

FLAMINEO

And safely.

FRANCISCO

Right; you shall see in the country in harvest time, pigeons,   125
though they destroy never so much corn, the farmer dare
not present the fowling-piece to them! Why? Because
they belong to the lord of the manor; whilst your poor
sparrows that belong to the Lord of heaven, they go to
the pot for't.   130

FLAMINEO

I will now give you some politic instruction. The Duke
says he will give you pension; that's but bare promise: get
it under his hand. For I have known men that have come
from serving against the Turk; for three or four months
they have had pension to buy them new wooden legs and   135
fresh plasters; but after 'twas not to be had. And this
miserable courtesy shows, as if a tormentor should give
hot cordial drinks to one three-quarters dead o'th' rack,
only to fetch the miserable soul again to endure more
dog-days.   140

Enter HORTENSIO, *a* YOUNG LORD, ZANCHE *and two more*

How now, gallants; what, are they ready for the barriers?

[*Exit* FRANCISCO]

YOUNG LORD

Yes: the lords are putting on their armour.

HORTENSIO

What's he?

FLAMINEO

A new upstart: one that swears like a falc'ner, and will lie
in the Duke's ear day by day like a maker of almanacs; and   145
yet I knew him since he came to th'court smell worse of
sweat than an under-tennis-court-keeper.

123 *do,—the* ed. (Q1, Q2 doe, the; Q3, Q4 do the; Lucas: doe–the)
127 *fowling-piece* light gun for shooting wild fowl
131 *instruction* Q1 (Q2, Q3, Q4 instructions)
132 *you* Q1 (Q2, Q3, Q4 you a)
133 *under his hand* i.e. a signed statement
137 *miserable* miserly, mean; compassionate
138 *cordial* for the heart; strengthening and restorative
140 *dog-days* see III.ii, 200 note.
141 *what,* Q4 (Q1, Q2, Q3 what)
144 *falc'ner* falconer

HORTENSIO

Look you, yonder's your sweet mistress.

FLAMINEO

Thou art my sworn brother; I'll tell thee, I do love that
Moor, that witch, very constrainedly: she knows some of   150
my villainy; I do love her, just as a man holds a wolf by the
ears. But for fear of turning upon me, and pulling out my
throat, I would let her go to the devil.

HORTENSIO

I hear she claims marriage of thee.

FLAMINEO

'Faith, I made to her some such dark promise, and in   155
seeking to fly from't I run on, like a frighted dog with a
bottle at's tail, that fain would bite it off and yet dares not
look behind him. [*to* ZANCHE] Now my precious gipsy!

ZANCHE

Ay, your love to me rather cools than heats.

FLAMINEO

Marry, I am the sounder lover; we have many wenches   160
about the town heat too fast.

HORTENSIO

What do you think of these perfum'd gallants then?

FLAMINEO

Their satin cannot save them. I am confident
They have a certain spice of the disease.
For they that sleep with dogs, shall rise with fleas.   165

ZANCHE

Believe it! A little painting and gay clothes
Make you loathe me.

FLAMINEO

How? Love a lady for painting or gay apparel? I'll unkennel
one example more for thee. Æsop had a foolish dog that let
go the flesh to catch the shadow. I would have courtiers be   170
better diners.

ZANCHE

You remember your oaths.

FLAMINEO

Lovers' oaths are like mariners' prayers, uttered in extremity; but when the tempest is o'er, and that the vessel

---

150 *constrainedly* in a constrained manner, without spontaneity
158 *gipsy:* an allusion to Zanche's dark skin and passionate nature
159 *cools . . . heats:* both verbs are used transitively and intransitively
160 *sounder lover* Q2, Q3, Q4 (Q1 sounder, lover)
171 *diners* ed. (Q1, Q2 *Diuers* [i.e. turned *n*]; Q3, Q4 *Divers*)

leaves tumbling, they fall from protesting to drinking. And   175
yet amongst gentlemen protesting and drinking go together,
and agree as well as shoemakers and Westphalia bacon. They
are both drawers on: for drink draws on protestation; and
protestation draws on more drink. Is not this discourse
better now than the morality of your sunburnt gentleman?   180

Enter CORNELIA

CORNELIA
    Is this your perch, you haggard? Fly to th'stews.
                                                    [*Strikes* ZANCHE]

FLAMINEO
    You should be clapp'd by th'heels now: strike i'th'court?
                                                    [*Exit* CORNELIA]

ZANCHE
    She's good for nothing but to make her maids
    Catch cold o'nights; they dare not use a bedstaff,
    For fear of her light fingers.
MARCELLO   You're a strumpet.   185
    An impudent one.
FLAMINEO   Why do you kick her? Say,
    Do you think that she's like a walnut-tree?
    Must she be cudgell'd ere she bear good fruit?
MARCELLO
    She brags that you shall marry her.
FLAMINEO   What then?

177–8 i.e. 'The shoemaker draws on shoes and salt things induce
     thirstiness.' (Sampson)
180 *morality* Q4 (Q1, Q2, Q3 mortality); *sunburnt gentleman* i.e.
     Francisco, disguised as Mulinassar: see Additional Notes, p. 149.
181 *haggard* wild hawk; wanton woman
182 *clapp'd by th' heels* fasten by the ankles in stocks or irons; *strike
     i'th' court?* see Textual Appendix–A.
184 *a bedstaff* Q1, Q2 (Q3 bed-staff; Q4 bed-staves): see Addditional
     Notes, p. 149.

───

173–5 Webster's simile is an imaginatively extended form of an expression
     found in George Pettie's translation of Guazzo's *Civil Conversation*
     (1581): 'The othes of lovers, carry as much credite as the vowes of
     Mariners.' Other dramatic references to mariners' oaths and their
     drinking habits will be found in R. R. Cawley, *The Voyagers and
     Elizabethan Drama*, pp. 194–200.
182 *strike i'th' court?* Lucas (*Webster*, i, 250) quotes from Stephen's *Com-
     mentaries on the Laws of England* (ed. 1914), IV, 156: 'By 33 Hen. VIII
     (1541), c. 12, malicious striking in the palace, which drew blood, was
     punishable with perpetual imprisonment and fine at the King's pleasure,
     and the loss of the striker's right hand.'

MARCELLO

I had rather she were pitch'd upon a stake　　　　190
In some new-seeded garden, to affright
Her fellow crows thence.

FLAMINEO　　　　　　　　You're a boy, a fool,
Be guardian to your hound, I am of age.

MARCELLO

If I take her near you I'll cut her throat.

FLAMINEO

With a fan of feathers?

MARCELLO　　　　　　　　And for you, I'll whip　195
This folly from you.

FLAMINEO　　　　　　　Are you choleric?
I'll purge't with rhubarb.

HORTENSIO　　　　　　　O your brother!

FLAMINEO　　　　　　　　　　　Hang him.
He wrongs me most that ought t'offend me least.
[*to* MARCELLO] I do suspect my mother play'd foul play
When she conceiv'd thee.

MARCELLO　　　　　　　　Now by all my hopes,　200
Like the two slaught'red sons of Œdipus,
The very flames of our affection
Shall turn two ways. Those words I'll make thee answer
With thy heart blood.

FLAMINEO　　　　　　　Do; like the gesses in the progress,
You know where you shall find me,—

MARCELLO　　　　　　　　　　　Very good.　205
　　　　　　　　　　　　　　　[*Exit* FLAMINEO]
And thou beest a noble friend, bear him my sword,
And bid him fit the length on't.

YOUNG LORD　　　　　　　Sir I shall.
　　　　　　　　　　　　[*Exeunt all but* ZANCHE]

---

190 *pitch'd* stuck, fastened
192 *You're* Q3, Q4 (Q1 Your; Q2 you'r)
196-7 Rhubarb, considered to be choleric itself, was a recognised
　antidote for an excess of the choleric humour. *Cf. The Duchess of
　Malfi*, II.v, 12-13.
197 *brother*! ed. (Qq brother.)　　203 *two* Q1b (Q1a 10)
204 *Do;* Q4 (Q1 Doe ; Q2 Doe,　; Q3 Do,); *gesses* ed. stopping-places
　on a royal progress: see Textual Appendix–A.
206 *noble friend* Q2, Q3, Q4 (Q1 noble, friend)

201-203 After Œdipus' sons Eteocles and Polynices had killed each other in
　single combat for the throne of Thebes, their bodies were burnt to-
　gether, but the flames were seen miraculously to part from one another.
　Webster may have found a reference to the legend in Pettie's translation
　of Guazzo's *Civil Conversation* (1581), Book II, p. 84.

Enter FRANCISCO *the Duke of Florence*

ZANCHE [*aside*]
  He comes. Hence petty thought of my disgrace!
  I ne'er lov'd my complexion till now,
  Cause I may boldly say without a blush,   210
  I love you.
FRANCISCO   Your love is untimely sown;
  There's a Spring at Michaelmas, but 'tis but a faint one.
  I am sunk in years, and I have vowed never to marry.

ZANCHE
  Alas! poor maids get more lovers than husbands. Yet you
  may mistake my wealth. For, as when ambassadors are sent   215
  to congratulate princes, there's commonly sent along with
  them a rich present; so that though the prince like not the
  ambassador's person nor words, yet he likes well of the
  presentment. So I may come to you in the same manner,
  and be better loved for my dowry than my virtue.   220

FRANCISCO
  I'll think on the motion.

ZANCHE
  Do, I'll now detain you no longer. At your better leisure
  I'll tell you things shall startle your blood.
  Nor blame me that this passion I reveal;
  Lovers die inward that their flames conceal.   225

FRANCISCO [*aside*]
  Of all intelligence this may prove the best,
  Sure I shall draw strange fowl, from this foul nest. *Exeunt.*

[Act V, Scene ii]

Enter MARCELLO *and* CORNELIA [*and a* PAGE, *who remains in the background*]

CORNELIA
  I hear a whispering all about the court,
  You are to fight; who is your opposite?
  What is the quarrel?

207 S.D. FRANCISCO i.e. disguised as Mulinassar
211 speech-prefix: Q3, Q4 *Fra.* (Q1, Q2 FLA.)
212 *but 'tis but* Qq (Sampson conjectured 'but 'tis'.)
221 speech-prefix: Q3, Q4 *Fra.* (Q1, Q2 FLA.); *motion* proposal;
    (sudden) impulse
226 speech-prefix: Q3, Q4 *Fra.* (Q1, Q2 FLA.)
S.D. PAGE: see Textual Appendix—A.
  2 *You are* Q2, Q3, Q4 (Q1 Your are)

MARCELLO   'Tis an idle rumour.

CORNELIA

Will you dissemble? Sure you do not well
To fright me thus; you never look thus pale,   5
But when you are most angry. I do charge you
Upon my blessing;——nay I'll call the Duke,
And he shall school you.

MARCELLO   Publish not a fear
Which would convert to laughter; 'tis not so.
Was not this crucifix my father's?

CORNELIA   Yes.   10

MARCELLO

I have heard you say, giving my brother suck,
He took the crucifix between his hands,   *Enter* FLAMINEO
And broke a limb off.

CORNELIA   Yes: but 'tis mended.

FLAMINEO

I have brought your weapon back.

                    FLAMINEO *runs* MARCELLO *through*

CORNELIA   Ha, O my horror!

MARCELLO

You have brought it home indeed.

CORNELIA   Help! oh he's murdered.   15

FLAMINEO

Do you turn your gall up? I'll to sanctuary,
And send a surgeon to you.
                                                            [*Exit*]

            Enter CARL[O,] HORT[ENSIO,] PEDRO

---

8 *school* teach, punish (Harrison)
10 *this crucifix:* It must hang round Cornelia's neck
16 *gall* Q2, Q3 (Q1 gaule; Q4 gill): *sanctuary* a place, such as a church,
   where, according to medieval ecclesiastical law, a fugitive from
   justice was entitled to immunity from arrest: *cf. The Duchess of
   Malfi*, IV.ii, 269

---

16 *gall.* 'It is . . . not quite clear whether the phrase here is figurative, of
   dying; or literal, because Marcello is vomiting from his wound. Probably
   the former.' (Lucas, *Webster*, i, 252). Gall was used to denote bitterness
   of spirit.
17 S.D. CAR[LO] i.e. Lodovico; PEDRO i.e. Gasparo: the presence of
   CARLO and PEDRO here confirms their identity as Lodovico and Gasparo
   since they, the human revengers of Brachiano's crimes, are thus permitted to witness the beginning of the great punishment of Brachiano,
   Vittoria and Vittoria's brothers. Marcello here interprets his own death
   as divine vengeance for his family's sin. This pattern of the presence of
   revengers at the death of one of their enemies and a man's acceptance
   of his death as part of a scheme of divine vengeance was common in
   Elizabethan and Jacobean revenge plays.

HORTENSIO   How? o'th' ground?

MARCELLO

O mother now remember what I told
Of breaking off the crucifix: farewell.
There are some sins which heaven doth duly punish   20
In a whole family. This it is to rise
By all dishonest means. Let all men know
That tree shall long time keep a steady foot
Whose branches spread no wider than the root.

CORNELIA

O my perpetual sorrow!
HORTENSIO   Virtuous Marcello.   25
He's dead: pray leave him lady; come, you shall.

CORNELIA

Alas he is not dead: he's in a trance.
Why here's nobody shall get anything by his death. Let me
call him again for God's sake.

LODOVICO

I would you were deceiv'd.   30

CORNELIA

O you abuse me, you abuse, me, you abuse me. How many
have gone away thus for lack of tendance; rear up's head,
rear up's head. His bleeding inward will kill him.

HORTENSIO

You see he is departed.

CORNELIA

Let me come to him; give me him as he is; if he be turn'd   35
to earth; let me but give him one hearty kiss, and you shall
put us both into one coffin: fetch a looking-glass, see if his
breath will not stain it; or pull out some feathers from my
pillow, and lay them to his lips,—will you lose him for a
little pains-taking?   40

HORTENSIO

Your kindest office is to pray for him.

CORNELIA

Alas! I would not pray for him yet. He may live to lay me
i'th' ground, and pray for me, if you'll let me come to him.

Enter BRACHIANO *all armed, save the beaver, with* FLAMINEO
[*and* FRANCISCO]

19 *breaking off* Q1 (Q2, Q3, Q4 breaking of)
24 *wider* Q4 (Q1, Q2, Q3 wilder)
30 speech-prefix: *Lodovico* ed. (Q1 CAR.; Q2, Q3 *Cor.*; Q4 *Hor.*)
39 *lose* Q4 (Q1, Q2, Q3 loose)
43 S.D. FRANCISCO i.e. disguised as Mulinassar

35–40 *cf. King Lear,* V.iii, 261–5.

BRACHIANO
Was this your handiwork?

FLAMINEO
It was my misfortune.   45

CORNELIA
He lies, he lies, he did not kill him: these have kill'd him,
that would not let him be better look'd to.

BRACHIANO
Have comfort my griev'd mother.

CORNELIA
O you screech-owl.

HORTENSIO
Forbear, good madam.   50

CORNELIA
Let me go, let me go.
She runs to FLAMINEO *with her knife drawn and coming to him*
lets it fall
The God of heaven forgive thee. Dost not wonder
I pray for thee? I'll tell thee what's the reason:
I have scarce breath to number twenty minutes;
I'd not spend that in cursing. Fare thee well—   55
Half of thyself lies there: and may'st thou live
To fill an hour-glass with his mould'red ashes,
To tell how thou shouldst spend the time to come
In blest repentance.

BRACHIANO   Mother, pray tell me
How came he by his death? What was the quarrel?   60

CORNELIA
Indeed my younger boy presum'd too much
Upon his manhood; gave him bitter words;
Drew his sword first; and so I know not how,
For I was out of my wits, he fell with's head
Just in my bosom.

PAGE   This is not true madam.   65

CORNELIA
I pray thee peace.
One arrow's graz'd already; it were vain
T'lose this: for that will nere be found again.

BRACHIANO
Go, bear the body to Cornelia's lodging:
And we command that none acquaint our Duchess   70
With this sad accident: for you Flamineo,

51 S.D. opposite 52–56 in Qq.
67 *graz'd* grassed i.e. lost in the grass

Hark you, I will not grant your pardon.

FLAMINEO   No?

BRACHIANO

Only a lease of your life. And that shall last
But for one day. Thou shalt be forc'd each evening
To renew it, or be hang'd.

FLAMINEO   At your pleasure.   75

> LODOVICO *sprinkles* BRACHIANO's *beaver with a poison*

Your will is law now, I'll not meddle with it.

BRACHIANO

You once did brave me in your sister's lodging;
I'll now keep you in awe for't. Where's our beaver?

FRANCISCO [*aside*]

He calls for his destruction. Noble youth,
I pity thy sad fate. Now to the barriers.   80
This shall his passage to the black lake further,
The last good deed he did, he pardon'd murther.   *Exeunt*

[Act V, Scene iii]

*Charges and shouts. They fight at barriers; first single
pairs, then three to three.*

Enter BRACHIANO *and* FLAMINEO *with others* [*including*
GIOVANNI, VITTORIA, *and* FRANCISCO]

BRACHIANO

An armourer! Ud's death, an armourer!

FLAMINEO

Armourer; where's the armourer?

BRACHIANO

Tear off my beaver.

FLAMINEO   Are you hurt, my lord?

BRACHIANO

O my brain's on fire,   *Enter* ARMOURER
The helmet is poison'd.

ARMOURER   My lord upon my soul—   5

BRACHIANO

Away with him to torture.   [*Exit* ARMOURER, *guarded*]
There are some great ones that have hand in this,
And near about me.

75 S.D. *beaver* lower part of the face-guard of a helmet
81 *black lake* i.e. the Styx (thought of as a lake or river)
S.D. *shouts* Q1, Q2 (Q3, Q4 *shoots*); FRANCISCO i.e. disguised as
    Mulinassar

VITTORIA   O my loved lord; poison'd?

FLAMINEO

Remove the bar: here's unfortunate revels,
Call the physicians; a plague upon you; *Ent[er]* 2 PHYSICIANS   10
We have too much of your cunning here already.
I fear the ambassadors are likewise poisoned.

BRACHIANO

Oh I am gone already: the infection
Flies to the brain and heart. O thou strong heart!
There's such a covenant 'tween the world and it,   15
They're loth to break.

GIOVANNI   O my most loved father!

BRACHIANO

Remove the boy away.
Where's this good woman? Had I infinite worlds
They were too little for thee. Must I leave thee?
What say yon screech-owls, is the venom mortal?   20

PHYSICIANS

Most deadly.

BRACHIANO   Most corrupted politic hangman!
You kill without book; but your art to save
Fails you as oft as great men's needy friends.
I that have given life to offending slaves
And wretched murderers, have I not power   25
To lengthen mine own a twelvemonth?
[*to* VITTORIA] Do not kiss me, for I shall poison thee.
This unction is sent from the great Duke of Florence.

FRANCISCO

Sir be of comfort.

BRACHIANO

O thou soft natural death, that art joint-twin   30

8 Q4 has '*Enter Vittoria*' to right of this line.
9 *bar:* either the barriers or some fastening of the beaver
15 '*tween* Q1, Q2, Q3 (Q4 'twixt)
16 Q4 has '*Enter Giovanni*' to right of this line.
20 *yon screech-owls* ed.: see Textual Appendix – A.
22 *without book* by heart
23 *men's* Qq: see Textual Appendix – A.
28 *unction* unguent, ointment (the poison); extreme unction: *cf.* V. iii, 38.
30 *art* Q1, Q4 (Q2, Q3 are)
31 *rough-bearded comet:* rough-bearded refers to the comet's shape; comets were supposed to presage disasters and evil.

27 In *Soliman and Perseda* (*circa* 1589–92) Soliman is killed by kissing the poisoned lips of Perseda who lies dying from the mortal wounds he has given her in single combat.

To sweetest slumber: no rough-bearded comet
Stares on thy mild departure: the dull owl
Beats not against thy casement: the hoarse wolf
Scents not thy carrion. Pity winds thy corse,
Whilst horror waits on princes.

VITTORIA   I am lost for ever.   35

BRACHIANO
How miserable a thing it is to die
'Mongst women howling!

> [*Enter* LODOVICO *and* GASPARO *disguised as Capuchins*]

What are those?

FLAMINEO   Franciscans.
They have brought the extreme unction.

BRACHIANO
On pain of death, let no man name death to me,
It is a word infinitely terrible.   40
Withdraw into our cabinet.

> *Exeunt omnes praeter* FRANCISCO *and* FLAMINEO

FLAMINEO
To see what solitariness is about dying princes. As heretofore they have unpeopled towns; divorc'd friends, and made
great houses unhospitable: so now, O justice! where are their
flatterers now? Flatterers are but the shadows of princes'   45
bodies, the least thick cloud makes them invisible.

FRANCISCO
There's great moan made for him.

FLAMINEO
'Faith, for some few hours salt water will run most plenti-
fully in every office o'th'court. But believe it; most of them
do but weep over their stepmothers' graves.   50

FRANCISCO
How mean you?

---

34 *Scents* Q4 (Q1, Q2, Q3 Sents); *corse* ed. (Q1, Q2, Q4 coarse; Q3
    course) corpse
35 *waits* Q3, Q4 (Q1 waights; Q2 waites); *princes* Qq (Hazlitt:
    princes')
37 *Franciscans:* see V, i, 16 note; members of the order of St. Francis;
    servants of Francisco (the pun is unknown to Flamineo)
37 s.d. *Capuchins* i.e. the Hungarians Carlo and Pedro
41 s.d. *Exeunt omnes praeter* Q4 (Q1, Q2, Q3 *Exeunt but*) 'All leave
    except'
46 *bodies, the* Q2, Q3, Q4 (Q1 bodies the)
50 *graves* Q1 (Q2, Q3, Q4 grave)

FLAMINEO

Why? They dissemble, as some men do that live within
compass o'th' verge.

FRANCISCO

Come you have thriv'd well under him.

FLAMINEO

'Faith, like a wolf in a woman's breast; I have been fed   55
with poultry: but for money, understand me, I had as good
a will to cozen him, as e'er an officer of them all. But I had
not cunning enough to do it.

FRANCISCO

What did'st thou think of him? 'Faith speak freely.

FLAMINEO

He was a kind of statesman, that would sooner have reckon'd   60
how many cannon-bullets he had discharged against a town,
to count his expense that way, than how many of his valiant
and deserving subjects he lost before it.

FRANCISCO

O speak well of the Duke.

FLAMINEO

I have done. Wilt hear some of my court wisdom?   65

                                        Enter LODOVICO

To reprehend princes is dangerous: and to over-commend
some of them is palpable lying.

FRANCISCO

How is it with the Duke?

LODOVICO   Most deadly ill.
He's fall'n into a strange distraction.
He talks of battles and monopolies,   70
Levying of taxes, and from that descends
To the most brain-sick language. His mind fastens
On twenty several objects, which confound
Deep sense with folly. Such a fearful end
May teach some men that bear too lofty crest,   75

52 *some men* an ironic understatement (Lucas)
55 *wolf* = lupus (ulcer)
62 *expense* ed. (Q1, Q2, Q3 expence; Q4 expences)
65 S.D. LODOVICO i.e. disguised as the Capuchin, Carlo

52–53 *within compass o'th' verge.* 'The *verge* was an area extending to a
   distance of twelve miles round the King's Court, which lay under the
   jurisdiction of the Lord High Steward (from Lat. *virga*, the steward's
   rod of office).' (Lucas, *Webster*, i, 253)
55–56. Ulcers were regularly treated by the application of the raw flesh of
   poultry or with raw meat to prevent them from feeding on the sick
   person's flesh. The historical Bracciano had raw meat applied to the
   malignant ulcer in his leg.

Though they live happiest, yet they die not best.
He hath conferr'd the whole state of the dukedom
Upon your sister, till the Prince arrive
At mature age.
FLAMINEO   There's some good luck in that yet.
FRANCISCO
See here he comes.

Enter BRACHIANO, *presented in a bed,* VITTORIA *and others*
              [*including* GASPARO].

                There's death in's face already.   80
VITTORIA
O my good lord!

*These speeches are several kinds of distractions and in the action
                should appear so*

BRACHIANO   Away, you have abus'd me.
You have convey'd coin forth our territories;
Bought and sold offices; oppress'd the poor,
And I ne'er dreamt on't. Make up your accounts;
I'll now be mine own steward.
FLAMINEO   Sir, have patience.   85
BRACHIANO
Indeed I am too blame.
For did you ever hear the dusky raven
Chide blackness? Or was't ever known the devil
Rail'd against cloven creatures?
VITTORIA   O my lord!
BRACHIANO
Let me have some quails to supper.
FLAMINEO   Sir, you shall.   90

---

77 *state* estate; power   81 S.D. opposite 82–88 in Q1
86 *too blame* Q1, Q2, Q4 (Q3 to blame) too blameworthy,
90 *quails* the birds (a delicacy); loose women

---

80 S.D. *presented in a bed* i.e. the traverse is drawn to discover Brachiano
   and the others on the inner stage; GASPARO i.e. disguised as the Capuchin
   Pedro
81ff. For critical comment on Brachiano's death scene, see: William Hazlitt,
   Lectures on the Dramatic Literature of the Age of Elizabeth (1821),
   pp. 129–32; W. W. Greg, 'Webster's "White Devil" ', *Modern Language
   Quarterly*, III (1900), p. 118; J. R. Mulryne, '*The White Devil* and *The
   Duchess of Malfi*', *Stratford-upon-Avon Studies 1: Jacobean Theatre*,
   p. 213; Irving Ribner, *Jacobean Tragedy: The Quest for Moral Order*
   (1962), pp. 104–5.

BRACHIANO
No: some fried dog-fish. Your quails feed on poison;—
That old dog-fox, that politician Florence,—
I'll forswear hunting and turn dog-killer;
Rare! I'll be friends with him: for mark you, sir, one dog
Still sets another a-barking: peace, peace,   95
Yonder's a fine slave come in now.

FLAMINEO   Where?

BRACHIANO
Why there.
In a blue bonnet, and a pair of breeches
With a great codpiece. Ha, ha, ha,
Look you his codpiece is stuck full of pins   100
With pearls o'th' head of them. Do not you know him?

FLAMINEO
No my lord.

BRACHIANO   Why 'tis the devil.
I know him by a great rose he wears on's shoe
To hide his cloven foot. I'll dispute with him.
He's a rare linguist.

VITTORIA   My lord here's nothing.   105

BRACHIANO
Nothing? rare! nothing! When I want money
Our treasury is empty; there is nothing.
I'll not be used thus.

VITTORIA   O! lie still my lord—

BRACHIANO
See, see, Flamineo that kill'd his brother
Is dancing on the ropes there: and he carries   110
A money-bag in each hand, to keep him even,
For fear of breaking's neck. And there's a lawyer
In a gown whipt with velvet, stares and gapes
When the money will fall. How the rogue cuts capers!

91 *dog-fish* 'technically the name of a kind of small shark, but common as a term of abuse' (Dent)
92 *politician* secretive, cunning person
99 *cod-piece* an appendage, often ornamented, to the close-fitting hose or breeches of the 15th–17th centuries
103 *rose* silk rosette or knot of ribbons
105 *linguist* master of language, eloquent disputant (Lucas)
113 *whipt* edged, trimmed; ornamented

91 *feed on poison.* The idea that quails fed on poison was an Elizabethan commonplace which has been traced back through Erasmus to Pliny. Dent comments: 'Surely the audience would think of Vittoria, advanced through the poisoning of Isabella, and now advanced again through that of Brachiano.' (p. 148)

It should have been in a halter.   115
'Tis there; what's she?
FLAMINEO   Vittoria, my lord.
BRACHIANO
Ha, ha, ha. Her hair is sprinkled with arras powder,
That makes her look as if she had sinn'd in the pastry.
What's he?
FLAMINEO
A divine my lord.   120
BRACHIANO
He will be drunk. Avoid him: th'argument is fearful when
churchmen stagger in't.
Look you; six gray rats that have lost their tails,
Crawl up the pillow; send for a rat-catcher.
I'll do a miracle: I'll free the court   125
From all foul vermin. Where's Flamineo?
FLAMINEO
I do not like that he names me so often,
Especially on's death-bed: 'tis a sign
I shall not live long: see he's near his end.
                    BRACHIANO *seems here near his end.*
    LODOVICO *and* GASPARO *in the habit of Capuchins present him in
        his bed with a crucifix and hallowed candle.*

LODOVICO
Pray give us leave: *Attende Domine Brachiane.*   130
FLAMINEO
See, see, how firmly he doth fix his eye
Upon the crucifix.
VITTORIA   O hold it constant.
It settles his wild spirits; and so his eyes
Melt into tears.
LODOVICO (*By the crucifix*)
Domine Brachiane, solebas in bello tutus esse tuo clypeo,   135
nùnc hanc clypeum hosti tuo opponas infernali.

118 *the pastry* place where pastry is made
122 *rats* Q1 (Q2, Q3, Q4 cats)   129 s.d. opposite 121–132 in Q1
130 'Listen Lord Brachiano.' *Brachiane* Q1, Q3, Q4 (Q2 *Brachiano*)
135–6. 'Lord Brachiano, you were accustomed in battle to be guarded
    by your shield, now you shall oppose *this* shield against your
    infernal enemy.'

---

117 *arras powder* or orris powder, made from orris root, smelt of violets. *Cf.
    The Duchess of Malfi,* II.ii, 59–60. Vittoria's hair has been sprinkled with
    the powder for her marriage earlier in the day. Dent (p. 150) remarks
    that the following comment by Brachiano is therefore doubly shocking,
    'though perfectly consistent with the implications of his speeches above.
    Throughout this episode . . . he associates her with falsehood and
    wantonness.'

GASPARO *(By the hallowed taper)*
Olim hastâ valuisti in bello; nùnc hanc sacram hastam vibrabis
contra hostem animarum.

LODOVICO
Attende Domine Brachiane si nunc quòque probas ea quæ acta
sunt inter nos, flecte caput in dextrum.   140

GASPARO
Esto securus Domine Brachiane: cogita quantum habeas
meritorum—denique memineris meam animam pro tua oppig-
noratam si quid esse periculi.

LODOVICO
Si nùnc quoque probas ea quæ acta sunt inter nos, flecte caput
in lævum.   145
He is departing: pray stand all apart,
And let us only whisper in his ears
Some private meditations, which our order
Permits you not to hear.

Here the rest being departed LODOVICO *and* GASPARO
discover themselves

GASPARO   Brachiano.
LODOVICO
Devil Brachiano. Thou art damn'd.
GASPARO   Perpetually.   150
LODOVICO
A slave condemn'd, and given up to the gallows
Is thy great lord and master.
GASPARO   True: for thou
Art given up to the devil.

137–8: 'Once you did prevail with your spear in battle; now you shall
    wield *this* sacred spear against the enemy of souls.'
139–40: 'Listen Lord Brachiano, if you now also approve what has
    been done between us, turn your head to the right.'
141–3: 'Be assured, Lord Brachiano: consider how many good deeds
    you have done – lastly remember that my soul is pledged for
    yours, should there be any peril.'
144–5: 'If you now also approve what has been done between us, turn
    your head to the left.'
149 S.D. opposite 148–150 in Q1

135–45 This passage, as A. W. Reed pointed out in *The Times Literary
    Supplement* (14th June, 1947) p. 295, is borrowed from Erasmus'
    Colloquy *Funus* in which the elaborate business of the death and burial
    of Georgius Balearicus who, trusting to his wealth, sought by purchase
    to retain his standing beyond the grave, is contrasted with the moving
    description of that of Cornelius Montius 'qui Christianeri more se ad
    mortem composuit.'

LODOVICO   O you slave!
   You that were held the famous politician;
   Whose art was poison.
GASPARO   And whose conscience murder.   155
LODOVICO
   That would have broke your wife's neck down the stairs
   Ere she was poison'd.
GASPARO   That had your villainous sallets—
LODOVICO
   And fine embroidered bottles, and perfumes
   Equally mortal with a winter plague—
GASPARO
   Now there's mercury—
LODOVICO   And copperas—
GASPARO   And quicksilver—   160
LODOVICO
   With other devilish pothecary stuff
   A-melting in your politic brains: dost hear?
GASPARO
   This is Count Lodovico.
LODOVICO   This Gasparo.
   And thou shalt die like a poor rogue.
GASPARO   And stink
   Like a dead fly-blown dog.
LODOVICO
   And be forgotten before thy funeral sermon.
BRACHIANO
   Vittoria! Vittoria!
LODOVICO   O the cursed devil,
   Come to himself again! We are undone.

               Enter VITTORIA *and the* ATTEND[ANTS]

GASPARO [*aside to* LODOVICO]
   Strangle him in private. [*to* VITTORIA] What? Will you call
                                             him again

157 *villainous sallets* see IV.ii, 60 note.
160 *copperas* sulphate of copper
168 *Come* Q1 (Q2, Q3, Q4 Comes)

---

158 *fine embroidered bottles.* One assumes that these were bottles made of
     patterned silver or glass bottles covered in decorated material or jewels.
160 *mercury:* 'corrosive sublimate, mercuric chloride; not the metal itself',
     since quicksilver is also mentioned (Lucas, *Webster*, i, 258), but Brown
     suggests that 'Gasparo repeats himself in trying to terrify Brachiano
     with words.' (p. 152 n.)

To live in treble torments? For charity,   170
For Christian charity, avoid the chamber.
                    Exeunt [VITTORIA *and* ATTENDANTS]
LODOVICO
You would prate, sir. This is a true-love knot
Sent from the Duke of Florence.   BRACHIANO *is strangled*
GASPARO   What, is it done?
LODOVICO
The snuff is out. No woman-keeper i'th' world,
Though she had practis'd seven year at the pest-house,   175
Could have done't quaintlier.
[*Enter* VITTORIA, FRANCISCO, FLAMINEO, *and* ATTENDANTS]
                    My lords he's dead.
OMNES
Rest to his soul.
VITTORIA   O me! this place is hell.   *Exit* VITTORIA
                    [*with* ATTENDANTS *and* GASPARO]
FRANCISCO
How heavily she takes it.
FLAMINEO   O yes, yes;
Had women navigable rivers in their eyes
They would dispend them all; surely I wonder   180
Why we should wish more rivers to the city
When they sell water so good cheap. I'll tell thee,
These are but moonish shades of griefs or fears,
There's nothing sooner dry than women's tears.
Why here's an end of all my harvest, he has given me nothing. 185
Court promises! Let wise men count them curs'd
For while you live he that scores best pays worst.
FRANCISCO
Sure, this was Florence' doing.

---

171 *avoid* empty, clear
171 s.d.: Q3, Q4 *Exeunt.* (Q1, Q2 [omit])
176 *done't* Q1 (Q2, Q3, Q4 don't); *quaintlier* more skilfully
176 s.d. ed. (Q3, Q4 *They return;* Q1, Q2 [omit])
178, 188, 198, 205, 217 speech-prefixes: Q3, Q4 *Fra.* (Q1, Q2 FLO.)
182 *cheap* bargain price
183 *moonish* like the moon, changeable

---

174 *woman-keeper* female nurse. At this time nurses were frequently sus-
     pected of strangling or smothering patients who were sick of the plague.
181 *more rivers to the city:* 'Certainly a reference to the New River project of
     Sir Hugh Myddleton to supply London with fresh water. The scheme
     was sanctioned in 1606 and after serious interruptions was completed
     in 1613.' (Sampson, p. 202)

FLAMINEO   Very likely.
Those are found weighty strokes which come from th'hand,
But those are killing strokes which come from th'head.   190
O the rare tricks of a Machivillian!
He doth not come like a gross plodding slave
And buffet you to death. No, my quaint knave,
He tickles you to death; makes you die laughing;
As if you had swallow'd down a pound of saffron.   195
You see the feat, 'tis practis'd in a trice:
To teach court-honesty, it jumps on ice.

FRANCISCO
Now have the people liberty to talk
And descant on his vices.

FLAMINEO   Misery of princes,
That must of force be censur'd by their slaves!   200
Not only blam'd for doing things are ill,
But for not doing all that all men will.
One were better be a thresher.
Ud's death, I would fain speak with this Duke yet.

FRANCISCO
Now he's dead?   205

FLAMINEO
I cannot conjure; but if prayers or oaths
Will get to th'speech of him: though forty devils
Wait on him in his livery of flames,
I'll speak to him, and shake him by the hand,
Though I be blasted.   *Exit* FLAMINEO

FRANCISCO   Excellent Lodovico!   210
What? Did you terrify him at the last gasp?

LODOVICO
Yes; and so idly, that the Duke had like
T'have terrified us.

FRANCISCO   How?
                    Enter [ZANCHE] *the Moor*

---

191 *a Machivillian* i.e. a Machiavellian, since Machiavelli was wrongly
       supposed to be the type of scheming villains
196 *feat* Q2, Q3, Q4 (Q1 seat)
199 *descant* comment on, criticize
200 *of force* of necessity   212 *idly* carelessly

194–5. This idea about the effects of immoderate taking of saffron was a
       commonplace of Elizabethan herbals.
196–207: 'You see, this feat, accomplished in such a short time, is to teach
       the kind of honesty found at court [i.e. that of the scheming 'politician']
       how dangerously insecure its footing is.' Cf. *The Duchess of Malfi*, V.
       ii, 327–9.

120   JOHN WEBSTER   [ACT V

LODOVICO   You shall hear that hereafter.
See! yon's the infernal that would make us sport.
Now to the revelation of that secret   215
She promis'd when she fell in love with you.
FRANCISCO
You're passionately met in this sad world.
ZANCHE
I would have you look up, sir; these court tears
Claim not your tribute to them. Let those weep
That guiltily partake in the sad cause.   220
I knew last night by a sad dream I had
Some mischief would ensue; yet to say truth
My dream most concern'd you.
LODOVICO   Shall's fall a-dreaming?
FRANCISCO
Yes, and for fashion sake I'll dream with her.
ZANCHE
Methought sir, you came stealing to my bed.   225
FRANCISCO
Wilt thou believe me sweeting? By this light
I was a-dreamt on thee too: for methought
I saw thee naked.
ZANCHE   Fie sir! as I told you,
Methought you lay down by me.
FRANCISCO   So dreamt I:
And lest thou shouldst take cold, I cover'd thee   230
With this Irish mantle.
ZANCHE   Verily I did dream,
You were somewhat bold with me; but to come to't.
LODOVICO
How? how? I hope you will not go to't here.
FRANCISCO
Nay: you must hear my dream out.
ZANCHE   Well, sir, forth.
FRANCISCO
When I threw the mantle o'er thee, thou didst laugh   235
Exceedingly methought.
ZANCHE   Laugh?

214 *the infernal* i.e. spirit; *us* Q4, Lucas (Q1, Q2, Q3, Sampson and
    Brown: up)
218 *et seq.*: speech-prefixes for Zanche: Q3, Q4 *Zan.* Q1, Q2 MOO.
    or MOORE.
231 *Irish mantle* kind of blanket or plaid worn by Irish peasants till the
    17th century, often (as implied here) with nothing underneath it
233 *go to't here* Q1b [go to͟t here] (Q1a go to it here; Q2 go to there;
    Q3, Q4 go to't there)

FRANCISCO   And cried'st out,
  The hair did tickle thee.
ZANCHE   There was a dream indeed.
LODOVICO
  Mark her I prithee, she simpers like the suds
  A collier hath been wash'd in.
ZANCHE
  Come, sir; good fortune tends you; I did tell you   240
  I would reveal a secret: Isabella
  The Duke of Florence' sister was empoison'd,
  By a fum'd picture: and Camillo's neck
  Was broke by damn'd Flamineo; the mischance
  Laid on a vaulting-horse.
FRANCISCO   Most strange!
ZANCHE   Most true.   245
LODOVICO
  The bed of snakes is broke.
ZANCHE
  I sadly do confess I had a hand
  In the black deed.
FRANCISCO   Thou kept'st their counsel,—
ZANCHE   Right.
  For which, urg'd with contrition, I intend
  This night to rob Vittoria.
LODOVICO   Excellent penitence!   250
  Usurers dream on't while they sleep out sermons.
ZANCHE
  To further our escape, I have entreated
  Leave to retire me, till the funeral
  Unto a friend i'th' country. That excuse
  Will further our escape. In coin and jewels   255
  I shall, at least, make good unto your use
  A hundred thousand crowns.
FRANCISCO   O noble wench!
LODOVICO
  Those crowns we'll share.
ZANCHE   It is a dowry,
  Methinks, should make that sunburnt proverb false,

---

238 *simpers:* ' "Simper" being an old alternate form of "simmer",
    play on the word was common.' (Dent)
243 *fum'd* perfumed
246 *bed* nest, thick entanglement
248 *kept'st* Q3, Q4 (Q1 kepts; Q2 keps't)
259 *sunburnt* dark-skinned; see V.i, 180. note, p. 149.

And wash the Ethiop white.

FRANCISCO   It shall, away!   260

ZANCHE

Be ready for our flight.

FRANCISCO   An hour 'fore day.

          Exit [ZANCHE] *the Moor*

O strange discovery! Why till now we knew not
The circumstance of either of their deaths.

      Enter [ZANCHE *the*] *Moor*

ZANCHE

You'll wait about midnight in the chapel?

FRANCISCO   There.

LODOVICO

Why now our action's justified,—

FRANCISCO   Tush for justice.   265

What harms it justice? We now, like the partridge
Purge the disease with laurel: for the fame
Shall crown the enterprise and quit the shame.   *Exeunt*

[Act V, Scene iv]

Enter FLAM[INEO] *and* GASP[ARO] *at one door, another
way* GIOVANNI *attended*

GASPARO

The young Duke. Did you e'er see a sweeter prince?

FLAMINEO

I have known a poor woman's bastard better favour'd. This

264 *chapel?* ed. (Qq Chappel.)
267 *laurel* (literally) laurel leaves; laurel wreath betokening a famous
  achievement; *fame* Q1 (Q2, Q3, Q4 same)
268 *quit* clear, rid, absolve [one] of
S.D. GASP[ARO] being still disguised as Pedro, here establishes his separate
  identity just as Lodovico, disguised as Carlo, had established his in the
  previous scene.

---

260 *And wash the Ethiop white.* This is probably derived from Jeremiah xiii,
  23: 'Can the Ethiopian change his skin, or the leopard his spots?' The
  phrase was used to express impossibility in Lucian, *Adversus Indoctum*,
  28. As a proverb it was particularly popular in the Elizabethan Age. (See
  R. R. Cawley, *The Voyagers and Elizabethan Drama*, pp. 37–38.)
266-7. The source of this statement is Pliny's *Natural History*, Book VIII,
  chapter xxvii: 'palumbes, graculi, merulae, perdices lauri folio annuum
  fastidium purgent.' Holland's translation (1601) reads: 'The Stock-
  doves, the Iaies, Merles, Blackbirds, Ousels, recover their appetite,
  which once in a year they loose, with eating Bay-leaves that purge their
  stomacke.' Partridges, omitted from this list, are included in the list
  which follows of birds which purge themselves with the herb pellitory.

is behind him. Now, to his face: all comparisons were hate-
ful. Wise was the courtly peacock, that being a great minion,
and being compar'd for beauty, by some dottrels that   5
stood by, to the kingly eagle, said the eagle was a far fairer
bird than herself, not in respect of her feathers, but in respect
of her long tallants. His will grow out in time.
My gracious lord.

GIOVANNI
I pray leave me sir.   10

FLAMINEO
Your Grace must be merry: 'tis I have cause to mourn; for
wot you what said the little boy that rode behind his father
on horseback?

GIOVANNI
Why, what said he?

FLAMINEO
'When you are dead father,' said he, 'I hope then I shall ride   15
in the saddle.' O 'tis a brave thing for a man to sit by himself: he may stretch himself in the stirrups, look about, and
see the whole compass of the hemisphere; you're now, my
lord, i'th'saddle.

GIOVANNI
Study your prayers sir, and be penitent;   20
'Twere fit you'd think on what hath former bin,
I have heard grief nam'd the eldest child of sin.

                                        Exit GIOV[ANNI]

FLAMINEO
Study my prayers? He threatens me divinely; I am falling
to pieces already; I care not, though, like Anacharsis I
were pounded to death in a mortar. And yet that death were   25
fitter for usurers' gold and themselves to be beaten together,
to make a most cordial cullis for the devil.

5 *dottrels* Q1b (Q1a dottrles) species of plover; fools, simpletons
8 *tallants* talons; talents   15–16 inverted commas ed.; (Qq (said he))
15 *I hope then I* Q1 (Q2, Q3, Q4 I hope that I)
21 *bin* Q1 (Q2, Q3, Q4 been): *cf. The Duchess of Malfi,* V.v, 53–4.
24 *to* Q1, Q2, Q3 (Q4 in)
26 *usurers'* ed. see Textual Appendix–A.
27 *cordial* see V.i, 138 note; *cullis* ed. (Q1a chullice; Q1b cullice)
   strengthening broth made by bruising meat

24 *Anarcharsis* was a Thracian prince of the 6th century B.C. It was, in
   fact, Anaxarchus who, by order of Nicocreon, was pounded to death in
   a mortar. The confusion of names belongs not to Webster, but his
   source, Nicholas de Montreux, *Honours Academie,* translated by R.
   Tofte (1610: '. . . *Anacharsis,* being pounded to death in a morter,
   iested at death.' (Dent, p. 156)

He hath his uncle's villainous look already,
In *decimo-sexto.* Now sir, what are you?   *Enter* COURTIER
COURTIER
It is the pleasure sir, of the young Duke   30
That you forbear the presence, and all rooms
That owe him reverence.
FLAMINEO   So, the wolf and the raven
Are very pretty fools when they are young.
Is it your office, sir, to keep me out?
COURTIER
So the Duke wills.   35
FLAMINEO
Verily, master courtier, extremity is not to be used in all
offices. Say that a gentlewoman were taken out of her bed
about midnight, and committed to Castle Angelo, to the
tower yonder, with nothing about her, but her smock:
would it not show a cruel part in the gentleman porter to   40
lay claim to her upper garment, pull it o'er her head and
ears; and put her in naked?
COURTIER
Very good: you are merry.   [*Exit*]
FLAMINEO
Doth he make a court ejectment of me? A flaming firebrand
casts more smoke without a chimney, than within 't. I'll   45
smoor some of them.

             Enter [FRANCISCO, *Duke of*] *Florence*

How now? Thou art sad.
FRANCISCO
I met even now with the most piteous sight.
FLAMINEO
Thou met'st another here, a pitiful
Degraded courtier.

---

29 *decimo-sexto* a book of very small pages, each being only $\frac{1}{16}$th of a
    full sheet of paper
31 *presence* presence or audience chamber
39 *nothing about* no money on; no clothes around
42 *naked* Q2, Q3, Q4 (Q1 nak'd)
44 *flaming firebrand:* 'with a play on his own name, Flamineo?'
    (Lucas)
46 *smoor* smother, suffocate
    S.D. FRANCISCO i.e. disguised as Mulinassar
49 *met'st* see Textual Appendix–A.

---

38 *Castle Angelo.* Vittoria was herself imprisoned in Castle Sant Angelo in
    Rome, 1581–2.

FRANCISCO   Your reverend mother   50
  Is grown a very old woman in two hours.
  I found them winding of Marcello's corse;
  And there is such a solemn melody
  'Tween doleful songs, tears, and sad elegies:
  Such as old grandames, watching by the dead,   55
  Were wont t'outwear the nights with; that believe me
  I had no eyes to guide me forth the room,
  They were so o'ercharg'd with water.
FLAMINEO   I will see them.
FRANCISCO
  'Twere much uncharity in you: for your sight
  Will add unto their tears.
FLAMINEO   I will see them.   60
FRANCISCO
  They are behind the traverse. I'll discover
  Their superstitious howling. [*Draws the traverse*]

> CORNELIA, [ZANCHE] *the Moor and 3. other Ladies*
> *discovered, winding* MARCELLO'S *corse. A song.*

CORNELIA
  This rosemary is wither'd, pray get fresh;
  I would have these herbs grow up in his grave
  When I am dead and rotten. Reach the bays,   65
  I'll tie a garland here about his head:
  'Twill keep my boy from lightning. This sheet
  I have kept this twenty year, and every day
  Hallow'd it with my prayers; I did not think
  He should have wore it.

65 *the bays* a garland of bay (or bay laurel) leaves such as was used
  to crown a poet or conqueror
67 *This sheet* i.e. her own winding-sheet
68 *year* ed. (Q1 yere; Q2 yeeres; Q3, Q4 years)

63ff. 'Partially because she was depicted without a real trace of melodrama,
    [Cornelia] remains . . . one of the most authentic pathological studies in
    the Jacobean drama.' (R. R. Reed, *Bedlam on the Jacobean Stage*
    (Cambridge, Mass., 1952), pp. 91–92). See also J. R. Mulryne, *op. cit.*,
    pp. 213–14. Cornelia's distribution of flowers recalls Ophelia's in
    Hamlet, IV.v, 175–83, but Dent (pp. 157–58) thinks that it hardly parallels
    Ophelia's in significance and suggests that it makes most sense if all
    three flowers are given to Flamineo.
67 *'Twill keep . . . lightning.* Holland's translation of Pliny's *Natural History*
    (1601), Book II, chapter lv reads: 'Of all those things which growe out of
    the earth, Lightning blasteth not the Laurell tree; . . .' and Book XV,
    chapter xxx: 'It is reported, that *Tiberius Caesar* the Emperor ever
    used to weare a chaplet thereof when it thundered, for feare of being
    strucken with lightning.'

ZANCHE   Look you; who are yonder?   70
CORNELIA
O reach me the flowers.
ZANCHE
Her ladyship's foolish.
WOMAN   Alas her grief
Hath turn'd her child again.
CORNELIA *to* FLAMINEO   You're very welcome.
There's rosemary for you, and rue for you,
Heart's-ease for you. I pray make much of it.   75
I have left more for myself.
FRANCISCO   Lady, who's this?
CORNELIA
You are, I take it, the grave-maker.
FLAMINEO   So.
ZANCHE
'Tis Flamineo.
                    [CORNELIA *takes his hand*]
CORNELIA
Will you make me such a fool? Here's a white hand:
Can blood so soon be wash'd out? Let me see: 80
When screech-owls croak upon the chimney tops,
And the strange cricket i'th' oven sings and hops,
When yellow spots do on your hands appear,
Be certain then you of a corse shall hear.
Out upon't, how 'tis speckled! H'as handled a toad sure.   85
Cowslip-water is good for the memory:
Pray buy me 3. ounces of't.
FLAMINEO
I would I were from hence.
CORNELIA   Do you hear, sir?
I'll give you a saying which my grandmother
Was wont, when she heard the bell toll, to sing o'er   90
Unto her lute—
FLAMINEO   Do and you will, do.
                    CORNELIA *doth this in several forms of distraction*
CORNELIA
Call for the robin red breast and the wren,

70, 72, 78 speech-prefixes for Zanche: Qq. MOO. or MOOR.
70 *yonder?* Q2, Q3, Q4 (Q1 yonder.)
84 *corse* ed. (Q1 Course; Q2, Q3, Q4 Coarse)
85 *H'as* ed. (Qq h'as) he has
91 S.D. opposite 93–95 in Q1; see Textual Appendix–A.

92–101 'No direct source has been suggested for any part of this beautiful
song.' (Dent, p. 159)

Since o'er shady groves they hover,
And with leaves and flow'rs do cover
The friendless bodies of unburied men.   95
Call unto his funeral dole
The ant, the field-mouse, and the mole
To rear him hillocks, that shall keep him warm
And (when gay tombs are robb'd) sustain no harm,
But keep the wolf far thence: that's foe to men,   100
For with his nails he'll dig them up again.
They would not bury him 'cause he died in a quarrel
But I have an answer for them.
Let holy church receive him duly
Since he paid the church tithes truly.   105
His wealth is summ'd, and this is all his store:
This poor men get; and great men get no more.
Now the wares are gone, we may shut up shop.
Bless you all good people.

                    Exeunt CORNELIA [,ZANCHE] *and Ladies*

FLAMINEO
I have a strange thing in me, to the which   110
I cannot give a name, without it be
Compassion; I pray leave me.   *Exit* FRANCISCO
This night I'll know the utmost of my fate,
I'll be resolv'd what my rich sister means
T'assign me for my service. I have liv'd   115
Riotously ill, like some that live in court.
And sometimes, when my face was full of smiles
Have felt the maze of conscience in my breast.
Oft gay and honour'd robes those tortures try,
We think cag'd birds sing, when indeed they cry.   120

---

96 *funeral dole* funeral rites
110 *to the* ed. (Qq to th')
114 *resolv'd* settled in my own mind; satisfied
117 *my* Q1 (Q2, Q3, Q4 his)
118 *maze* Q2, Q3, Q4 (Q1 mase) bewilderment
120 italics: ed. (Qq mark the line with inverted commas)

92–5. The belief that the robin would cover the face or whole body of a
    dead person was common in Europe in the sixteenth century. It is found
    in the 'babe in the wood' story of the murder of the orphan Pertillo by
    ruffians hired by his uncle Fallerio in Robert Yarington's *Two Lamen-
    table Tragedies* (1594–*circa* 1598). 'The wren appears here as well
    because she is, in popular belief, the robin's wife.' (Lucas, *Webster*, i,
    263)
100–101 *cf. The Duchess of Malfi*, IV.ii, 303–305.

Enter BRACHIA[NO'S] *Ghost. In his leather cassock and
breeches, boots, a cowl [and in his hand] a pot of lily-
flowers with a skull in't.*

Ha! I can stand thee. Nearer, nearer yet.
What a mockery hath death made of thee? Thou look'st sad.
In what place art thou? in yon starry gallery,
Or in the cursed dungeon? No? not speak?
Pray, sir, resolve me, what religion's best   125
For a man to die in? or is it in your knowledge
To answer me how long I have to live?
That's the most necessary question.
Not answer? Are you still like some great men
That only walk like shadows up and down,   130
And to no purpose: say:———
The ghost throws earth upon him and shows him the skull
What's that? O fatal! He throws earth upon me.
A dead man's skull beneath the roots of flowers.
I pray speak sir; our Italian churchmen
Make us believe, dead men hold conference   135
With their familiars, and many times
Will come to bed to them, and eat with them.   *Exit Ghost*
He's gone; and see, the skull and earth are vanish'd.
This is beyond melancholy. I do dare my fate
To do its worst. Now to my sister's lodging,   140
And sum up all these horrors; the disgrace
The Prince threw on me; next the piteous sight
Of my dead brother; and my mother's dotage;
And last this terrible vision. All these
Shall with Vittoria's bounty turn to good,   145
Or I will drown this weapon in her blood.   *Exit*

120 s.d. *cassock* long cloak; *cowl* ed. (Q1 coole; Q2 coule; Q3, Q4
    coul); *lily* ed. (Q1 *lilly*; Q2, Q3, Q4 *lilly*)
121 *stand* withstand: a word which recalls IV.ii, 50 'whether inten-
    tionally or no.' (Lucas)
122 *of thee* Q1 (Q2, Q3, Q4 thee)   132 *earth* Q1, Q2, Q3 (Q4 dirt)
136 *familiars* familiar spirits; close friends or relations

---

120 s.d. It was a common superstition that if a wicked man were buried in
    a Friar's *cowl* he would obtain remission for some part of his sins. A *pot
    of lily-flowers* was frequently used as a religious emblem to denote life in
    pictures of the Annunciation. The *skull* denoted death. 'Webster evi-
    dently intended a grotesque, though perhaps common, juxtaposition of
    symbols, . . .' (Dent, p. 161).
142-3 It was not unknown for villainous revengers, summing up the list of
    their wrongs before the final execution of vengeance, to include afflic-
    tions that they had brought upon themselves. Thus, in *Soliman and
    Perseda* the death of Erastus, carried out by Soliman's own command,
    is included in the final enumeration of his wrongs.

[Act V, Scene v]

Enter FRANCISCO, LODOVICO, *and* HORTENSIO [*over-hearing them*]

LODOVICO
My lord upon my soul you shall no further:
You have most ridiculously engag'd yourself
Too far already. For my part, I have paid
All my debts, so if I should chance to fall
My creditors fall not with me; and I vow   5
To quite all in this bold assembly
To the meanest follower. My lord leave the city,
Or I'll forswear the murder.
FRANCISCO   Farewell Lodovico.
If thou dost perish in this glorious act,
I'll rear unto thy memory that fame   10
Shall in the ashes keep alive thy name.
                    [*Exeunt* FRANCISCO *and* LODOVICO]

HORTENSIO
There's some black deed on foot. I'll presently
Down to the citadel, and raise some force.
These strong court factions that do brook no checks,
In the career oft break the riders' necks.   [*Exit*]   15

[Act V, Scene vi]

Enter VITTORIA *with a book in her hand,* ZANCHE;
FLAMINEO *following them*

FLAMINEO
What, are you at your prayers? Give o'er.
VITTORIA   How ruffin?
FLAMINEO
I come to you 'bout worldly business:

6 *quite* Q1, Q2 (Q3, Q4 quit) requite, repay
7 *To the* i.e. down to and including
8 *forswear* deny, repudiate
15 *career* see IV.iii, 94–95 note; *Exit.* Q3, Q4 (Q1, Q2 [omit])
1 *ruffin* cant term for the devil

Act V, Scene v: 'This brief scene is dramatically necessary, in order to account
for the entrance of Giovanni and the English ambassador after the triple
murder in the following scene.' (Sampson, p. 204)

Sit down, sit down. Nay, stay blouze, you may hear it,
The doors are fast enough.

VITTORIA   Ha, are you drunk?

FLAMINEO

Yes, yes, with wormwood water; you shall taste   5
Some of it presently.

VITTORIA   What intends the fury?

FLAMINEO

You are my lord's executrix, and I claim
Reward, for my long service.

VITTORIA   For your service?

FLAMINEO

Come therefore, here is pen and ink, set down
What you will give me.   10

VITTORIA

There.   *She writes*

FLAMINEO Ha! have you done already?
'Tis a most short conveyance.

VITTORIA   I will read it.

[*reads*] *I give that portion to thee, and no other*
Which Cain groan'd under having slain his brother.

FLAMINEO

A most courtly patent to beg by.

VITTORIA   You are a villain.   15

FLAMINEO

Is't come to this? They say affrights cure agues:
Thou hast a devil in thee; I will try
If I can scare him from thee. Nay sit still:
My lord hath left me yet two case of jewels

---

3 *blouze* beggar's trull; a fat, red-faced, slatternly wench
4 *fast* secure
5 *wormwood water* medicine made of the leaves and tips of artemisia
  absinthium, a plant proverbial for its very bitter taste; an emblem
  or type of what is bitter and grievous to the soul
6 *fury?* Q1 (Q2, Q3, Q4 Fury?): see IV.iii, 125 and 151 note.
8 *your service?* Q2, Q4 (Q1 your seruice ; Q3 you service?)
12 *conveyance* document by which property is transferred
13 *portion* part or share of an estate given by law to an heir
14 *which Cain groan'd under* i.e. God's curse: see Genesis iv, 11–15.
15 *patent* see V.i, 111 note.
18 *scare* Q3, Q4 (Q1, Q2 scarre)

18ff. An excellent analysis of the relationship between Flamineo and
  Vittoria as it is found in this scene, especially in the imagery, is given by
  B. J. Layman, 'The Equilibrium of Opposites in *The White Devil:*
  A Reinterpretation', *PMLA*, LXXIV (1959), 344–7.

Shall make me scorn your bounty; you shall see them. [*Exit*] 20

VITTORIA
Sure he's distracted.

ZANCHE   O he's desperate!
For your own safety give him gentle language.

He enters with two case of pistols

FLAMINEO
Look, these are better far at a dead lift,
Than all your jewel house.

VITTORIA   And yet methinks,
These stones have no fair lustre, they are ill set. 25

FLAMINEO
I'll turn the right side towards you: you shall see
How they will sparkle.

VITTORIA   Turn this horror from me:
What do you want? What would you have me do?
Is not all mine, yours? Have I any children?

FLAMINEO
Pray thee good woman do not trouble me 30
With this vain worldly business; say your prayers;
I made a vow to my deceased lord,
Neither yourself, nor I should outlive him,
The numb'ring of four hours.

VITTORIA   Did he enjoin it?

FLAMINEO
He did, and 'twas a deadly jealousy, 35
Lest any should enjoy thee after him,
That urg'd him vow me to it. For my death,
I did propound it voluntarily, knowing
If he could not be safe in his own court
Being a great Duke, what hope then for us? 40

VITTORIA
This is your melancholy and despair.

FLAMINEO   Away;
Fool that thou art to think that politicians
Do use to kill the effects of injuries
And let the cause live: shall we groan in irons,

21 *desperate*! Q2, Q3, Q4 (Q1 desperate)
22 s.d. Q1, Q2 (Q3, Q4 *And returns* . . .)
31 *worldly* Q2, Q3, Q4 (Q1 wordly)
32–33 *lord*, / *Neither* i.e. lord, [that] neither
42 *Fool that* ed.: see Textual Appendix–A.

23 *at a dead lift* in a tight corner. This phrase was originally applied to a
   horse which had to drag a dead weight that was too heavy for it. Here
   Flamineo is punning on *dead*.

Or be a shameful and a weighty burthen   45
To a public scaffold? This is my resolve:
I would not live at any man's entreaty
Nor die at any's bidding.

VITTORIA   Will you hear me?

FLAMINEO
My life hath done service to other men,
My death shall serve mine own turn; make you ready.   50

VITTORIA
Do you mean to die indeed?

FLAMINEO   With as much pleasure
As e'er my father gat me.

VITTORIA [*aside to* ZANCHE]   Are the doors lock'd?

ZANCHE
Yes madam.

VITTORIA
Are you grown an atheist? Will you turn your body,
Which is the goodly palace of the soul   55
To the soul's slaughter house? O the cursed devil
Which doth present us with all other sins
Thrice candied o'er; despair with gall and stibium,
Yet we carouse it off; [*aside to* ZANCHE] Cry out for help.
Makes us forsake that which was made for man,   60
The world, to sink to that was made for devils,
Eternal darkness.

ZANCHE   Help, help!

FLAMINEO   I'll stop your throat
With winter plums,—

VITTORIA   I prithee yet remember,
Millions are now in graves, which at last day
Like mandrakes shall rise shrieking.

FLAMINEO   Leave your prating,   65
For these are but grammatical laments,

---

48 *hear me* i.e. give me a hearing (with connotation of legal or judicial
   hearing): cf. *The Duchess of Malfi*, III.ii, 83.
54 *atheist* see IV.ii, 40 note.
58 *candied o'er* sugared over; *gall* bile; venom, poison; bitterness of
   spirit; *stibium* the poison antimony
65 *Like mandrakes* see III.i, 51 note.
66 *grammatical laments* laments made according to formal rules

---

56–58 i.e. 'O the cursed devil that presents all others sins to us under a
   sugar cover, [but] despair covered with bitterness and poison.' Cf. *The
   Duchess of Malfi*, I.ii, 196–8; IV.i, 19–20. *Despair* was considered one
   of the greatest sins because it meant denying the grace of God: cf. *The
   Duchess of Malfi*, IV.ii, 74–75.

Feminine arguments, and they move me
As some in pulpits move their auditory
More with their exclamation than sense
Of reason, or sound doctrine.
ZANCHE [*aside*]   Gentle madam   70
Seem to consent, only persuade him teach
The way to death; let him die first.
VITTORIA [*aside*]
'Tis good, I apprehend it.—
To kill oneself is meat that we must take
Like pills, not chew't, but quickly swallow it;   75
The smart o'th' wound, or weakness of the hand
May else bring treble torments.
FLAMINEO   I have held it
A wretched and most miserable life,
Which is not able to die.
VITTORIA   O but frailty!
Yet I am now resolv'd; farewell affliction.   80
Behold Brachiano, I that while you liv'd
Did make a flaming altar of my heart
To sacrifice unto you; now am ready
To sacrifice heart and all. Farewell Zanche.
ZANCHE
How madam! Do you think that I'll outlive you?   85
Expecially when my best self Flamineo
Goes the same voyage.
FLAMINEO   O most loved Moor!
ZANCHE
Only, by all my love let me entreat you;
Since it is most necessary none of us
Do violence on ourselves; let you or I   90
Be her sad taster, teach her how to die.
FLAMINEO
Thou dost instruct me nobly; take these pistols,
Because my hand is stain'd with blood already:
Two of these you shall level at my breast,
The other 'gainst your own, and so we'll die,   95
Most equally contented. But first swear
Not to outlive me.
VITTORIA and ZANCHE Most religiously.

69 *exclamation* formal declamation; emphatic or vehement speech
73 *apprehend* understand, feel the force of: *cf.* II.i, 243.
75 *chew't* chew it
89 *none* Q1 (Q2, Q3, Q4 one): see Textual Appendix–A.
95 *The other* ed. (Qq Th'other) i.e. the other pair (case) of pistols

FLAMINEO

   Then here's an end of me: farewell daylight;
   And O contemptible physic! that dost take
   So long a study, only to preserve   100
   So short a life, I take my leave of thee.

                                        Showing the pistols
   These are two cupping-glasses, that shall draw
   All my infected blood out.
   Are you ready?

VITTORIA and ZANCHE   Ready.

FLAMINEO

   Whither shall I go now? O Lucian thy ridiculous purgatory!   105
   to find Alexander the Great cobbling shoes, Pompey tagging
   points, and Julius Caesar making hair buttons, Hannibal
   selling blacking, and Augustus crying garlic, Charlemagne
   selling lists by the dozen, and King Pippin crying apples in
   a cart drawn with one horse.   110
   Whether I resolve to fire, earth, water, air,
   Or all the elements by scruples, I know not
   Nor greatly care.—Shoot, shoot,
   Of all deaths the violent death is best,
   For from ourselves it steals ourselves so fast   115
   The pain once apprehended is quite past.

      They shoot and run to him and tread upon him

VITTORIA

   What, are you dropp'd?

FLAMINEO

   I am mix'd with earth already. As you are noble
   Perform your vows, and bravely follow me.

VITTORIA

   Whither? to hell?

ZANCHE   To most assured damnation.   120

---

104 speech-prefix ed. (Qq *Both*)
105–6 see Textual Appendix–A. 105–110: see Additional Notes, p. 149.
107 *tagging points* 'fixing metal tags on the laces or points which
    largely did the work of buttons in Elizabethan dress' (Lucas)
108 *crying garlic* i.e. calling out the price of his garlic, like a street-
    vendor
109 *lists* strips of cloth   109–110: see Additional Notes, p. 149.
112 *by scruples* by small degrees or amounts
116 s.d. opposite 115–118 in Q1.

101–2 *Cupping-glasses* are surgical vessels used to draw off blood through
    the creation of a vacuum in them by means of heat. It was assumed that
    only *infected blood* would be drawn off, leaving the body healthy. *Cf.*
    The Duchess of Malfi, II.v, 23–6; Middleton and Rowley, *The Changeling*,
    ed. Patricia Thomson (The New Mermaids, 1964) V.iii, 149–53.

VITTORIA
O thou most cursed devil.
ZANCHE   Thou art caught—
VITTORIA
In thine own engine; I tread the fire out
That would have been my ruin.
FLAMINEO
Will you be perjur'd? What a religious oath was Styx that
the gods never durst swear by and violate? O that we had   125
such an oath to minister, and to be so well kept in our
courts of justice.
VITTORIA
Think whither thou art going.
ZANCHE   And remember
What villanies thou hast acted.
VITTORIA   This thy death
Shall make me like a blazing ominous star,—   130
Look up and tremble.
FLAMINEO   O I am caught with a springe!
VITTORIA
You see the fox comes many times short home,
'Tis here prov'd true.
FLAMINEO   Kill'd with a couple of braches!
VITTORIA
No fitter offering for the infernal Furies
Than one in whom they reign'd while he was living.   135
FLAMINEO
O the way's dark and horrid! I cannot see,
Shall I have no company?
VITTORIA   O yes thy sins
Do run before thee to fetch fire from hell,
To light thee thither.
FLAMINEO   O I smell soot,
Most stinking soot, the chimney is a-fire,   140
My liver's parboil'd like Scotch holy-bread;

122 *engine* contrivance
130 *star,*— ed. (Q1, Q2 starre,   ; Q3, Q4 star,)
131 *springe* snare for catching small game
132 *short home* i.e. without his tail, i.e. dead; *or* quickly home
133 *braches* bitches   134 *Furies* Q2, Q3, Q4 (Q1 furies)
140 *stinking* Q2, Q3, Q4 (Q1 sinking)
141 *parboil'd* Q2, Q3, Q4 (Q1 purboil'd) boiled through and through;
    holy bread Q4 (Q1, Q2, Q3 holly-bread)

141 *Scotch holy bread.* Cotgrave's *Dictionarie of the French and English
    Tongues* (1611) [quoted by Sampson, p. 205]: '*Pain benist d'Escosse–A*
    sodden sheepes liver.'

There's a plumber, laying pipes in my guts, it scalds;
Wilt thou outlive me?

ZANCHE   Yes, and drive a stake
Through thy body; for we'll give it out,
Thou didst this violence upon thyself.   145

FLAMINEO

O cunning devils! now I have try'd your love,
And doubled all your reaches. I am not wounded:

FLAMINEO *riseth*

The pistols held no bullets: 'Twas a plot
To prove your kindness to me; and I live
To punish your ingratitude; I knew
One time or other you would find a way   150
To give me a strong potion. O men
That lie upon your death-beds, and are haunted
With howling wives, ne'er trust them; they'll remarry
Ere the worm pierce your winding sheet; ere the spider
Make a thin curtain for your epitaphs.   155
How cunning you were to discharge! Do you practise at the
Artillery Yard? Trust a woman? Never, never; Brachiano
be my president: we lay our souls to pawn to the devil for
a little pleasure, and a woman makes the bill of sale. That
ever man should marry! For one Hypermnestra that sav'd   160
her lord and husband, forty-nine of her sisters cut their
throats all in one night. There was a shoal of virtuous horse-
leeches.
Here are two other instruments.

Enter LOD[OVICO], GASP[ARO, *disguised as*] CARLO, PEDRO
[*with others*]

---

147 *doubled all your reaches* i.e. 'matched, or been equal to, all your
    contrivances' (Brown)
149 *knew* Q1 (Q2, Q3, Q4 know)   156 *cunning* skilful
158 *president* precedent; (also with connotation 'president')
162-3 *horse-leeches* blood-suckers; *cf.* III.ii, 279.
164 S.D. Q1, Q2 *Enter Lod. Gasp. Pedro, Carlo*; Q3 *Enter Lod., Gasp.*;
    Q4 *Enter Lodovico and Gasparo:* see Additional Notes, p. 149.

144-5 'the traditional treatment of suicides, who were thus buried at cross-
      roads' (Lucas)
157 *Artillery Yard:* or Artillery Gardens, in Bishopsgate, was where,
    according to Stowe, *Annals* (1631), pp. 995-6, weekly exercise of arms
    and military discipline were revived in 1610. (Brown, p. 178 n.)
160 *Hypermnestra*, one of the fifty daughters of Danus who were forced to
    marry their uncle's fifty sons. Their father, having been warned by an
    oracle that one of his nephews would kill him, asked his daughters to
    kill their husbands on their wedding night. Forty-nine of them did as he
    wished. Hypermnestra alone spared her husband.

VITTORIA   Help, help!

FLAMINEO

    What noise is that? hah? false keys i'th' court.   165

LODOVICO

    We have brought you a masque.

FLAMINEO   A matachin it seems,

    By your drawn swords. Churchmen turn'd revellers.

CONSPIRATORS

    Isabella, Isabella!

              [They throw off their disguises]

LODOVICO

    Do you know us now?

FLAMINEO   Lodovico and Gasparo.

LODOVICO

    Yes, and that Moor the Duke gave pension to   170

    Was the great Duke of Florence.

VITTORIA   O we are lost.

FLAMINEO

    You shall not take justice from forth my hands;

    O let me kill her.——————I'll cut my safety

    Through your coats of steel. Fate's a spaniel,

    We cannot beat it from us. What remains now?   175

    Let all that do ill take this president:

    Man may his fate foresee, but not prevent.

    And of all axioms this shall win the prize,

    'Tis better to be fortunate than wise.

GASPARO

    Bind him to the pillar.

VITTORIA   O your gentle pity!   180

    I have seen a blackbird that would sooner fly

    To a man's bosom, than to stay the gripe

    Of the fierce sparrow-hawk.

GASPARO   Your hope deceives you.

VITTORIA

    If Florence be i'th' court, would he would kill me.

GASPARO

    Fool! Princes give rewards with their own hands,   185

    But death or punishment by the hands of others.

---

166 *matachin* a sword dance performed by masked dancers wearing
    fantastic costumes

168 speech-prefix: *Conspirators* Wheeler (Q1, Q2 CON.; Q3, Q4
    Gas.)

177, 179: italicized in Qq

182 *stay* wait for

184 *would he would* Q1, Q2 (Q3, Q4 he would not)

LODOVICO
Sirrah you once did strike me; I'll strike you
Into the centre.

FLAMINEO
Thou'lt do it like a hangman; a base hangman;
Not like a noble fellow, for thou seest   190
I cannot strike again.

LODOVICO   Dost laugh?

FLAMINEO
Wouldst have me die, as I was born, in whining?

GASPARO
Recommend yourself to heaven.

FLAMINEO
No I will carry mine own commendations thither.

LODOVICO
Oh could I kill you forty times a day   195
And use't four year together; 'twere too little:
Nought grieve's but that you are too few to feed
The famine of our vengeance. What dost think on?

FLAMINEO
Nothing; of nothing: leave thy idle questions;
I am i'th'way to study a long silence   200
To prate were idle; I remember nothing.
There's nothing of so infinite vexation
As man's own thoughts.

LODOVICO   O thou glorious strumpet,
Could I divide thy breath from this pure air
When't leaves thy body, I would suck it up   205
And breathe't upon some dunghill.

VITTORIA   You, my death's-man;
Methinks thou dost not look horrid enough,
Thou hast too good a face to be a hangman;
If thou be, do thy office in right form;
Fall down upon thy knees and ask forgiveness.   210

---

188 *Into* Q1 (Q2, Q3, Q4 Unto); *the centre* i.e. the heart
189 *hangman* i.e. executioner, whose prisoner is unable to resist him:
   cf. V.vi, 208 below.
196 *four year* Q3 (Q1, Q2 foure yeere; Q4 for years)
197 *grieve's* ed. (Q1, Q2 greeu's; Q3, Q4 griev's) grieves us
201 *idle* foolish, useless
206 *death's-man;* ed. (Q1, Q2 Deaths man; Q3 Deaths-man;   Q4
   deaths-man?)

---

199 *cf. The Duchess of Malfi,* IV.ii, 15–17.

LODOVICO
O thou hast been a most prodigious comet,
But I'll cut off your train: kill the Moor first.

VITTORIA
You shall not kill her first. Behold my breast,
I will be waited on in death; my servant
Shall never go before me.   215

GASPARO
Are you so brave?

VITTORIA   Yes I shall welcome death
As princes do some great ambassadors;
I'll meet thy weapon half way.

LODOVICO   Thou dost tremble,
Methinks fear should dissolve thee into air.

VITTORIA
O thou art deceiv'd, I am too true a woman: 220
Conceit can never kill me: I'll tell thee what;
I will not in my death shed one base tear,
Or if I look pale, for want of blood, not fear.

GASPARO
Thou art my task, black fury.

ZANCHE   I have blood
As red as either of theirs: wilt drink some?   225
'Tis good for the falling sickness. I am proud
Death cannot alter my complexion,
For I shall ne'er look pale.

LODOVICO   Strike, strike,
With a joint motion.   [*They strike*]

VITTORIA   'Twas a manly blow.
The next thou giv'st, murder some sucking infant,   230
And then thou wilt be famous.

FLAMINEO   O what blade is't?
A toledo, or an English fox?
I ever thought a cutler should distinguish
The cause of my death, rather than a doctor.

212 *train* comet's tail; train of servants, i.e. Zanche
220 *true* Q1c (Q1a treue; Q1b treu)
221 *Conceit* imagination; vanity; conception
224 speech-prefix: Q3, Q4 *Gas.* (Q1 CAR. ; Q2 *Cor.*); see note on
    164 s.d. above; *fury* Q1 (Q2, Q3, Q4 Fury)
226 *falling sickness* epilepsy

216ff. On the deaths of Vittoria and Flamineo see: J. R. Mulryne, *op. cit.*,
    pp. 212–13; Dent, p. 169; B. J. Layman, *op. cit.*, pp. 246–7.
232 *fox*: a common name for a sword in Elizabethan England, either because
    of the brown colour of the steel, or because the figure of a wolf on some
    blades was taken to be that of a fox.

Search my wound deeper: tent it with the steel   235
That made it.
FLAMINEO *(sic)* VITTORIA
O my greatest sin lay in my blood.
Now my blood pays for't.
FLAMINEO   Th'art a noble sister,
I love thee now; if woman do breed man
She ought to teach him manhood. Fare thee well.   240
Know many glorious women that are fam'd
For masculine virtue, have been vicious
Only a happier silence did betide them.
She hath no faults, who hath the art to hide them.
VITTORIA
My soul, like to a ship in a black storm,   245
Is driven I know not whither.
FLAMINEO   Then cast anchor.
Prosperity doth bewitch men seeming clear,
But seas do laugh, show white, when rocks are near.
We cease to grieve, cease to be Fortune's slaves,
Nay cease to die by dying. [*to* ZANCHE] Art thou gone?   250
[*to* VITTORIA] And thou so near the bottom? False report
Which says that women vie with the nine Muses
For nine tough durable lives. I do not look
Who went before, nor who shall follow me;
No, at myself I will begin and end.   255
While we look up to heaven we confound
Knowledge with knowledge. O I am in a mist.
VITTORIA
O happy they that never saw the court,
Nor ever knew great man but by report.   VITTORIA *dies*
FLAMINEO
I recover like a spent taper, for a flash   260
And instantly go out.
Let all that belong to great men remember th'old wives'
tradition, to be like the lions i'th' Tower on Candlemas day,

235 *tent* probe; apply a tent to it (A tent was a plug of soft material
    used for searching, cleaning or distending a wound.)
246 *anchor* Q4 (Q1 ancor; Q2, Q3 anclior)
247–50: These lines are preceded by inverted commas in Qq.
256–7; 259; 270–271: preceded by inverted commas in Qq.
259 *man* ed. (Q1 Man; Q2, Q3, Q4 Men)

---

263 *lions i'th'Tower.* Lions and, according to Stowe, other animals were
    kept in the Tower of London. There are records of lion-baiting for the
    amusement of the nobility in 1609 and 1610. The animals continued to
    be kept in the Tower till 1834 when they were removed to the Zoo.
    Candlemas day 2nd February: according to an old proverb, a fair and
    sunny Candlemas day foretold the quick flight of winter.

to mourn if the sun shine, for fear of the pitiful remainder of
winter to come.   265
'Tis well yet there's some goodness in my death,
My life was a black charnel. I have cought
An everlasting cold. I have lost my voice
Most irrecoverably. Farewell glorious villains,
This busy trade of life appears most vain,   270
Since rest breeds rest, where all seek pain by pain.
Let no harsh flattering bells resound my knell,
Strike thunder, and strike loud to my farewell.   *Dies*

    Enter [AMBASSADORS] *and* GIOVANNI. [GUARDS *follow.*]

ENGLISH AMBASSADOR
This way, this way, break ope the doors, this way.
LODOVICO
Ha, are we betray'd?   275
Why then let's constantly die all together,
And having finish'd this most noble deed,
Defy the worst of fate; not fear to bleed.
ENGLISH AMBASSADOR
Keep back the Prince: shoot, shoot—
           [GUARDS *shoot at conspirators*]
LODOVICO   O I am wounded.
I fear I shall be tane.
GIOVANNI   You bloody villains,   280
By what authority have you commited
This massacre?
LODOVICO   By thine.
GIOVANNI   Mine?
LODOVICO   Yes, thy uncle,
Which is a part of thee enjoin'd us to't:
Thou know'st me I am sure, I am Count Lodowick,
And thy most noble uncle in disguise   285
Was last night in thy court.
GIOVANNI   Ha!
GASPARO   Yes, that Moor
Thy father chose his pensioner.
GIOVANNI   He turn'd murderer?
Away with them to prison, and to torture;

267 *cought* Q1 (Q2, Q3, Q4 caught): possibly a pun is intended:
    coughed / caught
273 S.D. [AMBASSADORS] ed. (Q1, Q2 *Embassad:* Q3, Q4 *Embassador*)
282 *is a* Q1 (Q2, Q3, Q4 is)
286 speech-prefix: Q1, Q2 CAR.; Q3, Q4 *Gas.*

All that have hands in this, shall taste our justice,
As I hope heaven.

LODOVICO   I do glory yet   290
That I can call this act mine own. For my part,
The rack, the gallows, and the torturing wheel
Shall be but sound sleeps to me; here's my rest:
I limb'd this night-piece and it was my best.

GIOVANNI

Remove the bodies; see my honoured lord,   295
What use you ought make of their punishment.
Let guilty men remember their black deeds
Do lean on crutches, made of slender reeds.   [*Exeunt*]

Instead of an Epilogue only this of Martial supplies me:
        Haec fuerint nobis praemia si placui.   300

For the action of the play, 'twas generally well, and I dare
affirm, with the joint testimony of some of their own quality,
(for the true imitation of life, without striving to make nature
a monster) the best that ever became them: whereof as I make
a general acknowledgement, so in particular I must remem-   305
ber the well approved industry of my friend Master Perkins,
and confess the worth of his action did crown both the
beginning and end.

FINIS

292 *torturing* Q1, Q2 (Q3, Q4 torturious)
294 italics: ed. (Qq mark the line with inverted commas.); *limb'd* Q1,
    Q2, Q4 (Q3 limm'd) limned, i.e. painted; *night-piece* painting of
    a night scene
295 *lord* Qq: see Textual Appendix–A.
296 *you ought make* Q1, Q2, Q3 (Q4 we ought to make)
300 : 'These things will be our reward, if I have pleased.' (Martial II.
    xci, 8.)
302 *quality* profession

---

306 *Master Perkins* i.e. Richard Perkins, was the most famous 'straight' actor
    in the Queen's Men. In 'The Red Bull Company and the Importunate
    Widow', *Shakespeare Survey* 7 (Cambridge, 1954), p. 59 Professor C. J.
    Sisson comments '. . . Richard Perkins, at the peak of his career, when
    he gave his great performance in *The White Devil* at the Red Bull, was
    barely 30 years of age. A professional actor of that age would probably
    have had 14 years of experience on the public boards.' We know, in fact,
    that Perkins had belonged to Worcester's Men in 1602. Since Webster
    refers to his action as having crowned 'both the beginning and end' of
    the play, we assume that he took the part of Flamineo. For further
    details of Perkins' career, see G. E. Bentley, *The Jacobean and Caroline
    Stage*, ii (1941), pp. 525–6.

ADDITIONAL NOTES

1   *the famous Venetian Curtizan:* The real Vittoria Accoramboni, born in Gubbio, came of a noble Roman family. It has been suggested that Webster may have confused her with the Venetian born Bianca Capello, the heroine of Thomas Middleton's *Women Beware Women* (*c.* 1620–27) who, after the murder of the husband with whom she eloped to Florence, became the mistress and then the wife of Francisco de Medicis, Bracciano's brother-in-law. (See F. L. Lucas, *Webster*, i, 89, 194.) Venice was famous for its courtesans, and many English readers would be familiar with the personal account of them given by Thomas Coryate in *Coryat's Crudities* (1611). Thus, as Dr. Gunnar Boklund points out, once Webster had decided to present Vittoria as a famous courtesan–which neither she nor Bianca Capello really was –'the transfer from Rome to Venice would follow naturally . . .' (*The Sources of 'The White Devil'*, (Uppsala, 1957), p. 138.)

3   [DRAMATIS PERSONÆ] Q1 and Q2 omit the names of the characters. Q3 and Q4 supply a list of 'The Persons' which is reproduced here with the addition of characters omitted by that list but included in the action of the play (e.g. the Cardinal of Arragon, Doctor Julio, the Matrona and such 'extras' as Lawyers). The 'ghost characters' Christophero, Guid-Antonio, Ferneze and Jaques the Moor are each mentioned once in the stage directions (see II. i; II. ii [first dumb show] and V. i, 42) but have no speaking parts. It may be supposed that either Webster intended to make these small parts and then changed his mind, or that each originally had something to say which was later removed from the play (see Brown, p. 31); or it may be that these parts gave importance as well as 'something to do' to minor members of an acting company. Their presence or absence in a production of the play today will depend on the producer's ideas for the disposition of 'Attendants' and on his resources in the cast.

12   I. ii, 31 *wage all downward.* According to R. Stanyhurst's Description of Ireland, given in Holinshed's *Chronicles* (1577), some of the wild Irish would play away their clothes, truss themselves in straw or leaves and then, for lack of other stuff, would pawn the locks of hair on their foreheads, their finger or toe nails and their testicles, which they would lose or

redeem at the courtesy of the winner. Thus F. L. Lucas explains the allusion here as meaning that Camillo would be as ready as an Irish gambler to stake his virility (having none) but Dent (p. 79) finds this interpretation far-fetched and suggests that Flamineo 'probably means that Camillo has ventured all his amourousness, has lost brains, beard, "back", etc.'

25 I. ii, 325–7. Thomas Coryate's description of Venice, published in *Coryat's Crudities* (1611), was the most detailed account of the city that had hitherto been given in English. Coryate's personal investigation into the courtesans' way of life contained an idea similar to Flamineo's here: 'There is one most notable thing more to be mentioned concerning these Venetian Cortezans, with the relation whereof I will end this discourse of them. If any of them happen to haue any children (as indeede they haue but few, for according to the old prouerbe the best carpenters make the fewest chips) they are brought vp either at their owne charge, or in a certaine house of the citie appointed for no other vse but onely for the bringing vp of the Cortezans bastards, which I saw Eastward aboue Saint *Markes* streete neare to the sea side.'

26 II. i, 14–18. Isabella here refers to a test to prove the genuineness of powdered unicorn's horn by its ability to prevent the spider–supposedly poisonous–from leaving the circle. The belief in the efficacy of the unicorn's horn as an antidote to poison is as old as the legend of the unicorn itself. In the sixteenth century the supposed horn, both whole and powdered, was more expensive than gold. In his *Historie of Foure-Footed Beastes* (1607) Edward Topsell declared that there were only twenty whole horns in Europe. Sir Thomas Browne, in *Pseudodoxia Epidemica* (1646) Book III, chapter xxiii declared that 'many in common use and high esteeme are no hornes at all', but Birch's *History of the Royal Society*, i (1756) records how on 24th July, 1661 the test to which Isabella refers was actually made with powdered horn and a spider. See Brown, p. 32 n.

37 II. i, 253–63. Isabella deliberately repeats Brachiano's own cruelly ironic method of swearing divorce by a wedding ring in II. i, 194–205. It is a measure of Brachiano's callousness that he, in turn, is prepared to echo the sentiment, though not the words, of his wife's former pleas to him. The quotation from Virgil that she makes–*manet alta mente repostum* (l. 262)–is cited by two sixteenth-century accounts of the capture and trial of Count Lodovico as part of his

Page

reply to the question of the *rettori* whether he can throw any light on the murders of Vittoria and Flamineo. See Gunnar Boklund, *op. cit.*, pp. 50–51; 63; 83–84; 128 ff. and *cf.* Introduction, p. xii above.

38 II. i, 284. Spanish flies were used medicinally. They were applied externally, to raise blisters and thus act as a counter-irritant; and a drug prepared of their wings was taken internally, but was dangerous if taken in any but the smallest quantities. Some of their poison might be absorbed through the skin, but Webster's image of their secret working is an exaggeration, perhaps 'suggested by the fact that they were both medicinal *and* poisonous.' (Brown, p. 47 n.)

39 II. i, 298. *lamprey.* Observation of the row of seven branchial openings found on each side, behind the lamprey's head, and which convey water to and from its gills, gave rise to the idea, discussed by Sir Thomas Browne in *Pseudodoxia Epidemica*, Book III, chapter xix, that the lamprey had nine eyes. Webster also refers to this fish in *The Duchess of Malfi*, I.ii, 255. The notion that lampreys are full of eyes on both sides is mentioned in John Marston's *The Malcontent*, I, i, 335.

39 II. i, 300–301. Ireland was said to breed no poison because St. Patrick collected all the venomous beasts in the island and cast them into the sea at Clew Bay, Co. Mayo. A Spaniard, Don Diego, was notorious for having broken wind in St. Paul's, sometime before 1598. According to Thomas Nashe, 'The Irishman will drawe his dagger, and bee ready to kill and slay, if one breake winde in his company.' (*Pierce Pennilesse his Supplication to the Devil* (1592))

40 II. i, 324. *Inopem me copia fecit:* 'Abundance has made me destitute.' This is Narcissus' complaint to his own reflection in Ovid's *Metamorphoses*, III, 466. Lucas suggests that this means that Camillo's having so fair a wife has left him worse off than having no wife at all. Brown paraphrases Monticelso's comment as 'the plentiful sexual satisfaction others have received has meant that he has received none at all.' Dent (p. 97) thinks that Brachiano is the stag, behaving traditionally after satisfying his lust; his loss of horns signifies the consequences of his hours with Vittoria. 'Thus *copia* in the tag may refer to the virile activity of Brachiano, and at the same time glance at the plenty of horns thereby transferred to the cuckolded Camillo.'

44 II. ii, A DUMB SHOW. The earliest use of the dumb show in sixteenth-century drama was that of preparing an audience for the significance or the main action of the following play.

(See *Gorboduc* and *cf. Hamlet*, III. ii.) Later, in such plays as Peele's *Battle of Alcazar* and Greene's *Friar Bacon and Friar Bungay*, dumb shows provided the dramatist with a means of cramming more action into the play without producing more dialogue and of providing variety of action by showing the audience, as well as characters on the stage, something that is happening elsewhere. Webster's use of the dumb show here is closely parallel to Greene's use of it in *Friar Bacon and Friar Bungay* (*circa* 1589) II.iii and IV.iii. In the latter scene two young men see in Bacon's magic glass, how their fathers meet and kill each other. For comment on the effect of Webster's two dumb shows in this scene, see H. Fluchère, *Shakespeare and the Elizabethans* (New York, 1956), pp. 112–13 and J. R. Mulryne, '*The White Devil* and *The Duchess of Malfi*', *Stratford-upon-Avon Studies I: Jacobean Theatre*, pp. 203–204.

51   III. ii. Vittoria's arraignment takes place in the papal consistory. The most famous scene in the play, it has attracted the attention of many critics whose comments examine both the total effect of the scene and the light it throws on the character of Vittoria. See Charles Lamb, *Specimens of English Dramatic Poets . . .* (1808), pp. 229–30; William Hazlitt, *Lectures on the Dramatic Literature of the Age of Elizabeth* (1821), pp. 126–7; J. A. Symonds, 'Vittoria Accoramboni, and the Tragedy of Webster', *Italian Byways* (1883), p. 177; W. W. Greg, 'Webster's *White Devil*', *Modern Language Quarterly*, III (1900), 118–19; P. Haworth, 'Prelude to the Study of Webster's Plays', *English Hymns and Ballads . . .* (Oxford, 1927), pp. 82–84; M. C. Bradbrook, *Themes and Conventions of Elizabethan Tragedy* (Cambridge, 1935), pp. 93 (on the borrowings from Jonson's *Sejanus* in the trial scene); 119; W. Farnham, *Shakespeare's Tragic Frontier* (Berkeley and Los Angeles, 1950), p. 29; Clifford Leech, *John Webster: A Critical Study* (1951), pp. 36–39; G. Baldini, *John Webster e il linguaggio della tragedia* (Rome, 1953), pp. 80–95; Hereward T. Price, 'The Function of Imagery in John Webster', *PMLA*, LXX (1955), 724–5; B. J. Layman, 'The Equilibrium of Opposites in *The White Devil*: A Reinterpretation', *PMLA*, LXXIV (1959), 339–40; H. Bruce Franklin, 'The Trial Scene of Webster's *The White Devil* examined in terms of Renaissance Rhetoric', *Studies in English Literature*, I, 2 (1961), 35–51.

55   III. ii, 79 *character*. This kind of analysis, based on the classical models of Theophrastus, was found in many literary forms in the seventeenth century. Among collections of 'characters'

the most celebrated is that of Sir Thomas Overbury and it is
of particular interest here because Webster almost certainly
contributed to the second edition. (*Cf.* Introduction, p. vii
above) Webster used the analytical technique to give several
different types of 'character' in his work. For example, in
The Duchess of Malfi Antonio gives a full-length portrait in
his idealized 'character' of the Duchess (I. ii, 109–31); Delio
gives a brief, humorous 'character' of Bosola to Silvio (III.
iii, 40–46) while Delio and Silvio combine to produce an
amusing 'character' of Malateste for Ferdinand (III.iii,
12–33). Dent (p. 104) has pointed out that Monticelso's description of a whore, composed wholly of metaphors and
similes and without any direct description of the whore's
activities, 'has little in common with the prose characters of
Hall, Overbury or Webster himself.' Its rhetoric is intended
to impress the audience on stage and in the theatre. For
comment on Webster's affinities with the mannered prose of
the character writers, see W. A. Edwards, 'John Webster',
Determinations, ed. F. R. Leavis (1934), pp. 158–65 and M. C.
Bradbrook, *Themes and Conventions of Elizabethan Tragedy*,
pp. 108–109.

55   III. ii, 81. *coz'ning alchemy.* From the Middle Ages onwards
cheats had extracted money from their avaricious victims by
claiming the ability to produce the philosopher's stone
which would turn base metals into gold. The methods by
which these alchemists propagated their fraud seem to have
varied little down the centuries, as a comparison of Chaucer's
Canon's Yeoman's Tale, John Lyly's *Gallathea* and Ben
Jonson's *The Alchemist* will show.

55   III. ii, 89–91. This may have been an allusion to Sir Walter
Raleigh's loss of his estate of Sherborne through a clerk's
omission of ten words from an early transfer to his wife.
The judgment taking the estate from Lady Raleigh was
made in 1609. (See G. V. P. Akrigg, 'Webster and Raleigh',
Notes and Queries, CXCIII (1948), 427–8.) Brown (pp.
69–70 n.) quotes from Florio and from *The Atheist's
Tragedy* to show that the idea was quite a common one.

67   III. iii. 28. *Those weights ... death with.* This is 'the *peine
forte et dure* inflicted by English law up to 1772 on those
who refused to plead guilty or not guilty, when charged
with felonies other than treason.' (Lucas) If the victim remained silent and was pressed to death, his goods could
not be confiscated, because he had not been convicted.
Cf. Richard II, III.iv,72—*Queen.* O I am pressed to
death through want of speaking.—and see Clifford Dobb,

'London's Prisons', *Shakespeare Survey* 17 (1964), p. 89
and Plate XIII.)

80 IV. ii, 54–55. R. R. Cawley, *The Voyagers and Elizabethan
Drama* (Boston and London, 1938), p. 262 cites three English
travellers who described the punishment of debtors in Russia
by beating on the shins: Richard Chancellor, whose account
of his accompanying Sir Hugh Willoughby to Russia in
1553 was published by Richard Hakluyt (1589); Edward
Webbe, who published a 'newly enlarged' description of the
'Rare and wonderfull' things he had seen and passed 'in
his troublesome trauailes' in 1590; and Giles Fletcher
whose work *Of the Russe Common Wealth* appeared in
1591.

82 IV. ii, 85. *the devil in crystal*. More than one meaning may be
suggested for this phrase which probably alludes to the title
of the play. Witches were supposed to be able to make
devils appear in their crystals. According to Dent (p. 125)
'To behold the devil in crystal appears to have meant,
generally, simply to be deceived, as by the apparent reality
of an illusion.' G. V. P. Akrigg, 'John Webster's "Devil in
Crystal" ', *Notes and Queries*, N.S. I, (1954), p. 52 suggested
that the image might well refer to a type of small shrine of
rock crystal in which the figure of a saint was enclosed. 'If
we take it that Webster had these Renaissance crystal shrines
in mind, his metaphor gains in effect. Not only is Brachiano
repeating the "white devil" theme, he is saying that he has
given to the devil Vittoria the worship one gives to a saint
set in her crystal shrine.'

98 V. i, 68–70. The anonymous play *Arden of Feversham* (*circa*
1585–92), based on a true murder story of the reign of
Edward VI demonstrates a genuine belief in the efficacy of
strange methods of poison. In 1598 Edward Squire, employed in Queen Elizabeth's stable, was executed for having
attempted to poison the pommel of her saddle in the previous
year with a drug which he had received from the Spanish
Jesuits.

98 V. i, 71–73. The original game of tennis was played indoors
(lawn tennis dates only from 1873) on a court whose two
sides were called the service side and the hazard side. The
hazard is one of the openings, of which there are two on the
hazard side and one on the service side, on the inner wall of
the court into which a winning stroke may be played. The
game, which originated in France and is known to have been
played in Canterbury in 1396, is still played on the Royal
Tennis Court built by Henry VIII at Hampton Court in

1530. Used metaphorically, *hazard* means peril or jeopardy. Both senses are implicit here.

103　V. i, 180. *sunburnt gentleman.* It was assumed, on the basis of the Song of Solomon i, 6——'I am black, because the sun hath looked upon me'——for instance, that dark skin was the result of excessive exposure to the sun. Bishop Hall expressed this theory in his *Contemplations*, ii (1614), Book V, pp. 121–2: 'A man may passe through Æthiopia vnchaunged: but he cannot dwell there, and not be discoloured.' *Cf.* V.iii, 259.

103　V. i, 184. *a bedstaff.* C. B. Wheeler notes, 'According to Johnson, "a wooden pin stuck anciently on sides of the bedstead to hold the clothes from slipping"; it would be a handy weapon.' *O.E.D.* says that there is no corroborative evidence for Dr. Johnson's definition. Lucas (*Webster*, i, 250) defines it as either one of the staves which supported the bedding, or a staff used for making a bed, especially when it stood in a recess. As well as meaning a staff with which Cornelia might beat her maids, the phrase here also refers to a lover who might keep the maids warm at night.

134　V. vi, 105–10. Lucian's purgatory, described in his *Menippos*, in fact included different examples of the ridiculous fates of the famous, e.g. Philip, King of Macedon 'sitting in a little corner, cobbling old shoes to get somewhat towards his living' (Hickes' version, published in Oxford in 1634, as quoted by Sampson, p. 204). Rabelais used the same idea in the thirtieth chapter of *Pantagruel*, where he sees 'Alexander as a clothes patcher, Hannibal a kettle maker and seller of eggshells.' (Dent, p. 165). H. Dugdale Sykes pointed out a parallel with *Love's Labour's Lost*, IV.iii, 166–9 where the listing of notables and their activities is again different from Webster's.

134　V. vi, 109. *King Pippin* i.e. Pepin III, king of the Franks, known as 'The Short' who was the most famous monarch of that name. His coronation, performed by St. Boniface, was a ceremony new to France. By wresting the exarchate of Ravenna from Aistulf, King of the Lombards and conferring it on the Pope, Pepin became the veritable creator of the Papal state. Upon his death in 768 his Kingdom was divided between his sons Charles (Charlemagne) and Carloman. Webster is also punning on the name pippin as a type of apple.

136　V. vi, 164 s.d. Q1, Q2 *Enter Lod. Gasp. Pedro, Carlo.* The confusion of this entry and in the use of the disguise names of the conspirators in the speech-prefix at l. 224 below which is found in Q1 and Q2 is eliminated in Q3 and Q4, and all previous editors, except Brown, have followed the assumption of Q3 and Q4 that, in the fifth act, Lodovico is disguised as Carlo and Gasparo as Pedro, the supposed Hungarians who have entered the strict order of Capuchins. Dr. Brown feels that this confusion, with the facts that at V. i, 62 Lodovico welcomes Francisco and Gasparo who are supposed to have travelled to Padua with him, that more than two conspirators are necessary to execute the murders of the last scene and that more than two remain alive at the end, means that Carlo and Pedro are separate conspirators, not to be identified with Lodovico and Gasparo. (p. 126 n.) Yet, Brown is prepared to consider the entry of Isabella at III.ii (she was murdered in II.ii) as an irrational slip: 'anyone familiar with the *dramatis personæ* might have made it, but it is easier to imagine the author doing so (correcting his manuscript confidently and, perhaps, in haste), than an 'editor' (reconstructing the action as he worked from scene to scene.)' (p. lxvii n.) It seems to me equally possible to accept that, sure in his own mind of the separate identity of Lodovico and Gasparo, Webster was quite capable of confusing their disguise names. If he did make some hasty additions to his manuscript before sending it to the printer, as Dr. Brown suggests, he may well have added the duplicate names (though in the reverse of the proper order) to identify them for the printer. The variation between real and disguise names in speech-prefixes is comparable with the variation between *Zan.* and *Moo.* for Zanche in V.iv.

Collations and general notes on the text

To the Reader: 12 *rhoncos* ed. (Q1a Rhonoas; Q1b Rhoncos)
19 *critical* ed. (Q1a critticcall; Q1b critticall)

I. i, 30 *either* Q2, Q3, Q4 (Q1 eather)
48 *and so* Q1 (Q2, Q3, Q4 and)
54 *grown* Qq (Dodsley ii and iii, Scott, Hazlitt: grow)
59 S.D. [*A sennet sounds.*] Brown (Qq *Enter Sennet.*) A
sennet, being a flourish of trumpets, may sound but not
enter; so Brown suggests that the original direction may have
implied that the trumpeters appear on stage. 'But, more
probably, the copy read simply "Senate" (a 17th-century
spelling) and so gave rise to' the literally impossible stage
direction of Qq. (p. 11 n.)

I. ii, 14 *Zanche* Q1b (Q1a *Zawche*)
22 *whereas* Dodsley (Qq where a)
24 *there* Q2, Q3, Q4 (Q1 their)
39 *pursued* Q2, Q3, Q4 (Q1 peursued)
40 *3 or 4* Q1, Q2, Q3 (Q4 three or four)
48 *it* Q1, Q2, Q3 (Q4 him)
56 *There* Q4 (Q1, Q2, Q3 Their); '*T had* Q3, Q4 (Q1, Q2
T' had)
76 '*Twere* Q3, Q4 (Q1 T'weare; Q2 T'were)
79 *leon* Qq, Dodsley ii and iii, Scott, Lucas, Harrison, Brown
(Dyce, Wheeler: lyam; Hazlitt, Sampson: leam)
87 *entertainment:* Qq, Dyce, Hazlitt, Sampson, Harrison,
Brown (Dodsley ii and iii, Scott: entertainment. ; Wheeler,
[conjecture of Lucas]: entertainment?)
109 S.D. is placed in the margin of Q1, with an asterisk to
indicate the position of the entry in the text after 'cuckold-
maker'.
118 ff. Compositor B, who set up this passage, was unable to
distinguish all Flamineo's asides to Vittoria. Since he used
dashes for those he did distinguish, I have preferred the
augmentation of these, where necessary, to the introduction
of brackets.
133 *Is* Q4 (Q1, Q2, Q3 is)
150 *Shalt* ed. (Qq Shal't)

163 *off.* Q3, Q4 (Q1, Q2 of:)

178 *In troth* Q4 (Q1 Introth; Q2 Introath; Q3 In troath); *jailer* ed. (Q1 iaylor; Q2 Iaylor; Q3 Jaylor; Q4 Gaoler)

197 *Loose* Qq (Brown conjectures 'Lose'; but Qq reading may suggest the binding force of lovers' vows.)

216 *sir.* Qq, Dodsley ii and iii, Scott, Sampson, Brown (Dyce, Hazlitt, Wheeler, Lucas, Harrison: sir?)

226 *there* Q2, Q3, Q4 (Q1 their)

252 *scandal,* Q1 (Q2, Q3 scandal;   ; Q4 scandal.). It follows from these variants that 'Give' in the following line is either indicative, i.e. 'I'll give', according to the reading of Q1, or imperative, according to the reading of Q2, Q3 and Q4.

262 *Till* ed. (Q1 tell; Q2, Q3, Q4 till).

264 *with all* Q3, Q4 (Q1, Q2 all; MS. interlineation in Garrick copy of Q1: all ⋏ with; ; Sampson all [with])

266 *rather than* Q3, Q4 (Q1, Q2 rather; MS. interlineation in Garrick copy of Q1: rather ⋏ than)

270 *frequently* Q2, Q3, Q4 (Q1 ftequeuently)

274 *dream'd'st* ed. (Q1, Q2 dreamd'st; Q3, Q4 dream'st)

286 *In great men's.* Wheeler (Qq, Sampson: In great mens. ; Dodsley ii and iii, Scott, Dyce, Hazlitt, Harrison: In great men's— ; Lucas: In great mens ...; Brown: In great men's, —)

288 *May'st* Q4 (Q1, Q2 Maiest ; Q3 Mayest)

310 (*the university judge me,*) Q3, Q4 (Q1, Q2 the university judge me,)

325 *pitiful* Q3, Q4 (Q1 pittful ; Q2 pittiful)

335 *We are* ed. (Q1 Wee are; Q2 Weare ; Q3, Q4 W'are)

II.i, 4 *were't* ed. (Qq wer't)

27 *you that have* Lucas, Brown (Q1, Dodsley iii, Sampson: you have ; Q2, Q3, Q4, Scott, Harrison: you having ; Dodsley ii, Dyce, Hazlitt: you, having ; Wheeler: you, [who] have)

29 *And have to* Qq (Dyce: And to ; Hazlitt, Harrison: And having to)

38 *petty* Q1, Q2, Q4 (Q3 pretty)

40 *sceptre* ed. (Q1 Scepter; Q2, Q3, Q4 Scepters)

51 *prey* Q2, Q3, Q4 (Q1 pery)

54 *is lord of* Qq (Garrick copy of Q1 has MS interlineation is ⋏ the lord of which is accepted by Dodsley ii and iii, Scott and Sampson.)

78 *Your new-plough'd forehead. Defiance!—and I'll* ed.

(i–Q1, Q2,   Sampson Your new plow'd fore-head defiance, and I'le
ii–Q3   Your new-plow'd forehead defiance, and i'le
iii–Q4   Your new-plow'd forehead defiance; and i'le
iv–Dodsley ii, Scott
Your new-plow'd forehead–defiance. I'll
v–Dyce, Wheeler
Your new-ploughed forehead–defiance! and
I'll
vi–Hazlitt   Your new-plowd forehead–defiance! and I'll
vii–Lucas   Your new-plow'd [forehead. Defiance!–and]
I'll
viii–Harrison Your new-plowd forehead. Defiance! and I'll
ix–Brown   Your new-plough'd forehead–Defiance!–
and I'll)

84, 92 speech-prefix: Q1 FLAN.; Q2, Q3 *Flam.*; Q4 *Fra.*
85 *'Bout* Q3, Q4 (Q1, Q2 Bout)
90 (*'Bout . . . mean,*) ed. No brackets in Qq.
92 *words* Q1, Q2 (Q3 wounders ; Q4 wonders)
94 s.d. In Q1, Q2, Q3 this entrance is in the margin, opposite l. 93; in Q4 it is opposite l. 94. As Brown points out, the
position in Q1, Q2, Q3 is suspect for it is as near to l. 95 as
the text-space in Q1 permitted. (p. 37 n.) The compositors
of Q1 'set their material within as few pages as possible, and
in consequence both sometimes misplaced a direction in
order to fit it in within the text-space to the right of the
dialogue and so avoid using an extra line or so of type.'
(p. lxiv)
105 *Be* ed. (Q1, Q2 be ; Q3, Q4 by)
110 *coz?* ed. (Q1 cous. ; Q2 Cou· ; Q3 Cu'z: ; Q4 Cuz!)
118 *make* Q1, Q2, (Q3, Q4 makes)
125 *Forward* Qq (MS. interlineation in Garrick copy of Q1:
⋏ A Forward)
153 *reck'nings* Q4 (Q1, Q2, Q3 reckonings)
156 *two* Q1, Q2 (Q3, Q4, Dodsley ii, Scott, Dyce, Hazlitt,
Wheeler, Harrison: now two; Dodsley iii: now too; MS.
interlineation in Garrick copy of Q1 reads '⋏ these two' and
this is accepted by Sampson.)
167 *withered* ed. (Q1 whithered; Q2, Q3, Q4 wither'd)
169 *helmet lovely*, MS. correction in Garrick copy of Q1;
Q2, Q3, Q4 (Q1 Helmet, louely)
170 *interview* ed. (Q1 enterueiw ; Q2 enterueew ; Q3, Q4
enterview)
208 *Never?* ed. (Qq never.)
208b *Never!* ed. (Q1, Q2, Q3 Never? ; Q4 Never.)

228 *given* Qq (Garrick copy of Q1 has MS. interlineation given ⋏ me which is accepted by Hazlitt.)

233 *No though* Qq. (Lucas suggests the possible reading 'Not though'.)

240 *with* Qq (MS. interlineation in Garrick copy of Q1: ⋏ & with)

246 *a-dying* ed. (Qq a dying)

276–7: In Qq the reader's attention was called to these lines by the use of quotation marks, viz: ,,ISA. Unkindness...
,, Those are . . .

277 *speak.* Q1b speake. (Q1a speake,)

302 *Anthony's* Q4 (Q1 *Anthony*; Q2, Q3 *Anthonies*)

306 *and love* Q1a (Q1b & love); *abhominable* Q1, Q2 (Q3, Q4 abominable). The Q1, Q2 spelling, as Brown suggests, indicates that 'Webster may have remembered the absurd etymology, *ab homine* (*cf. Love's Labours' Lost*, V.i, 26–27.)'

307 *loathsome* ed. (Q1a le- / than; Q1b, Q2, Q3 loth- / some ; Q4 lothsome) Brown remarks that it is hard to see how 'loathsome' in the copy could have been misread as 'lethan'. He further suggests that, if Q1b is not authoritative, Symonds' conjecture 'lethal' (i.e. deadly) is very attractive. (pp. 49–50 n.)

309 *thee* Q1b, Q2 (Q1a, Q3, Q4 the)

312 *Camillo?* Q1b (Q1a *Camillo,*)

333 *need* ed. Q1 neede (Q2, Q3, Q4 needs)

345 *one* Q2, Q3, Q4 (Q1 one,)

365 *turn'd* Qq (Sampson; A. H. Thorndike, *Webster and Tourneur* (1912) and Harold Jenkins, *Review of English Studies*, N.S. XII (1961), 292–4 suggest 'turned'.)

381 *our* Q1, Q2, Q3 (Q4 your)

II, ii, 3 *murder* Qq (Lucas: murder[s])

13 *there* Q3, Q4 (Q1, Q2 their)

18 *stol'n* ed. (Q1, Q2 stolne; Q3, Q4 stoln)

DUMB SHOW: CHRISTOPHERO and GUID-ANTONIO of the Qq are 'ghost characters' (see Additional Notes, p. 145 above). Sampson substitutes 'Gasparo, Antonelli' for Guid-Antonio; Brown substitutes 'another' for Christophero and omits Guid-Antonio; *express'd* ed. (Q1a *expresse*; Q1b *exprest*).

SECOND DUMB SHOW: *strip* Q1, Q2 (Q3, Q4 stript); *under* Q1, Q2 (Q3, Q4 upon); *makes shows* Q3, Q4, Dyce, Wheeler, Brown (Q1, Sampson: makes shewes; Q2 makes showes; Dodsley ii and iii, Scott: makes shew; Hazlitt, Harrison: makes shews; Lucas: makes [shewe]); *Cardinal . . .* VITTORIA: *mes co* Q1, Q2, Q3 (Q4 come); *wonder* Q1, Q4

(Q2, Q3 wonders); *commands* Q1, Q2, Q3 (Q4 command); *apprehends* Q1, Q2, Q3 (Q4 apprehend); *go* Q1, Q4 (Q2, Q3 goes). I agree with J. R. Brown that, though Compositor A did confuse singular and plural verbs elsewhere, the changes from singular to plural in this passage seem appropriate and 'instead of emending the verbs it is probably better to clarify the terse style by adding subjects.' (p. 58 n.)

III.i, 10 s.d. *a* LAWYER Qq. Brown (p. 60 n.) thinks that this lawyer is so different from the lawyer in III.ii that they may not only be two distinct characters; this should perhaps have been called 'Courtier'.
48 *reward* Q1, Q2 (Q3, Q4 rewards)
50 *physic on* Lucas, Brown (Q1 physicke: Or; Q2 Phisicke: Or ; Q3 Physick or ; Q4 Physick, or)
64–5 *him? / He's* ed. (Q1, Q2, Q3 him, he's ; Q4 him? he's)

III.ii, 8 *gentlewomen* Q1, Q2, Q3 (Q4 gentlewoman). Previous editors, except those of Dodsley iii, have accepted the Q4 reading, since the arraignment is of Vittoria alone; but Brown thinks that 'gentlewomen' might 'just possibly be right'. (p. 65 n.) Though the case proceeds only against Vittoria, Zanche is also implicated, and comes under sentence of the court, though Monticelso's pronouncement against her is interrupted and left unfinished. (See III.ii, 262–4.)
22 *God* Q1, Q2, Q3 (Q4 God's)
36 *pothecary's* ed. (Q1 Poticaryes; Q2, Q3, Q4 Apothecaries)
74–77: Q1 punctuation:

> Out-brau'd the stars with seuerall kind of lights,
> When shee did counterfet a Princes Court.
> In musicke banquets and most ryotous surfets
> This whoore, forsooth, was holy.

Q2, Q3 punctuation alters 76 to:

> In Musicke, Banquets, and most ryotous surfets:

Q4 punctuation alters 75–77 to:

> When she did counterfeit a Princes Court,
> In Musick, Banquets, and most Riotous surfets:
> This Whore, forsooth, was holy.

The punctuation of Q1 clearly gives two separate statements about Vittoria, the first being a rhetorical question which, in modernization, needs a question mark. In Q2, Q3 the colon after *surfeits* weakens the force of the pause after *court*, and suggests that this was a mistake, the intention being to give

a description of what was known of Vittoria's way of life and
then a brief comment on her in 77. This impression is con-
firmed by Q4's change of the point to a comma. In modernization of Q4's punctuation it is the colon after *surfeits* that
becomes a question mark. Lucas prints Monticelso's speech
as a single sentence with a comma after *Court*, no pause
after *surfets* and the question mark after *holy*. Brown interprets it as a rhetorical question and a short comment,
with no pause after *court* and the question mark after *surfeits*.
I have preferred the simplest modernization of Q1, since the
colon in Elizabethan and Jacobean punctuation frequently
carried the force of the modern point and, moreover, this
passage was set up by compositor A who elsewhere used a
colon for a question mark: e.g. I.ii, 299: Q1 man: Q2, Q3,
Q4 man?

80 *nostril* Q1 (Q2, Q3, Q4 nostrils)

94 *fill'd* Q4 (Q1, Q2, Q3 fild)

95 *emptied* Q2, Q4 (Q1 empted; Q3 emptyed)

102 *gentlewoman?* Q2, Q3 (Q1 gentlewoman;   ; Q4 gentlewoman,)

104 *poison.* Q1, Q4 (Q2, Q3 poison: ; Dodsley ii and iii,
Dyce *et al*: poison—)

108–9 Q1 punctuation:

> You know what Whore is next the deuell; Adultry.
> Enters the deuell, murder.

Q2 punctuation:

> You know what Whore is next the Diuell; adultery,
> Enters the Diuell, murder.

Q3 punctuation:

> You know what whore: is next the Divel adutlery,
> Enters the Divel, murder.   (*sic*)

Q4 alters sense and punctuation:

> You know a Whore is next the Devil: Adultery
> Enters, the Devil and Murder.

Brown has noted that compositor A had a tendency 'to end
a line with . . . a colon or full stop where a comma is required.' Q2 is, therefore, right to put a comma after *adultery*.
Obviously some pause was needed between *is* and *next*;
probably the semi-colon which Q1 compositor A mistakenly
placed instead of a comma, after *devil*.

123 *cunning* Q2, Q3, Q4 (Q1 conning)

135 *virtue to the point.* Qq, Sampson (Dodsley ii and iii,
Scott: virtue. To the point; ; Dyce, Hazlitt, Wheeler,
Harrison: virtue. To the point. ; Lucas: vertue—To the
point! ; Brown: virtue—to the point!)

138 *At* Q2, Q3, Q4 (Q1 at)

139 *spirit—* ed. (Q1 spirit   ; Q2, Q3, Q4 spirit.)

211 *you your* Qq. Hazlitt, followed by Wheeler and Harrison, omitted the *you* and, as Brown notes, the emendation is attractive in view of compositor A's clearly erroneous *you, you* of I.i, 19; 'but the irregular metre and the sentiment may seem to require the emphatic, repetitive phrasing.' (p. 76 n.)

227–8 *as long / As to my thoughts* Lucas (Qq *as loving / As to my thoughts*) Lucas's emendation is obviously supported by reference to Webster's source for these lines, Jonson's *Sejanus* (1605), II, 453–6:

Agrippina. Yea had Sejanus both his ears as long
            As to my inmost closet: I would hate
            To whisper any thought, or change an act,
            To be made Juno's rival.

Webster borrowed other words of the wounded Agrippina in the same scene: see III.ii, 223–9, 267 notes.

237 *months* ed. (Q1a mouthes ; Q1b, Q2 monthes ; Q3, Q4 moneths)

245 *repetition* Q1b (Q1a repetion)

261 *To princes; here's* Brown (Q1 To Princes heares; your   ; Q2 To Princes, heare your ; Q3 To Princes hear your   ; Q4 To Princes, hear your   ; Dodsley ii and iii, Hazlitt, Harrison: To princes. Hear your   ; Dyce: To princes: hear your   ; Sampson: To princes: heare your   ; Wheeler: To princes: here's your   ; Lucas: To Princes; [heare] your)

284 *on* Q2, Q3, Q4 (Q1 one)

290 *thy* Q1, Q2 (Q3, Q4 my)

292 S.D. [*with* ZANCHE, *guarded*] Brown. Q1, Q2, Q3 align the directions *Enter Brachiano. Exit Vittoria.* Q4 has Vittoria's exit in the margin opposite l. 292; then marks 'Act.3. Scen.3.' which commences with Brachiano's entry.

302 *feign* Q4 (Q1 faine ; Q2 fayne ; Q3 fain)

309 *you must* Qq. Swinburne suggested to Sampson that this should be 'you now must' and Wheeler accepted this.

314 *Is dead.* Qq (Lucas: Is dead?)

III.iii: This scene is not marked in Qq, and Dyce commented: 'This is not a new scene; for Lodovico and Marcello are still on the stage and speak presently.' The division, suggested by W. W. Greg, first appeared in Sampson's edition of the play. Sampson made Flamineo's first speech a soliloquy, with Marcello and Lodovico entering at l. 7. Wheeler followed this. Lucas, followed by

Brown, placed the entry of Marcello and Lodovico with Flamineo's.

22 *Yon* Hazlitt, Lucas, Harrison, Brown (Q1, Q2, Q3, Dodsley ii and iii, Scott: You ; Q4, Dyce, Sampson, Wheeler: Your)

26 *line* Q2, Q3, Q4 (Q1 liue); s.d. is opposite ll. 28 and 29 in Q1 (Q2, Q3, Q4 [omit])

33 s.d. is not in Qq. J. R. Brown notes: 'The break in the consecutive prose of Q suggests that Compositor B intended to place a stage-direction here (he broke prose for directions at l. 7 above, and at I.ii,' 185 and 187, . . .). (pp. 85–86 n.)

39 *happened* Q1, Q2 (Q3, Q4 hapned)

67 *overtake* Qq. J. R. Brown conjectures 'o'ertake.'

79 *gentle* ed. (Qq gentile ; Dodsley ii and iii, Dyce: genteel)

81 s.d. Q1, Q2, Q3 have *Enter Antonelli* opposite l. 93; Q4 has *Enter Antonelli and Gasparo* opposite ll. 93–94.

88 *girn, rogue* Brown (Q1a grine rouge ; Q1b, Q2 gue ; Q3, Q4 Rogue) The two different readings of Q1 have puzzled editors and produced a variety of suggested emendations and even attempts to find a meaning for one or other of the variants. The meaning of *girn* as a snarl, or the act of showing the teeth in a disagreeable way is still found in the Scottish and Ulster dialects. Brown found a close parallel to the usage here, which includes a quibble on the other meaning of 'snare, trap, wile,' in Marston's *Antonio and Mellida* (1602), III.ii, which confirms his reading. His explanation of the Q1b variant is most convincing: 'gue' is probably an ill-executed miscorrection of an obscure passage (i.e. intending to read the commoner spelling 'rogue' and dropping (either intentionally or by accident) the puzzling 'grine') . . .(p. 90 n.)

93 *lives* ed. (Q1a liues.   ; Q1b, Q2 liues   ; Q3, Q4 lives.).

110 *Wilt* ed. (Qq Wil't)

114 *Ha, Ha!* Q2, Q3, Q4 (Q1 Ha, ha?)

131 *learnt* Q1, Q4 (Q2, Q3 learn't)

IV.i, 2 *bride's* ed. (Q1 brids ; Q2, Q3 Brides ; Q4 brides)

38 *I will* Q1b (Q1a I'le)

42 *heats* Q4 (Q1, Q2, Q3 heat's); s.d. Q1b places opposite ll.43–44; (Q1a *Enter Mont.* opposite l. 43)

45–46 Brown remarks that no satisfactory typographical reason suggests itself for the line-arrangement of Q1. 'Monticelso should, perhaps, pause while silently pointing out details in his book to Francisco.' (p. 94 n.)

47 *take* Q1, Q2, Q3 (Q4 take them)
48 *Next* Q1, Q2 (Q3, Q4 The next)
56 *are for* Q1, Q2 (Q3, Q4 are)
61 *conscience' sake* ed. (Qq conscience sake)
64 *Murderers.* Q1, Q2, Lucas, Brown (Q3, Q4 Murderers: ;
Dodsley ii and iii, Scott, Hazlitt, Harrison: Murderers? ;
Dyce, Wheeler: Murderers! ; Sampson: Murderers—)
73 *Dearly* ed. Q1 Deerely (Q2 Deere ; Q3, Q4 Dear)
78 *justice'* ed. (Q1 Iustice ; Q2, Q3, Q4 Justices)
83 *bribe* Q1, Q2 (Q3, Q4 bribes)
101 *I ha't* — ed. (Q1a I---d'foot ; Q1b I---ha'te ; Q2 I——
hau't ; Q3, Q4 I hav't—)
107 *which have cause* Q1, Q2, Hazlitt, Harrison, Brown (Q3,
Q4, Dodsley ii and iii, Scott, Dyce, Sampson, Wheeler:
which yet have cause ; Lucas suggests: which have [a]
cause)

IV.ii, 36 *mellow?* ed. (Qq *mellow.*)
41 *Ud's death* Q4 (Q1 Vdsdeath ; Q2 Vds'death ; Q3
Uds' death)
44 *That—? what do* Brown (Q1a, Q4, Sampson: What?
what do ; Q1b, Q2, Q3 That? what do ; Lucas: That! what
do)
46 *off* Q1b (Q1a of)
49 *What* Q1, Q2 (Q3, Q4 What of)
68–69. W. W. Greg suggested a new scene here ('Webster's
"White Devil",' p. 123) but indicated that the characters
simply pass from the outer to the inner stage, having drawn
the traverse. Sampson and Wheeler marked a new scene.
90 *We'll* ed. (Q1a Well ; Q1b, Q2 Wee'l ; Q3 Weel ; Q4
We'l)
136 *is t'express* Q1, Q4 (Q2, Q3 is't express)
141 *For* ed. (Qq for ; Brown conjectures 'fore)
182 *Ay, ay* ed. (Qq I, I)
190 *turn'd* Q2, Q3, Q4 (Q1 turne'd)
196 *wooden* Q3, Q4 (Q1 wodden ; Q2 woodden)
199 *Stay–ingrateful Rome!* Brown (Q1, Q2, Q3, Sampson:
Stay ingratefull Rome. ; Q4, Lucas: Stay, ingrateful
Rome! ; Dodsley ii, Scott: Stay, ungrateful Rome. ;
Dodsley iii, Dyce, Hazlitt: Stay, ingrateful Rome— ; Dyce
queried: Stay in ingrateful Rome! ; Brereton: Stay in
gratefull Rome! ; Wheeler: Stay! ingrateful Rome—;
Harrison: Stay—ingrateful Rome—)
226-7 *top o' th' which* Q1, Q2 (Q3, Q4 top, which)
234 *particle* Q1, Q2, Q3 (Q4 particular)

IV.iii, S.D. *Enter* LODOVICO, GASPARO, ed. (Qq *Enter Francisco, Lodovico, Gasper.*)

22 *Who's* Lucas (Qq *et al*: Whose)

35 speech-prefix: Qq *A Car.* (Brown: *Con.* i.e. Conclavist)

40 *sure* Q1, Q2 (Q3, Q4 surely)

61 *My* Q1b (Q1a MON. My)

83–4 Q1, Q2, Q3 have duplicate S.D. *Enter Monticelso* opposite these lines.

89c speech-prefix: Q3, Q4 *Mon.* (Q1, Q2 [omit])

90 *How* Q3, Q4 (Q1, Q2 MONT. How)

99 *dost* ed. (Qq do'st)

120 *melancholic* Q1, Q2, Q3 (Q4 melancholy)

121 *Dost* ed. (Qq Do'st)

125 *With all* Q3, Q4 (Q1, Q2 Withall)

128 *damnable* Q2, Q3, Q4 (Q1 damable)

134 *confirm* Qq (Dyce, Sampson: confirm [him])

150 *now. Now to* Qq. Sampson conjectured: Now to; Brereton thought that this was probably right and that the full stop before 'Now' should also be omitted.

151 *Furies* Q2, Q3, Q4 (Q1 furies): *cf.* 125 and see notes.

V.i, S.D. *[Enter* FLAMINEO *and* HORTENSIO.] ed. (Sampson: *[Then re-enter Flamineo and Hortensio.]*; Lucas: *[Flamineo, Marcello and Hortensio remain.]*; Brown: [FLAMINEO *and* HORTENSIO *remain.]* *cf.* note on V.i, 61 below.

30 speech-prefix: Q2, Q3, Q4 *Fla.* (Q1 FLV.)

47 *those two* Qq (Lucas conjectured, and Brown accepts: these two)

61 S.D. *and* [HORTENSIO]. ed. (Qq *and Marcello.*) If Qq are right, Marcello must have entered at the beginning of the scene and his name should be added—as it was by Hazlitt, Dyce, Sampson and Lucas—to the original entry. Since Marcello's presence is not required, and he would be silent if he were on stage, it seems simpler to assume that there was some scribal confusion of names.

120 *pitiful* Q4 (Q1 pittifull. ; Q2, Q3 pittifull)

144 *falc'ner* ed. (Q1 Falckner ; Q2, Q3, Q4 Falconer)

159 *Ay* ed. (Qq I)

167 *loathe* Q1, Q2, Q3 (Q4, Sampson: love)

172 *oaths.* Brown; Qq, Sampson: oathes. (Lucas: oathes? ; Dodsley ii and iii, Scott, Dyce, Hazlitt, Wheeler, Harrison: oaths?)

182 *court?* Q2, Q3, Q4, Dodsley ii and iii (Dyce, Hazlitt, Sampson, Wheeler, Lucas, Brown: court! ; Q1 Court.)

204 *Do; like* Q4 (Q1, Sampson, Lucas: Doe like ; Q2 Doe,

like ; Q3, Dodsley ii and iii, Scott, Dyce, Hazlitt, Wheeler, Harrison: Do, like ; Brown: Do—like) *gesses* ed. (Q1 geesse ; Q2, Q3 gesse ; Q4 gess) *Gesses* is a form of the word *gestes*, stopping-places on a royal progress. That this meaning was assumed here by earlier scholars is made clear by the notes of the Johnson and Steevens edition of Shakespeare (1778) on *The Winter's Tale*, I.ii, 41. The first edition (1773) gave a quotation from Strype's *Memorials of Archbishop Cranmer* (1694) to establish the meaning of 'gest' in its context: 'The archbishop intreats Cecil, "to let him have the new-resolved-upon *gestes*, from that time to the end, that he might from time to time know where the king was." (Samuel Johnson and George Steevens, *The Plays of William Shakespeare* (1773), iv, 261.) A reference to gestes as 'ordinary resting and baiting places' of quails, was also given (from Holland's Pliny). The 1778 edition added to these two quotations others from Dekker's *Match me in London*, Greene's *Friar Bacon and Friar Bungay* and this passage from *The White Devil* in which the line is printed:

Do like the gests in the progress,

In the fourth edition (1793) Malone added to these notes the gloss:

Gests, or rather *gists*, from the Fr. *giste*, (which signifies a bed, and a lodging-place,) were the names of the houses or towns where the king or prince intended to lie every night during his PROGRESS. They were written in a scroll, and probably each of the royal attendants was furnished with a copy.

Lucas suggested 'gestes' or 'gesses'. Brown reads 'geese' and notes '*geese* was often used for "prostitutes" . . . Royal progresses were reputed to be occasions for licentiousness . . . and so prostitutes were readily found in the course of one; . . .' (p. 135 n.)

V.ii, S.D. [*and a* PAGE, *who remains in the background*] ed. The Page speaks at l. 65 but, since this is to contradict Cornelia's account of Marcello's murder, as Lucas points out, he 'must at least have watched through the doorway at the beginning of this scene.' (John Webster, *The White Devil* (1958), p. 219). In his text Lucas makes the Page enter, as do Q3, Q4, Sampson and Brown, at l. 43.
38 *pull out* Q1, Q2, Q3 (Q4 pull)
49 *O you* Q1, Q2 (Q3, Q4 O yon)
82: the line is indented in Q1, Q2.

V.iii, 9 *revels* Q3, Q4 (Q1 reuls ; Q2 reuels)

15 *'tween* Q1, Q2, Q3 (Q4 'twixt)

20 *yon screech-owls* ed. (Q1 yon scritch-owles ; Q2 you scritch-owles ; Q3 yon scritch owl ; Q4 you, Scrietch-owl)

40 *infinitely* Qq (Garrick copy of Q1 has MS interlineation ⋏ most infinitely.)

50 *weep* Q1, Q2, Q3 (Q4 weep as)

79 s.d. *presented* Q1b (Q1a *preseuted*)

81 s.d. Q1 (Q2, Q3, Q4 [omit]); *appear so* Q1b [appeare so] (Q1a apeare)

124 *rat-catcher* ed. (Q1 Rat-cather ; Q2, Q3, Q4 Rat-catcher)

129 s.d. Q1b *Gasparo* (Q1a *Gasparoe*)

145 *lævum* Q3, Q4 (Q1 *leuum* ; Q2 *læuum*)

148 s.d.: in the margin, to the right of ll. 149–51 in Q1; *Gasparo* Q1b ; (Q1a *Gasparoa or*)

160 *mercury* ed. (Q1 Mercarie ; Q2, Q3, Q4 Mercury)

161 *pothecary* ed. (Q1 potticarie ; Q2 Apothecarie; Q3, Q4 Apothecary)

167 *Vittoria! Vittoria!* Q2, Q3, Q4 (Q1 *Vittoria? Vittoria!*); *cursed devil,* Q1b (Q1a cursed, devil)

185 *has* Q1b, Q4 (Q1a as ; Q2, Q3 ha's)

186 *wise men* Q3, Q4 (Q1, Q2 wisemen)

195 *swallow'd down* Q1, Q2, Q3 (Q4 swallowed)

211 *Did you* ed. (Q1, Q2, Q3 did you ; Q4 didst thou)

236c speech-prefix: Q4 *Fra.* (Q1, Q2, Q3 *Fla.*)

248 *counsel,*— Brown (Q1, Q2, counsell, ; Sampson: counsell. Q3, Q4 counsel. ; Dyce, Lucas: counsell?)

256 *your* Q1, Q2, Q3 (Q4 our)

264 *chapel?* Dyce, Lucas (Q1, Q4 Chappel. ; Q2, Q3 Chappell. ; Brown: chapel.)

V.iv, 25 *to* Q1, Q2, Q3 (Q4 in)

26 *usurers'* Brown (Q1, Q2 Vsurers ; Q3, Q4 Usurers ; Sampson, Lucas: usurers,—)

29 *decimo-sexto* Q2, Q3, Q4 (Q1 *dicimo-sexto*)

30 *young Duke* Q1, Q2 (Q3, Q4 Duke)

46 *smoor* ed. (Q1 smoore ; Q2, Q3 smoo're ; Q4 smother)

47 *art* Q2, Q3, Q4 (Q1 hart)

49 *met'st* Q2, Q3, Brown (Q1, Sampson: metst ; Q4, Dodsley ii and iii, Scott, Dyce, Hazlitt, Wheeler, Lucas, Harrison: meet'st)

55 *grandames* Q1, Q2, Q3 (Q4 Grandams)

75 *make* Qq (Sampson queried: 'take')

81 *screech-owls* ed. (Q1 scritch-howles ; Q2 scritch-owles ; Q3 scritch-owls; Q4 Scrietch-owls)

86 *Cowslip-water* Q4 (Q1 Couslep-water ; Q2 Couslip-water; Q3 Cowslip water)

91 *lute*— ed. (Q1, Q2, Q3 lute   ; Q4 Lute.)

91 s.d. Brown notes that there is little authority for the position of this direction in Q1, for l. 93 is the first position in the text-space after l. 70 where there is room for it. 'It seems best to place the direction where Cornelia hears Flamineo's name and begins her long speech (*cf.* Brachiano's distraction of v. iii).' (pp. 163–4 n.) The fact that the direction might indeed be intended to apply specifically to the dirge would not detract from its poetry. Indeed the effect of the pathos of the words and the pathos of the distracted speaker (who, in fact, interrupts the dirge herself at ll. 102–3) should be doubly moving.

94 *flow'rs* ed. (Q1, Q2 *flowres* ; Q3, Q4 *flowers*)

100 *thence:* Q1, Q2, Q3 (Q4, Sampson, Lucas, Brown: thence,)

108 *up shop* Q1, Q2 (Q3, Q4 up)

V.v, 11 *the ashes* Q1, Q2, Q3 (Q4 thy ashes)

15 *necks* Q1, Q2, Q3 (Q4 neck)

V.vi, s.d.: in margin to left of 1–5 in Q1; ZANCHE Q4 (Q1, Q2, Q3 *Zanke*)

13–14 are in roman type in Qq.

16 speech-prefix: Q1 FLV.; Q2, Q3, Q4 *Fla.* ; *They* ed. (Q1 the ; Q2, Q3, Q4 they)

27 *they* Q2, Q3, Q4 (Q1 the)

30 *Pray thee* Q1b (Q1a Pray theee ; Q2, Q3 Pray thee, ; Q4 Prethee)

42 *Fool that* Wheeler, Lucas (Q1 Foole, thou ; Q2 Foole thou ; Q3, Q4 Fool thou). Though retaining the reading of Q3, Q4, Brown finds Wheeler's emendation attractive, 'especially since Compositor A clearly omitted short words on other occasions.' (p. 171 n.). It could be added that the comma after 'Foole' might even have been intended by Compositor A to supply 'that': *cf.* V.vi, 32–33.

89 *none* Q1 (Q2, Q3, Q4 one). Brown points out that 'none' makes good sense if interpreted according to ll. 74–7: i.e. *none* must do violence by botching the task. (p. 174 n.) Previous editors have accepted the reading of Q2, Q3, Q4.

98 speech-prefix: Q1, Q2 VIT. & MOO. Q3, Q4 *Vit.* and *Zan.*

105 *purgatory! to* Dyce, Hazlitt, Sampson, Wheeler, Harrison, Brown (Q1 Purgatory to ; Q2, Q3, Q4 Purgatory, to ; Dodsley ii and iii, Scott: O Lucian, to thy ridiculous purgatory? to ; Lucas: Purgatory—to)

123 *been* Q4 (Q1 bene ; Q2, Q3 bin)

130 *me* Q1, Q2, Q3 (Q4 me,)

136 *way's* Q4 (Q1 waies ; Q2 waiees ; Q3 ways)

140 *chimney is* Q3, Q4 (Q1 chimneis ; Q2 chimnie is)

144 *Through* Qq, Dodsley ii and iii, Scott, Hazlitt, Sampson, Harrison, Brown (Dyce, Wheeler, Lucas: Thorough)

157 *woman? Never* ed. (Q1 woman; neuer   ; Q2 woman? neuer ; Q3, Q4 woman? never)

167 *Churchmen* ed. (Q1 Chuch-men ; Q2, Q3, Q4 Church-men)

184 *be* Q1, Q2, Q3 (Q4 were)

187 *Sirrah* Q3, Q4, (Q1, Q2 Sirha); *I'll strike* Qq (Wheeler: [now] I'll strike)

203 *own thoughts* Q1, Q2, Q3 (Q4 thoughts)

212 *off* Q3, Q4 (Q1, Q2 of)

232 *A toledo* Qq (Wheeler: [Is't] a toledo)

258–9 Sampson wondered whether this speech should be assigned to Zanche; but she is dead by l. 250.

262 *wives'* ed. (Q1 wides ; Q2 wiues ; Q3, Q4 wives)

272 *flattering* Q1, Q2 (Q3, Q4 flatting)

274 *ope* Q1, Q2 (Q3, Q4 open)

276 *constantly* Q1, Q2, Q3 (Q4 instantly)

284 *Count* Q2, Q3, Q4 (Q1 Cout)

295 *lord* Qq (Dyce, Sampson, Wheeler: lords)

TEXTUAL APPENDIX – B

Variant readings which affect the verse structure of the play

I.i, 1–5 Q1, Q2 print as prose.
44a and b. Aligned in Qq, Lucas; a single line of verse in Sampson and Wheeler; two lines in Brown.

I.ii, 49b–50 Qq and Hazlitt print as one line.
53–54a. Qq print as one line.
57–58. Qq, Hazlitt, Harrison print as three lines, dividing at ... *flaw* / ... *in't* / ... *matter?* / ; Lucas prints as four lines, dividing ... *flaw* / ... *loathes* / ... *in't* / ... *matter?* /
64–65a. Qq, Hazlitt print as one line.
69a–b. Qq and Lucas print as two lines; Sampson, Wheeler and Brown print as a single line of verse.
178–9. Dyce and Wheeler print as prose.
197–199. Qq print as three lines, dividing .. *eternally.* / ... *heart-whole.* / ... *physicians.* / .

201–202a. Qq print as one line.

211b–212. Q2, Q3, Q4 and Hazlitt print as one line.

230. Qq and Lucas print as two lines, dividing . . . *tree.* /. *This* . . .; Sampson, Wheeler and Brown print as a single line.

245–6. Dyce and Wheeler print as one line.

261–262a. Qq, Hazlitt and Lucas print as one line.

272a–b. Qq and Lucas print as two lines; Sampson, Wheeler and Brown print as one line.

275. Qq and Lucas print as two lines, dividing . . . *Duchess,* / *She* . . .; Sampson, Wheeler and Brown print as one line.

282a–b. Qq and Lucas print as two lines; Sampson, Wheeler and Brown print as one line.

323a–b. Qq and Lucas print as two lines; Sampson, Wheeler and Brown print as one line.

333a–b. Qq, Lucas, Sampson and Brown print as two lines; Sampson and Brown accept the punctuation of Q2, Q3, Q4: . . . *to be barren.* ; Wheeler prints as a single line of verse.

II.i, 8–10. Sampson prints as three lines, dividing . . . *here.* / . . . *away!* / . . . *you* / ; Wheeler prints as three lines, dividing . . . *here.* / . . . *seen.* / . . . *you,* / ; Brown prints as three lines, dividing . . . *fitted.* / . . . *away—* / . . . *you* /.

10–11. Qq divide . . . *mildly* / *Let* . . .

19. Qq and Lucas print as two lines, dividing . . . *gone.* / *Void.* . . and which are interrupted by the stage direction for the entrance of Brachiano and Flamineo.

52. Qq. and Lucas print as two lines, dividing . . . *Yes.* / *You* . . . ; Wheeler and Brown print as one line.

67. Qq and Lucas print as two lines, dividing . . . *then.* / *True:* ; Wheeler and Brown print as one line.

82–83a. Q1, Q2, Q3 divide . . . *a* / *Lyon*; Q4 prints as a single line.

108–9: aligned in Qq and Lucas; a single line of verse in Sampson and Wheeler; two lines in Brown.

173–174a. Q1a prints as one line; Q1b, Q2, Q3, Q4 divide . . . *complain* / *Unto your* . . . .

208a–b. Brown prints as two lines.

258–9. Qq and Lucas divide . . . *me?* / . . . *dotage* / ; Sampson and Brown divide . . . *separation.* / . . . *dotage* / ; Wheeler prints as a single line of verse.

278–81. Qq and Lucas print as three lines, dividing . . . *lord.* / . . . *here.* / . . . *signet.* / ; Sampson and Wheeler print as two lines of verse, dividing . . . *commission?* / . . . *signet.* / .

310–311a. Qq print as one line.
311b–312: aligned in Qq.

II.ii, 46–7. Qq print as one line.

III.i, 9b–10. Qq, Hazlitt and Harrison print as one line.
31a–b. Qq, Lucas and Brown print as two lines; Sampson
and Wheeler print as a single line of verse.
62–3. Qq print as one line.

III.ii, 12a–b. Qq and Wheeler print as two lines; Sampson and
Brown print as a single line of verse.
17. Qq and Lucas print as two lines, dividing . . . *sir.* / *By*
. . . ; Sampson, Wheeler and Brown print as a single line of
verse.
23a–b. Qq and Lucas print as two lines; Sampson, Wheeler
and Brown print as a single line of verse.
61–2. Wheeler divides . . . *trade* / *Instructs* . . .
66–8. Qq, Hazlitt and Harrison print as four lines,
dividing . . . *see* / . . . *ashes.* / . . . *do't.* / . . . *resolved* / .
77a–b. Qq and Lucas print as two lines.
109–10. Qq and Hazlitt divide . . . *husband* / *Is* . . .
123a–b. Qq, Wheeler, Lucas and Brown print as two lines;
Sampson prints as a single line of verse.
139a–b. Qq, Sampson, Lucas and Brown print as two lines;
Wheeler prints as a single line of verse.
157. Qq and Lucas print as two lines, dividing . . . *was.* /
And . . .
167. Qq and Lucas print as two lines, dividing . . . *Ha?* /
Your . . .
170a–b. Qq and Lucas print as two lines; Sampson, Wheeler
and Brown print as a single line of verse.
178a–b Qq and Lucas print as two lines; Sampson, Wheeler
and Brown print as a single line of verse.
216–217a. Qq, Lucas and Brown print as two lines; Sampson and Wheeler print as a single line of verse.
243. Qq and Lucas print as two lines, dividing . . . *lord.* /
Nay . . . ; Sampson, Wheeler and Brown print as a single line
of verse.
263. Qq and Lucas print as two lines, dividing . . . *Moor.* / *O
I am* . . . ; Sampson, Wheeler and Brown print as a single
line of verse.
263–5. Qq print as four lines, dividing . . . *again.* / . . . *that?* /
. . . *whores.* / . . . *Rome* / .
267–8. Qq and Lucas align 267 and 268a, making 268b a
separate line.

271–2. Qq align 271, 272 a–b, making 271c a separate line; Lucas aligns and divides . . . *her.* / . . . *hence* / . . . *justice*, / Sampson divides 270–2: . . . *thus.* / *hence.* / . . . *justice*, / .

286–7: aligned in Qq; two lines in Lucas, Sampson, Wheeler and Brown.

311a–b: aligned in Qq and Lucas; a single line of verse in Sampson and Wheeler; two lines in Brown.

313–4: aligned in Qq and Lucas; a single line of verse in Sampson.

313–5: a single line of verse in Wheeler.

317–18. Qq divide . . . *Lady*; / *Thou* . . . ; Sampson prints as a single line of verse.

321–22. Qq print as one line.

323a–b. Qq and Lucas print as two lines; Sampson, Wheeler and Brown print as a single line of verse.

325a–b. Qq and Lucas print as two lines; Sampson, Wheeler and Brown print as a single line of verse.

328. Brown prints as two lines, divided . . . *tears.* / *I am* . . .

III.iii, 63a–b. Qq and Lucas print as two lines; Sampson, Wheeler and Brown print as a single line of verse.

69a–b. Qq and Lucas print as two lines; Sampson, Wheeler and Brown print as a single line of verse.

72–73. Qq align 72 and 73a, making 73b a separate line.

76–77. Qq, Harrison and Brown print as two lines; Sampson, Wheeler and Lucas print as one line.

77–78a: aligned in Qq.

80a–b: aligned in Qq and Lucas; a single line of verse in Brown; Sampson and Wheeler print as two lines.

89a–b: aligned in Qq and Lucas; a single line of verse in Sampson and Wheeler; Brown prints as two lines.

100a–b: aligned in Qq and Lucas; a single line of verse in Sampson and Wheeler; Brown prints as two lines.

109a–b. Qq and Lucas print as two lines; Sampson, Wheeler and Brown print as a single line of verse.

117. Qq and Lucas align 117a–b, making 117c a separate line; Sampson, Wheeler and Brown print as a single line of verse.

121a–b. Qq and Lucas print as two lines; Sampson, Wheeler and Brown print as a single line of verse.

123–6. Wheeler prints as five lines, dividing . . . *good* / . . . *shows!* / . . . *rogues* / . . . *scape* / . . . *dangers.* / .

125a–b. Qq and Lucas print as two lines; Sampson and Brown print as a single line of verse.

IV.i, 3a–b. Qq and Lucas print as two lines; Sampson, Wheeler and Brown print as a single line of verse.

4a–b. Qq and Lucas print as two lines; Sampson, Wheeler and Brown print as a single line of verse.

37a–b. Qq and Lucas print as two lines; Sampson, Wheeler and Brown print as a single line of verse.

45–6. Qq, Hazlitt, Lucas, Harrison and Brown print as two lines; Dyce, Sampson and Wheeler print as one line.

47–8. Q1, Q2, Hazlitt, Lucas, Harrison and Brown print as two lines; Q3, Q4, Dyce, Sampson and Wheeler print as one line.

51. Brown prints as two lines, dividing ... *commodities: / for* ...

67a–b. Qq and Lucas print as two lines; Sampson, Wheeler and Brown print as a single line of verse.

72a–b. Qq and Lucas print as two lines; Sampson, Wheeler and Brown print as a single line of verse.

IV.ii 11a–b. Qq and Lucas print as two lines; Sampson, Wheeler and Brown print as a single line of verse.

15–17. Qq and Lucas print as three lines, dividing ... *Look./ ... Vittoria / ... not. /* ; Sampson prints as three lines of verse, dividing ... *Ha! / ... respected / ... messenger? /* ; Dyce, Hazlitt and Harrison prints 16–17 as prose; Wheeler and Brown print 16–17 as prose and divide 15–17 ... *Look / ... respected / Vittoria— /* .

18–19. Wheeler divides ... *No? / Who* ...

19a–b. Qq and Lucas print as two lines; Wheeler and Brown print as a single line of verse; Sampson prints 19b as a single verse line.

22–3. Qq divide ... *Florence? / This* ...

29. Wheeler prints as prose.

37. Dyce and Wheeler print as prose.

40. Qq, Hazlitt, Harrison and Wheeler print as one line; Sampson and Lucas print as two lines of verse, dividing ... *atheists / For* ...; Dyce and Brown print as two lines of prose.

44a–b. Qq and Lucas print as two lines; Sampson, Wheeler and Brown print as a single line of verse.

49–50. Wheeler divides ... *blood-hound: / Do* ...

55–6. Sampson and Wheeler divide ... *whole. / methodi- cally. /* .

102a–b. Qq and Lucas print as two lines; Sampson, Wheeler and Brown print as a single line of verse.

109. Brown prints as two lines, dividing ... *nostrils. / What* ...

125–6. Qq and Lucas divide ... *Lethe. / Vittoria! My* ...

132a–b. Qq and Lucas print as two lines; Sampson, Wheeler and Brown print as a single line of verse.

135a–b. Qq and Lucas print as two lines; Sampson, Wheeler and Brown print as a single line of verse.

143–4. Wheeler divides ... *bonfire. / ... Never. /* .

160–2. Qq, Lucas and Sampson align and divide ... *world, /* ... *them / ... do't /* ; Hazlitt prints as verse, dividing ... *world, / ... use / ... do't. /* ; Wheeler prints as verse, dividing ... *out? / ... groats / ... do't. /* ; Brown prints 160b–162 as prose.

165–68. Wheeler prints as three lines, dividing ... *rage, /* ... *commit / ... hard./*

177–80. Q1, Q2, Q3 align and divide ... *men! / ... in our /* ... *Sweetest. /* ; Q4 aligns as three lines, dividing ... *men! /* ... *infancy. / ... Sweetest. /* ; Lucas prints as four lines, dividing ... *safely. / ... sister, / ... infancy. / ... Sweetest. /* ; Sampson and Brown print as verse, dividing ... *safely. /* ... *sister, / ... infancy. / ... Sweetest. /.* Brown adds a note that the line arrangement of Q1, Q2, Q3 'may well be right in view of Flamineo's frequent use of prose fragments in this scene.' (p. 110 n.)

180–1. Wheeler prints as a single line of verse.

188–90. Qq and Brown print as three lines; Sampson, Wheeler and Harrison print as two lines, dividing ... *So, / ... about.* /. Lucas prints as two lines, dividing ... *Lord / ... about.* /.

193a–b. Qq and Lucas print as two lines; Sampson, Wheeler and Brown print as a single line of verse.

199b–200. Qq prints as a single line; Dyce, Hazlitt and Harrison divide ... *Barbary, / For* ... ; Brown prints as two lines of prose; Lucas aligns 199a–b and divides ... *deserves / To* ... ; Sampson and Wheeler print as verse, dividing ... *deserves / To* ... .

IV.iii, 6–16. Wheeler prints as ten lines, dividing ... *knights / ... cloak / ... next / ... Fleece; / ... Ghost; / ... Annunciation; / ... Garter, / ... could / ... institutions, / ... time /* .

17a–b. Qq and Lucas print as two lines; Sampson, Wheeler and Brown print as a single line of verse.

18a–b. Qq print as two lines; Sampson, Wheeler, Lucas and Brown print as a single line of verse.

17–18. Q1a aligns and divides ... *discovery. / ... Lodowick? / ... lord. / ... dinner time; /* ; Q1b aligns and divides ... *discovery. / ... lord. / ... dinner time; /*

22a–b. Qq and Lucas print as two lines; Sampson, Wheeler and Brown print as a single line of verse.

47–9. Qq and Lucas print as four lines, dividing . . . *my lord.* / . . . *Ha?* / . . . *Giovanni* / . . . *father.* / ; Sampson, Wheeler and Brown divide . . . *her?* / . . . *Brachiano.* / . . . *father.* / .

89. Qq print as two lines, dividing . . . *lord?* / . . . *you* / .

129–30. Lucas divides . . . *reason* / *Of* . . .

134–5. Qq align and divide . . . *Sir.* / . . . *me sir?* / ; Lucas aligns and divides . . . *rest.* / . . . *me sir?* / ; Sampson prints as two lines of verse, dividing . . . *rest.* / . . . *me sir?* / ; Brown prints as three lines, dividing . . . *rest.* / *Sir .*/ . . . *sir?* /

134–9. Wheeler divides . . . *rest.* / . . . *sent you* / . . . *travel,* / . . . *intelligence.* / . . . *commanded.* /

138–9. Qq align as one line; Lucas and Brown divide . . . *creature* / *Ever* . . . ; Dyce, Hazlitt, Sampson and Harrison print 138b and 139 as a single line of verse.

V.i, 24: aligned with 23 in Qq and Lucas.

25–8. Qq align and divide . . . *ever to* / . . . *they ser-* / . . . *penance.* / . . . *is.* / .

61a–b. Qq and Lucas print as two lines; Sampson, Wheeler and Brown print as a single line of verse.

84. Qq and Lucas print as two lines, dividing . . . *lust.* / . . . *Flamineo* . . .

85a–b. Qq and Lucas print as two lines; Sampson, Wheeler and Brown print as a single line of verse.

166–7. Dyce, Hazlitt, Harrison and Brown print as prose.

211b–213. Qq divide . . . *sown;* / . . . *sunk* / ; Lucas and Brown divide 211–12 at . . . *sown;* / and print 212–13 as prose; Dyce, Hazlitt, Sampson, Wheeler and Harrison print 211b–213 as prose.

221–3. Qq, Hazlitt, Sampson, Lucas, Harrison and Brown print as prose; Dyce prints as four lines, dividing . . . *motion.* / . . . *now* / . . . *leisure* / . . . *blood.* / ; Wheeler prints as three lines of verse, dividing . . . *now* / . . . *leisure* / . . . *blood.* / .

V.ii, 14–15. Qq and Lucas print as four lines; Sampson, Wheeler and Brown print as two lines of verse.

24–5. Wheeler divides . . . *Oh!* / *My perpetual* . . .

27. Qq, Sampson, Lucas and Brown print as a single line; Dyce, Hazlitt, Wheeler and Harrison print as prose continuous with 28–29.

48–51. Wheeler prints as two lines of verse, dividing . . . *-owl!* / . . . *me go.* /

49–50: aligned in Qq and Lucas; Sampson and Brown print as two lines.

65–66. Qq and Lucas align and divide . . . *madam.* / . . . *peace.* / ; Wheeler and Brown divide . . . *bosom.* / . . . *peace.* / ; Sampson divides . . . *madam.* / . . . *peace.* / .

74–75a. Qq print as prose.

V.iii, 5–6. Wheeler divides . . . *My lord* / . . . *torture.* / ; Brown divides . . . *poison'd.* / . . . *torture.* / .

35a–b: aligned in Qq and Lucas; Brown prints as two lines.

42–46. 'This speech may be rendered into a kind of verse whose lines end in *see, princes, towns, unhospitable, now, bodies, invisible.*' (Sampson, p. 142)

52–53. Q1, Q4 print as prose; Q2, Q3 print as verse, dividing . . . *live* / *Within* . . .

64–68. Qq and Lucas align and divide . . . *done.* / . . . *wisdom?* / . . . *some* / . . . *Duke?* / ; Sampson, Wheeler and Brown print 65–67 as continuous prose and 68a–b as a single line of verse; Dyce prints 65–67 as prose; Hazlitt and Harrison print 65b [*Wilt* . . .] – 67 as prose.

80. Qq and Lucas print as two lines; Sampson, Wheeler and Brown print as a single line of verse.

94–99. Wheeler divides . . . *sir,* / . . . *peace,* / . . . *Where?* / . . . *pair* / . . . *ha, ha, ha!* /

96–97. Qq and Lucas print as two lines; Sampson and Brown print as a single line of verse.

114. Brown conjectures that this should be two lines.

115–116a. Dyce, Hazlitt, Wheeler and Harrison print as one line.

117–124. Dyce, Hazlitt, Sampson and Lucas print 117–19 as verse, dividing . . . *powder,* / . . . *pastry.* / . . . *he.* / ; Qq and Brown print 117–19 as prose; Harrison divides 121–4; . . . *th'argument* / . . . *in't.* / . . . *tails,* / . . . *rat-catcher:* / ; Wheeler divides 117–24 . . . *hair* / . . . *look* / . . . *he?* / . . . *him:* / . . . *in't.* / . . . *tails,* / . . . *rat-catcher:* / ; Q1, Q2, Q3 print 121–4 as prose; Q4 prints 121–6 as verse. Sampson notes 'The presence of the marginal note is perhaps responsible for the irregular line-arrangement' of Q1, Q2 and Q3.

149–50. Wheeler divides . . . *Devil* / . . . *Perpetually.* /

150. Qq print as two lines, divided . . . *Brachiano.* / *Thou* . . . probably because of the stage direction printed in the margin.

156–157a. Qq print as prose.

158. Q1 and Lucas print as two lines, dividing . . . *bottles,* // *And* . . .

160. Qq and Lucas print as two lines, dividing . . . *copperas* / *And* . . . ; Sampson, Wheeler and Brown print as a single line of verse.

164–7. Wheeler divides... *stink* / ... *forgotten* / ... *devil* / ;
Brown divides... *stink* / ... *forgotten* / ... *Vittoria?* / ...
devil / .

166. Dyce, Hazlitt and Harrison print as two lines, dividing
... *forgotten* / *Before* ...

169. Hazlitt and Brown print as two lines, dividing ...
private. / *What?* ...

173a–b. Qq and Lucas print as two lines; Sampson, Wheeler
and Brown print as a single line of verse.

174–6 Brown conjectures these lines should be prose.

185. Brown conjectures this line should be prose.

203–5. Sampson prints as two lines, dividing ... *I* / ...
dead? / ; Wheeler prints as two lines, dividing ... *death,* /
... *dead?* / .

213. Qq and Lucas print as two lines, dividing... *How?* /
You ... ; Sampson, Wheeler and Brown print as a single
line of verse.

223a–b. Qq and Lucas print as two lines; Sampson, Wheeler
and Brown print as a single line of verse.

229a–b. Qq and Lucas print as two lines; Sampson, Wheeler
and Brown print as a single line of verse.

234a–b. Qq and Lucas print as two lines; Sampson, Wheeler
and Brown print as a single line of verse.

236. Qq and Lucas print as two lines, dividing... *Laugh?* /
And ... ; Sampson, Wheeler and Brown print as a single
line of verse.

245. Qq print as two lines, dividing... *strange!* / *Most* ...;
Lucas, Wheeler and Brown print as a single line of verse.

245–6. Sampson divides ... *horse.* / ... *broke./* .

247–8. Q1, Q2, Q3 and Lucas print as three lines, dividing
... *hand* / ... *deed.* / ... *Right,* / ; Q4 prints as two lines,
dividing... *deed* / ... *Right:* / ; Sampson, Wheeler and
Brown print as two lines of verse, dividing ... *hand* / ...
Right, / .

264a–b. Qq print as two lines, dividing ... *midnight* / *In*
... ; Sampson, Wheeler, Lucas and Brown print as a single
line of verse.

265a–b. Qq and Lucas print as two lines; Sampson, Wheeler
and Brown print as a single line of verse.

V.iv, 9: printed as a separate line in Qq, Lucas and Brown; Dyce,
Hazlitt, Sampson, Wheeler and Harrison print as prose,
continuous with 2–8.

32–34. Q1, Q2 and Q3 divide ... *reverence.* / ... *when* / ...
out? / , printing 32b–34 as prose; Q4 prints 32a as a separate

line and 32b–34 as prose; Lucas and Brown divide . . .
reverence. / . . . raven / . . . young. / ; Hazlitt and Harrison
print 32b–34 as prose; Sampson and Wheeler print as
verse, dividing . . . *raven / . . . young. / . . . out? / .*
70–72. Wheeler divides . . . *wore it. / . . . flowers. / . . . grief /*
86–91. Q1 and Q2 divide . . . *oun- / . . . sir? / . . . grandmother /*
. . . *lute / . . . do. /* ; Q3 divides . . . *ounces / . . . sir? /*
. . . *grandmother / . . . lute / . . . do. /* ; Q4 divides
. . . *of't. / . . . sir? / . . . grandmother / . . . lute / . . . do. /* ;
Dyce, Hazlitt and Harrison divide . . . *memory: / . . . of't. /*
. . . *hence / . . . sir? / . . . grandmother / . . . o'er / . . . lute /*
. . . *do. /* ; Sampson and Lucas divide . . . *memory: / . . .*
of't. / . . . sir? / . . . grandmother / . . . o'er / . . . do. / ;
Brown prints 86–87 as prose and then divides . . . *sir? /*
. . . *grandmother / . . . o'er / . . . do. /* as verse.
102–3. Brown conjectures these lines should be prose.
122. Brown prints as two lines, dividing . . . *thee? / Thou . . .*
139. Brown conjectures that this should be two lines, dividing . . . *melancholy. / I do . . .*

V.vi, 1a–b. Qq and Lucas print as two lines; Sampson, Wheeler
and Brown print as a single line of verse.
10–11. Sampson and Wheeler print as a single line of verse.
15a–b. Qq, Lucas and Brown print as two lines; Sampson
and Wheeler print as a single line of verse.
26–27a. Qq print as prose; Dyce *et al* print as verse, dividing
. . . *see / How . . .*
51a–b. Qq and Lucas print as two lines; Sampson, Wheeler
and Brown print as a single line of verse.
51b–52a. Q1, Q2, Q3 divide . . . *pleasure / As* . . . ; Q4 prints
as one line.
52a–b: aligned in Q1, Q2, Q3 and Lucas; Sampson and
Wheeler print as a single verse line; Brown prints as two
lines.
71–3. Wheeler divides . . . *teach / . . . good, / . . . take. /.*
105–10. Sampson comments. 'Possibly as verse with lines
ending in *now, purgatory, shooes, Cæsar, blacking, Charle-
maigne, Pippin, horse.*' (p. 172 n.)
139b–140. Qq and Hazlitt print as one line.
164a–b. Qq and Lucas print as two lines; Brown prints as a
single line of verse; Dyce, Hazlitt, Sampson, Wheeler and
Harrison print 156–164 as continuous prose.
167–8. Q1, Q2 and Q3 align and divide . . . *swords. / . . .*
Isabella, / ; Q4 aligns and divides . . . *revellers. / . . .*
Isabella! /

187–8. Q1, Q2 and Q3 print as two lines; Q4 prints as one line.

187–91. Wheeler divides . . . *you* / . . . *a hangman,* / . . . *fellow*; / . . . *laugh?* / .

193–4. Wheeler divides . . . *carry* / *Mine* . . .

215–16. Qq and Lucas divide . . . *brave?* / . . . *death* / ; Sampson, Wheeler and Brown divide . . . *me.* / . . . *death* / .

217–19. Qq divide . . . *weapon* / . . . *tremble,* / .

235–6. Qq print as one line.

279a–b. Qq and Lucas print as two lines; Sampson, Wheeler and Brown print as a single line of verse.

282–3. Q1, Q2 divide . . . *Mine?* / . . . *to't.* / ; Q3, Q4 divide . . . *Yes.* / . . . *to't.* / .

286–7. Qq divide . . . *Ha!* / . . . *pensioner.* / .